Liberation Theology

OTHER BOOKS BY RONALD H. NASH

Christianity and the Hellenistic World

Christian Faith and Historical Understanding

The Concept of God

Social Justice and the Christian Church

The Word of God and the Mind of Man

Freedom, Justice and the State

Ideas of History (editor)

The Light of the Mind: St. Augustine's Theory of Knowledge

The Case for Biblical Christianity (editor)

The Philosophy of Gordon H. Clark (editor)

The New Evangelicanism

Dooyeweerd and the Amsterdam Philosophy

Liberation Theology

Edited by **Ronald Nash**

A Mott Media Book

BAKER BOOK HOUSE
Grand Rapids, Michigan 49516

Contents

Introduction

Liberation theology is the most widely discussed theological movement of the decade. While liberation theology has taken a variety of forms that speak to the oppression of several different classes of people (including blacks and women), the liberation theology in view in this book is the movement among Latin American Catholics and Protestants that seeks radical changes in the political and economic institutions of that region along Marxist lines. But of course, Europe also has its stock of Christian theologians who believe that a hybrid social theology resulting from a cross between Christianity and Marxism is both desirable and necessary. And as a growing number of North American theologians translate their theoretical displeasure and distrust of capitalism into action, the language and literature of liberation theology becomes increasingly more prominent.

Liberation theology began sometime in the mid-1960s. Most lists of the major proponents (and representative books) include the following:[1] Rubem Alves, *A Theology of Human Hope* (1969); Helder Camara, *Church and Colonialism* (1969); Paulo Freire, *Pedagogy of the Oppressed* (1970); Gustavo Gutiérrez, *A Theology of Liberation* (1973); José Miranda, *Marx and the Bible* (1974); Hugo Assmann, *Theology for a Nomad Church* (1975); José Míguez-Bonino, *Doing Theology in a Revolutionary Situation* (1975); Juan Luis Segundo, *The Liberation of Theology* (1976); Eduardo Frei, *Latin America: The Hopeful Option* (1978); and Jon Sobrino, *Christology at the Crossroads: A Latin American Approach* (1978).

The fundamental objective of liberation theology is Christian action on behalf of the poor and oppressed. As Gustavo Gutiérrez put it, "To believe is . . . to be united with the poor and exploited of this world from within the very heart of the social confrontations and 'popular' struggles for liberation."[2] Liberation theology urges the elimination of oppression and poverty through a replacement of the economic and political structures alleged to be their causes. If it proves necessary, the revolution may use violence. Not only is this revolutionary activity recommended and promoted by the theologians, they insist that the Church should be at the very center of the revolutionary activity. Gutiérrez declares:

> It is becoming more evident that the Latin American peoples will not emerge from their present status except by means of a profound transformation, a *social revolution*, which will qualitatively change the conditions in which they now live. The oppressed sectors within each country are becoming aware—slowly, it is true—of their class interests and of the painful road which must be followed to accomplish the breakup of the status quo.[3]

Consequently, liberationists believe, the Christian church must become a part of the revolutionary process including its violence. According to Gutiérrez, "The Church's *mission* is defined practically and theoretically, pastorally and theologically in relation to this revolutionary process."[4]

One of the more unusual features of liberation theology's brief history has been its relative immunity to any serious, concentrated, and systematic critique—a fact that can hardly be attributed to the movement's lack of difficulties. This book is an attempt to remedy this critical silence. The ten contributors to this volume come from both sides of the Atlantic and represent a wide spectrum of ecclesiastical fellowships including Roman Catholic, Anglican, Lutheran, Presbyterian, Reformed, and Baptist. The contributors readily acknowledge that liberation theologians have made a number of contributions to the church's understanding of its contemporary mission. But they agree that liberation theology is a movement replete with problems and that it is time that those difficulties be discussed.

NOTES

1. The books are listed in the order of the publication in English. Full bibliographic information is included at the end of this book.

2. Gustavo Gutiérrez, "Freedom and Salvation: A Political Problem," in G. Gutiérrez and R. Schaull, *Liberation and Change*, ed. R. H. Stone (Atlanta: John Knox, 1977) p. 92.

3. Gustavo Gutiérrez, *A Theology of Liberation* (Maryknoll, Orbis, 1973) p. 88.

4. Ibid., p. 138.

WHAT IS
LIBERATION THEOLOGY?

Harold O. J. Brown

Harold O. J. Brown

Harold O. J. Brown is Professor of Biblical and Systematic
Theology at Trinity Evangelical Divinity School. He is currently on
leave while he serves as pastor of the Reformed Church in Klosters,
Switzerland. Educated at Harvard College, Harvard Divinity School
and Harvard Graduate School (where he earned his Ph.D.),
Dr. Brown has also studied at universities in Germany and Austria.
He has also served as associate editor of *Christianity Today* and is
a co-founder of the Christian Action Council as well as its current
chairman. He is the author of several books including *Christianity
and the Class Struggle, The Protest of a Troubled Protestant, The
Reconstruction of the Republic,* and *Heresies: The Image of Christ
in the Mirror of Heresy and Orthodoxy.*

WHAT IS LIBERATION THEOLOGY? — A Hermeneutical Battlefield.

Christianity is the most theological of all the world's religions. It has produced not one "Christian theology," but a whole array of "theologies." Ancient and medieval Christianity produced a variety of doctrinal systems over the centuries, but it was meager compared to the profusion that came with the Protestant Reformation. There came a time when it seemed as though every minister called himself a" theologian" and produced his own "theology." Reportedly 8000 theologians subscribed to the Lutheran Formula of Concord in 1577.[1] This does not take into account Reformed theologians, theologians in the Church of England, or the so-called radicals—Anabaptists and others. Among the bewildering variety of theological fads that come and often (fortunately) also go, liberation theology occupies a distinctive place. In the Library of Congress cataloging system, liberation theology comes between the "death of God theology" and process theology—one an evanescent movement that flourished briefly in the 1960s, the other a twentieth century version of one of the most tenacious adversaries of orthodox, biblical religion—pantheism.[2]

In addition to being theologically prolific, Christianity is a religion where almost everything depends on the concept of the Word of God and on the particular words in which the Word of God first comes to us and then is explained and interpreted. Despite the fact that it is very much dependent on words and their meanings (as well as on the Word), Christian theology has not always taken the trouble to establish a precise, scientific language suited to its own special needs as it tries to communicate eternal truths in the context of a world that is always in transition. Expressions such as "sin," "salvation," "church," "redemption," and "Lord's Supper" have taken on a special, religious significance in English. Yet each of them was in common secular use in the original languages of the Bible at the time that it was written. The tendency of Christianity to take over secular terms and to use them in an exclusive sense often makes them seem exclusively religious. In our own twentieth century, so long after

5

the Bible was written in what was, at the time, ordinary everyday language, there are very few English-speaking readers who are aware of the extensive associations, of the rich spectrum of meanings, that characterized many of the most important terms of Christianity. Thus very few modern readers realize that the Greek term *Christos* (Christ) as well as the Hebrew *mashiach* (Messiah) both mean "annointed one." Admittedly, to call Jesus the Christ is to say much more than that he was ritually annointed, but it does also say that, which is something that most modern speakers of English and other languages seldom notice. Both "Christ" and "Messiah" have become highly technical terms with a special religious significance. When we say "sin," we always think of a religious transgression, not realizing that in the Greek of New Testament times it could also be used simply for missing the target.

Sometimes the honest efforts of modern readers to get a feeling for the original languages leads to misunderstandings of another kind. The real meaning of words in everyday use is sometimes not precisely understood by breaking them down into component parts—a favorite technique of many of the scholars who contributed to Gerhard Kittel's famous *Theological Dictionary of the New Testament.*[3] Although the English verb "to understand" is composed of two words (the verb "to stand" and the preposition "under"), knowing this does not really help us to see what "understand" means. It certainly has little to do with either "standing under" (in the sense of" beneath") or with "under standing" (in the sense of "insufficiently"). The importance of the Word in Christianity—of the Bible as God's Word written, acknowledged by orthodox theologians as infallible and inerrant, but also of Christ the Lord, designated as the living Word of God—virtually guarantees that both Christian thinkers and those trying to make sense out of their remarks will run into trouble when words are used ambiguously or, worse still, slyly ride piggyback on linguistic or cultural associations that have nothing much to do with their actual meaning.

Liberation theology, then, is in large measure a quest in hermeneutics, in the interpretation of biblical revelation, or more generally, of the Christian message. If this were *all* that it is, then there would be no need to criticize its motivation, regardless of whether we agreed with its conclusions. But it is evident that the

movement quickly slips from an interpretation of *biblical* revelation
to an interpretation of revelations of quite a different kind, produced
by analyzing history from one particular philosophical perspective
and measuring it according to one presuppositional yardstick. The
perspective, more or less conscious, more or less openly acknowledged, is Marxist; the yardstick is the axiom, "God is on the side
of the oppressed."

THE IMPORTANCE OF SEMANTICS

Liberation theology, as already indicated, appears in the cataloging system between the death of God and process theology. Another
close relative is existentialist interpretation, a school inspired and
led by the celebrated New Testament scholar Rudolf Bultmann
(l886-1976). The semantic aspect has been both positive and negative.
On the one hand, it has helped Christians to recover some of the
full range of meaning, some of the depth and color, of powerful
expressions that had been largely sanitized by being given a single,
narrow, technical religious interpretation. Salvation is one such word.
Although the angelic prophecy states that Mary's child will be called
Jesus "because he will save his people from their sins" (Matt. 1:19),
very few English readers realize that the name Jesus is derived from
the Hebrew word *yeshuah*, "salvation." And even fewer recognize
that the root verb *yasha*, from which the noun is derived, is frequently
used in a down-to-earth military sense to mean deliver or rescue by
armed force.[4] Salvation, in the Old Testament as well as in the New,
frequently has a largely spiritual significance, but the worldly concept of deliverance from evil as such, not just from spiritual evil,
is never absent. From a New Testament perspective, it really is not
correct to speak of "saving one's soul" as though salvation has no
necessary reference to physical deliverance—i.e., the rescue of body
as well as soul—from all evil, including present physical dangers as
well as the peril of eternal damnation.

If we glance for an instant at the neighbor of liberation theology,
namely death of God theology, we see a dramatic illustration of the
danger that results from taking a valid biblical theme and making
it the key to one's understanding of the whole message of Scripture.

Traditional theology tells us that Jesus Christ possesses deity, i.e., is God. It also tells us that Jesus died for us on the cross. The theology of the death of God ties these two legitimate doctrines together to produce an illegitimate conclusion: God has died, on the cross, and consequently God is now dead. This entirely overlooks the triumphant way the story of Jesus' death continues in the very texts that teach us about both his deity and his death. Those texts speak of the resurrection, which authenticated the victory of Jesus over the power of death and sin. Since his resurrection, Jesus appears to believers as *Christos Pantokrator*, Christ the Ruler of All, Jesus King Most Wonderful. In seeking not to trivialize the message of the death of Christ, the death of God theology radicalizes and distorts it, claiming that God, who died in Jesus Christ, subsequently was also dead and remains dead. The logical conclusion of all this is that man, following the death and consequent disappearance of God, is himself absolutized. It is man, not Christ, who demands to be seen as "king" and "ruler of all."

The theology of existentialist interpretation also takes a valid insight and, by making it the sole and unique measuring stick, distorts the full meaning of Scripture and finally makes the New Testament message unrecognizable. Bultmann proclaimed that the goal of the New Testament is to make it possible for us to have a new and authentic self-understanding. According to this new self-understanding, man no longer sees himself as under the bondage of sin, the "rudiments of the world" (Col.2:8), but discovers the possibility of authenticity. Unfortunately, for Bultmann, the important thing is the act of looking, not whether the object at which one is looking is in fact the truth. What is important is not the external, formal conformity of the New Testament message to truth, but the fact that it permits us to understand ourselves in a new way.[5] Orthodox Christianity is also willing to state that the gospel permits us to understand ourselves in a new way, but by this it means something quite different. Jesus permits us to see ourselves in a new light, subjectively speaking, because objectively speaking he has transferred us "from the power of darkness . . . into the kingdom" (Col. 1:13). A related current in modern theology, called the theology of hope, emphasizes the future, but not in the traditional Christian sense of an eager awaiting of the return of Christ, but rather as simply a quality or way of hoping. It is not that one hopes for something specific, such as the second coming of Christ, but rather that one adopts a fundamental attitude of hopefulness, without stressing any specific doctrinal or historical content of that hope. The theology of revolution, stressing that Paul and his friends have indeed "turned the world upside down"(Acts 17:6), becomes preoccupied with the act of turning upside down, and not with Paul's reason—the news of an objective event, the Resurrection, the truth of which great reality totally changed our perspective on the world and its values. Paul stressed the revolutionary act of God; to change the emphasis to the revolutionary activities of men is to falsify the original message.

THE ROOTS OF LIBERATION THEOLOGY

Liberation theology has three roots: a linguistic root, a political root, and a nationalistic or ethnic root. Of these, the linguistic root is the most legitimate, although it is made to produce more than it really can sustain. The biblical language of salvation indeed has a "liberation" aspect—the deliverance of captive and of oppressed peoples from degrading servitude. Indeed, the story of the Exodus is the story of a military triumph, one might even say of God's right hand that "dashed in pieces the enemy" (Ex. 15:6, from the passage known as *The Song of Moses*). Even the New Testament, which is more otherworldly than the Old and far more interested in life beyond the grave, speaks of salvation in terms of victory—victory over Satan and over the power of sin and death. There is a concrete and tangible side to biblical salvation that orthodox Christians cannot and ought not deny. The legitimacy of this aspect of salvation causes many theologically conservative Christians to draw back and hesitate to reject liberation theology out of hand. It would be wrong to deny this aspect of biblical salvation, but it is perverse to make it the fundamental aspect which is what most, if not all, that is called liberation theology actually does.

The political root is important, sometimes so important that it causes critics to take liberation theology as political ideology in theological language. This criticism is noted by José Miguez-Bonino, one of the foremost architects of liberation theology, who puts it perhaps even better than his critics might:"The text of Scripture and tradition [Bonino has the critics of liberation theology say] is forced into the Procrustean bed of ideology, and the theologian who has fallen prey of this procedure is forever condemned to listen only to the echo of his own ideology. There is no redemption for this theology, because it has muzzled the Word of God . . . "⁶ In the context, Bonino acknowledges "that the criticism is not without significance,"⁷ although he ultimately rejects it. Bonino makes no bones about the Marxist basis of liberation thought, saying only that the "Marxist scheme cannot be taken as a dogma, but rather as a method."⁸ Elsewhere he notes: "The thought of these men is characterized by a strict scientific ideological analysis, avowedly Marxist."⁹

Where do the liberation theologians derive the right to call this Marxist "scientific-ideological analysis" a "theology" at all? They do so on the basis of a number of presuppositions of varying reliability. First, they presuppose God. In so doing, they are in company with Christian believers throughout the centuries. Second, they presuppose or stipulate that God is *par excellence* "the God of the oppressed" and is "on the side of the oppressed." Although there are many examples of oppression, oppressors, and oppressed people in the Bible, the concept of oppression is not a biblical category, but rather one that is drawn from the nonbiblical atheistic ideology of Marxism. It is not too much to call it a "Procrustean bed," precisely as Bonino puts it, one that will result in the mutilation, indeed in the decapitation, of the gospel placed upon it. Borrowing its ideological analysis from Marxism creates a fundamental link between liberation theology and Marxism, even when the advocates of liberation theology explicitly reject Marxism, at least as a "dogma." How do they come by the right to make this presupposition? They have, in effect, accepted another source of revelation. Neither the *sola Scriptura* of Reformation Protestantism nor the "two sources" of Tridentine Catholicism (the Catholicism of the Council of Trent, substantially modified by the Second Vatican Council), namely, Scripture and sacred tradition, is sufficient to justify so fundamental an assumption. Liberation theology has taken as its primary source of revelation the consciousness and experience of the oppressed classes. It was Friedrich Daniel Schleiermacher

(1768-1834), the most influential Protestant thinker since the Reformation, who made human religious consciousness a *source* of religious knowledge.[10] (More traditional theology sees the healthy religious consciousness as an intuitive or emotive way of understanding what has been revealed in Scripture, not of creating new revelation.) Schleiermacher extolled those human spirits in which the aesthetic sense is sufficiently developed to have a "feeling and taste for the infinite." For liberation theologians, the important question is not the intensity of feeling but the severity of one's oppression; it is not sensitivity but suffering that creates the religious consciousness that authorizes them to graft onto the simple gospel a specific political ideology and then to maintain that this grafting is necessary if the gospel is to be understood, and—even more important for them—put into practice.

Formally speaking, such a grafting combines a mistake of classical heresies with one of classical liberalism. Like many heresies, it absolutizes a fundamentally nonbiblical standard, the feelings and experience of oppressed peoples. Because this standard is drawn from human feelings and experience—although limited to those of a particular group or class—liberation theology also resembles classic Protestant liberalism after Schleiermacher: it has made human feelings and human sensitivity a source of divine revelation that can be placed alongside Scripture. But to place any other authority, even such apparently trustworthy ones as common tradition or the orthodox creeds, alongside of the Scripture and on a par with it is ultimately to deny the finality of Scripture and thus to undermine the reliability and consistency of a faith that claims to be based on the Word of God. No matter how much liberation theologians can say that is incisive, challenging, or perhaps even correct, it is important to note that this fundamentally false principle of accepting another source of knowledge in effect denies the sovereignty and sufficiency of biblical revelation. Another prominent liberation theologian, Gustavo Gutiérrez, expresses this fundamental duality quite candidly. At the same time, he points us to the third root of this theology, the root that we have called nationalistic or ethnic. He states that his work is "based on the Gospel and the experiences of men and women committed to the process of liberation in the oppressed and exploited land of Latin America."[11]

Liberation Theology

Luther's Reformation was sparked by his awareness of a very negative force that, in Luther's eyes, jeopardized the very foundations of the Christian faith. He called it the "Babylonian captivity of the church" under the false and avaricious papal system. Liberation theology—perhaps the most important new movement in theology since Schleiermacher—is sparked by a more positive perception: the sense that there is a third force in the world, the so-called "third world." Contrasted with the "first world" of European and North American capitalism as well as with the "second world" of Communism, this "third world" definitely is a force worthy of notice and respect. But whether its men and women have experiences that can produce doctrines worthy of being called divine revelation is quite another matter. Latin Americans are not the only distinct group whose "experiences" have been hailed as a source of religious truth and as the foundation of a special kind of liberation theology. Blacks have been so hailed, for example, by the spokesman for black liberation theology, James H. Cone.[12] The same thing has been done for the largest "minority," in fact a majority, women, by Rosemary Radford Reuther.[13] Although even a modest knowledge of history and sociology would lead one to suspect that the experiences of groups so overlapping and yet diverse as Latin Americans, blacks, and women could produce any kind of unified theology, it almost seems as though there is a common pedagogy of the oppressed, to borrow a term from Paulo Freire.[14] Critics of liberation theology suspect that the apparent unity lies less in the fact of oppression and the shared experience it is supposed to bring than in the shared acceptance of Marxist optics, which necessarily imparts a certain sameness to the experiences examined through them.

For liberation theology, the parallel to Luther's "Babylonian captivity" lies in the assumption of a certain Babylonian captivity of the Christian mind, not to the strictures of the hierarchy but to the structures of traditional Western theology. All Christian thought for centuries has been in bondage to specifically Western ways of thinking—always one-sided, in this view, and quite frequently wrong. There is a measure of justification in this assumption. (It often overlooks the contributions of Eastern theology, specifically, Greek and Russian, and even these would probably be suspect as "Western" by comparison with all non-European thought.) We may well suppose, indeed we should, that the entire Holy Scripture is a precious message to us from God, in verbal form, and that it must be handed down from generation to generation intact and unaltered, "the faith once delivered to the saints" (Jude v. 3). But is it necessary to suppose that this message, this faith, must be delivered in a package together with two thousand years of Western intellectual history? Indeed, it is sometimes shocking to notice the way in which new Christians in Asian lands, with an intellectual tradition older than that of Europe, are forced to study not only great Western Christians such as Augustine and Aquinas, Luther and Calvin, but also prominent Western anti-Christians, such as Kant and Hegel, Nietzsche and Freud, before they can be certified as "theologians," while their own intellectual history is neglected if not dismissed as irrelevant. The charge of liberation theology is that the Christian theological tradition has accumulated too many Western barnacles, which must be scraped before the ship of the church can sail effectively. The difficulty is that Latin America, both its governing classes and its oppressed, is also Western—as are the blacks whose religion Cone cites and the women adduced by Reuther. If an excessively Western orientation has given Christian theology a skewed perspective, reorienting itself about the perspective of Latin Americans, blacks, or women—or all three at once—does not seem enough to unskew it. After all, Latin America has a longer Western European cultural tradition than North America. Cone's blacks are American Christian blacks, and Rosemary Reuther is just as much a Roman Catholic born and reared as the pope.

If liberation theology is supposed to be more authentically human and hence more truly catholic than the orthodoxy of white European and North American males, it is perplexing that it has so far received no contribution from those elements of Christendom that must be considered at least as oppressed, albeit in different ways and for different reasons, as Latin Americans, American blacks, and women. We speak of the Christians in countries where religious freedom is curtailed, such as the Soviet Union, and particularly of Christians whose religion *and* their nationality—such as the Uniates of the Ukraine, the Catholics of Lithuania, the Lutherans of Latvia and Estonia—combine to make them the target of effective, skillful, and persistent oppression. One cannot demand that liberation theologians—Latin Americans, blacks, and women—think *like* Ukrainians, Lithuanians, or Latvians, but one might at least expect them sometimes to think *of* them. Until they do so, it will appear that liberation theology, to borrow the phraseology of Jacques Ellul, is making a distinction between the "interesting poor" and the "uninteresting poor." Doing so, it must forfeit its claim to speak for the oppressed.

THE VISION OF LIBERATION THEOLOGY

If liberation theology, far from being the recovery of a sound Christian center, looks like an even more eccentric expression of the Christian faith than the orthodoxy it denigrates, why is it so attractive? Is it, as Raffaelo Balestrini said in another connection, "the sign of a widespread and fundamental degeneracy"? It is tempting to the orthodox to dismiss liberation theology, its apparent excesses and its sometimes painfully trenchant criticisms, as simply a consequence of theology forsaking its only reliable source in an authoritative Bible. But it is important to recognize that it is indeed a *sign*, or a *symptom*, rather than a cause. The church's message, through nearly two thousand years of theological introspection and almost five hundred years of Protestant-Catholic polemics, has become so intellectualized that it sometimes begins to sound like footnotes to footnotes. Unfortunately—and perhaps even more seriously—the church's practice sometimes seems as far from that of Christ and his disciples as Jesus' donkey is from the limousines of certain cardinals or the private jet planes of television preachers. The vision of liberation theology is to make an old message understandable, and thus both acceptable and effective. But this vision is blurred, because the liberationists—as they so readily acknowledge—have put on the spectacles of an ideology that has indeed succeeded in changing the world, but not in understanding it, and moreover of an ideology that by virtue of its fundamentally atheistic orientation can never consider the Gospel of Christ as more than the ramblings of a deluded "idealist."[15] Because its vision is thus affected, it has lost sight of two fundamental realities: first, that God is no respecter of persons (Acts 10:34), and second, that

biblical salvation involves resurrection and return, not revolution—
the resurrection of the dead and the return of Jesus Christ. Because
God is no respecter of persons, he can indeed be the God of the
oppressed, but not of the oppressed *only*, and certainly not of
oppressed Latinos only, yet not of oppressed Lithuanians. Because
of its Marxist optics, liberation theology assumes that the Western,
somewhat capitalist, somewhat free economic system is by its very
nature oppressive, and hence that all who live under it are either
oppressing or oppressed. At the same time it appears all but blind
to what the late President Charles deGaulle, with his usual *franchise*,
called "the most odious of tyrannies known to man."

Whatever value there is in liberation theology—and as a corrective to the smug self-sufficiency of bourgeois Christianity its value
may be significant—its adequacy is marred by a most fundamental
blindness, one to which we have already alluded, but not yet clearly
stated. It is this blindness that makes liberation theology appear not
as helpfully corrective, but as dangerously defective. In affirming
that salvation, to be truly and effectively *human* salvation, must
include many kinds of human liberation, liberation theology has
obscured if not denied the fact that only one kind of liberation
deserves being called salvation, because only one kind of oppression is so totally beyond mere human correction that it requires a
divine conquest. We speak of bondage not to the powers of this
world, the powers of politics and of the marketplace, but to the
power of sin and death. We may paraphrase the question of Jesus:
What does it profit a man if he liberate the whole world, yet fail
to be liberated himself? This is the question that liberation theology
has not answered; still worse, it is one they have not yet asked.

NOTES

1. Compare the present author's recent work, *Heresies: The Image of Christ in the Mirror of Heresy and Orthodoxy* (Garden City: Doubleday, 1983).

2. It must be acknowledged that process theologians generally do not want to be called pantheists, preferring the expression *panentheist*. See Ronald Nash, *The Concept of God* (Grand Rapids: Zondervan, 1983), chapter 2.

3. (Grand Rapids: Eerdmans, 1965ff). The approach of this great *Dictionary* has been analyzed and criticized by James Barr in *The Semantics of Biblical Language* (London: Oxford, 1961).

4. Even the Greek New Testament verb *sodzo*, "save," is used in many passages in a purely secular sense, as "to save from shipwreck."

5. For more on this aspect of Bultmann's thought, see Ronald Nash, *Christian Faith and Historical Understanding* (Grand Rapids: Zondervan, 1983).

6. José Miguez Bonino, *Doing Theology in a Revolutionary Situation* (Philadelphia: Fortress, 1975) p. 87.

7. Ibid.

8. Ibid., p. 35.

9. Ibid., p. 71.

10. See Ronald Nash, *The Word of God and the Mind of Man* (Grand Rapids: Zondervan, 1982) chapter 2.

11. Gustavo Gutiérrez, *A Theology of Liberation*, tr. and ed. by Sister Caridad Inda and John Eagleson (Maryknoll: Orbis, 1973) p. ix.

12. See his programmic volume, *God of the Oppressed* (New York: Seabury, 1975).

13. See her *Liberation Theology: Human Hope Confronts Christian History and American Power* (New York: Paulist, 1972).

14. Paulo Freire, *Pedagogy of the Oppressed* (New York: Seabury, 1970).

15. In Marxist terminology, religion is a form of idealism.

A THEOLOGY
OF DEVELOPMENT
FOR LATIN AMERICA

Michael Novak

Michael Novak

Michael Novak is Resident Scholar in Philosophy, Religion and Public Policy at the American Enterprise Institute in Washington, D.C. He has published several influential books including *The Spirit of Democratic Capitalism*, *Belief and Unbelief*, *The Experience of Nothingness*, *Ascent of the Mountain*, *Flight of the Dove*, and *The Rise of the Unmeltable Ethnics*. Mr. Novak was educated at Holy Cross Seminary, Stonehill College and Gregorian University in Rome. He did his graduate studies in history and philosophy of religion at Harvard University. He has taught at Union Theological Seminary, Stanford University, the State University of New York, Syracuse University, and the University of California at Santa Barbara. For two years, in 1981 and again in 1982, Mr. Novak was appointed by President Reagan as the Chief of the U.S. Delegation to the U.N. Human Rights Commission Meeting in Geneva. He has published scores of articles in *The New Republic*, *Commentary*, *Harper's*, *National Review*, *The Atlantic*, and other journals.

A THEOLOGY OF DEVELOPMENT FOR LATIN AMERICA*
— Liberation from Private Property

DEMOCRATIC CAPITALISM

Of all the systems of political economy which have shaped our history, none has so revolutionized ordinary expectations of human life—lengthened the life span, made the elimination of poverty and famine thinkable, enlarged the range of human choice—as democratic capitalism.

What do I mean by "democratic capitalism"? I mean three systems in one: a predominantly market economy; a polity respectful of the rights of the individual to life, liberty, and the pursuit of happiness; and a system of cultural institutions moved by ideals of liberty and justice for all. In short, three dynamic and converging systems functioning as one: a democratic polity, an economy based on markets and incentives, and a moral-cultural system which is pluralistic and, in the largest sense, liberal. Social systems like those of the United States, West Germany, and Japan (with perhaps a score of others among the world's nations) illustrate the type.

In the conventional view, the link between a democratic political system and a market economy is merely an accident of history. My argument is that the link is stronger: political democracy is compatible in practice only with a market economy. In turn, both systems nourish and are best nourished by a pluralistic liberal culture.

DO DEVELOPED NATIONS CAUSE POVERTY?

On few continents of the planet is the socialist myth more vigorous than in Latin America, where it seems well suited to the political culture, if badly suited to the moral culture, of traditional societies. The vision of socialism legitimates an authoritarian (even a

*From Michael Novak's *The Spirit of Democratic Capitalism* (New York: Simon & Schuster, 1982). Reprinted by permission of Simon & Schuster, a Division of Gulf & Western Corporation.

totalitarian) order. It ensures order and stability. In Cuba and Nicaragua, it permits the abrogation of elections and the suppression of dissent. It legitimates the wholesale indoctrination of populations in a millenarian vision. It unites the political system, the economic system, and the moral-cultural system under one set of authorities. It now inspires the most heavily armed states on the continent.

Yet one attraction of socialism may also be that it provides an excuse. Confronting the relatively inferior economic performance of their continent, the Catholic bishops of Latin America do not now blame themselves for the teachings about political economy which Latin American Catholicism has nourished for four hundred years. Conveniently, socialist theory allows them to blame the United States and other successful economic powers. No passion better fits the fundamental Marxist stencil, which offers a universally applicable paradigm: *If I am poor, my poverty is due to malevolent and powerful others.*

The use of this stencil illustrates a transformation in socialist theory. Whereas Marx based the promise of socialism upon the predicted failures of democratic capitalism, the new socialists attack its successes, to which they attribute their own failures. Democratic capitalism, they say, is responsible for the poverty of the third world. It typically creates a "center" which oppresses "the periphery," offers reform and development which either don't work or take too long, imposes unfavorable terms of trade on third world nations, and acts through multinational corporations which are outside the law.

It is odd, on the face of it, to blame the poverty of the rest of the world on democratic capitalism. Such poverty, after all, is hundreds of years older than its purported cause. Two hundred years ago, Latin America was poorer than it is today; but so was North America. At that time, Adam Smith drew attention to the two contrasting experiments taking place in "the New World," one on the southern continent and one on the northern, one based on the political economy of southern Europe, the other launching a new idea.

In those early days, Latin America seemed to have greater physical resources than North America. Much of its gold, silver, and lead ended up in the ornate churches and chapels of the Catholic church in Spain and Portugal. Columbus himself, seeking gold and other precious resources, sailed under a Spanish flag. By contrast, the first settlers in New England discovered a relatively harsh agricultural environment. Such riches as they won from North America consisted of tobacco, furs, corn, and later cotton, which they traded to Europe for manufactured goods.

In 1800, there were about 4 million European settlers in the United States, about 900,000 blacks, and an estimated 1 million "Indians". The population of South America was then 3 times larger, numbering 19 million, of which the original population of Indians, estimated at between 25 and 50 million in 1500, had been dramatically reduced. By 1940, the populations of the United States and Latin America were about equal, some 130 million each. By 1977, the population of the United States had reached a relatively stable 220 million but that of Latin America had shot up to 342 million.

In computing average per capita income, population is important in three ways. First, every newborn child lowers the average per capita income. Second, as the cohorts of those under age eighteen increase in proportion, the relative number of productive workers decreases. Third, rapidly increasing populations indicate that many parents have decided in favor of larger families, through whatever combination of motives. This is an admirable preference. But it has, in some but not all respects, economic costs. Those who make that choice cannot properly blame others for its consequences. Since 1940, the population of the United States has grown by 90 million, that of Latin America by 210 million.

In the nineteenth century, on both continents, independence was relatively new. Both had recently been colonies of the greatest powers in Europe. All through the nineteenth century, trade between Latin America and North America was negligible. Nearly all trade between either continent was transatlantic trade with Europe. In North America, the vast majority of persons became owners of their homes and lands; not so in Latin America. The moral-cultural system of North America placed great emphasis on building and working for the future. The moral-cultural system of Latin America favored other values. Either choice has its own costs and its own rewards.

Consider what might have been. Suppose that Latin America had developed industries and manufacturing before the United States. Clearly, the resources were available. Latin America is rich in oil, tin, bauxite, and many other important minerals. Its farmlands and tropical gardens are luxuriant. Why, then, didn't Latin America become the richer of the two continents of the New World? The answer appears to lie in the quite different nature of the Latin American political system, economic system, and moral-cultural system. The last is probably decisive. Latin America might have been economically active, progressive, and independent. Indeed, Latin America had the advantage of remaining outside World Wars I and II. It might long ago have placed the United States in its economic shadow. It might yet do so, if it were to organize itself to use its own great wealth in an appropriate way. Yet its Catholic bishops do not blame the Catholic church, the systems of political economy they long supported, or the past values and choices of its peoples. They blame the United States.

Specific emphasis is placed upon practices of trade. During the nineteenth century, trade between Latin America and the United States was minimal. Between 1900 and 1950, trade did begin to grow, but by 1950 the total historical investment of U.S. companies in Latin America totaled only $4.6 billion. During World War II, Western Europe lay in rubble, its economies broken, and Japan lay economically prostrate. After the war, trade between the United States and Latin America grew. Still, by 1965, the total value of all U.S. investments in Latin America was $11 billion. By 1965, investments by Western European nations and Japan, just beginning to revive after World War II, were not of great significance. It seems preposterous to believe that such small sums are responsible for the poverty or the dependence of Latin America. They are neither a high proportion of the wealth of the investing nations nor a high proportion of Latin America's internally generated wealth. The total U.S. investment of $11 billion averages out to $44 per capita for the 250 million Latin Americans of 1965. Moreover, U.S. investments in Western Europe and Japan during the same period were many times higher, without producing similar "dependence." Is it supposed that such investments in Latin America should have been forbidden altogether?

Traditional Catholic ignorance about modern economics may, in fact, have more to do with the poverty of Latin America than any other single factor. Consider the economic history of traditional Latin cultures.

LATIN CATHOLIC ECONOMICS

Max Weber observed that capitalism seemed to succeed first and most steadily in Protestant lands. He traced the origins of the modern capitalist ethos to Calvinism. Unfortunately, scholars also observed that capitalism was retarded for ideological reasons in certain Calvinist lands, too—Calvin's Geneva, for one. The empirical picture is a bit more complicated than Weber thought.

Hugh R. Trevor-Roper, for example, discovered that many of the great entrepreneurs of the sixteenth and seventeenth centuries are to be distinguished less by the fact that many were Calvinists than by the fact that nearly all were immigrants. Among them were some Calvinists, but also others who were Jewish or Catholic. Thus, Trevor-Roper asks, what made these entrepreneurs migrate? Why did they find some cities and some regimes hospitable and others (including Calvinist ones) inhospitable? The details of Trevor-Roper's argument are rich and the scholarship he cites broad. The basic picture he draws indicts Catholic Counter Reformation economies, particularly that of the Castilian monarchy of Spain, then at the zenith of its imperial power.

Trevor-Roper uncovers many surprising patterns of fact. He discovers the remote origins of capitalism, both as a system of production and as a technique of financing, in Catholic cities like Antwerp, Liege, Lisbon, Augsburg, Milan, Lucca. "These were the centers of European capitalism in 1500," Trevor-Roper writes. Yet between 1550 and 1620 these centers were "convulsed, and the secret techniques of capitalism were carried away to other cities, to be applied in new lands."[1] Why?

For Trevor-Roper, the decisive factor was a new alliance of church and state, more intolerable with each passing year, which drove the new class of Catholic businessmen in some cases out of their church but in many more cases out of their native cities and homelands. They sought out cities no longer under the control of princes and bishops; they sought self-governing cities of a republican character. A sharp contrast arose between such cities and the religio-economic shortsightedness of the Spanish Empire. Made rich by silver from South America, the Spaniards, who represented the dominant Catholic state, misperceived the basis of their new economic strength. Officials of church and state grew ever more numerous. They produced little, being parasitic upon the producers, whom they gouged and regulated until the latter emigrated. With relative suddenness, then, the strongholds of the Counter Reformation economically declined and northern European centers of commerce gained the ascendancy. Trevor-Roper concludes: "The Calvinist and for that matter the Jewish entrepreneurs of northern Europe were not a new native growth: they were an old growth transplanted. Weber, in seeing the 'spirit of Capitalism' as something new, whose origins must be sought in the sixteenth century, inverted the problem. The novelty lay not in the entrepreneurs themselves, but in the circumstances which drove them to emigrate."[2]

The Counter Reformation state impugned the religious value of commerce. It banned or restricted enterprise in the private sector. It licensed certain entrepreneurs to develop state monopolies; it favored state mercantilism over private mercantilism. "It was a change," Trevor-Roper reports, "which occurred predominantly in countries of the Spanish clientele."[3]

At the time of America's founding—Latin America and North America alike—Spain and Portugal were the world's dominant and most active powers. But the philosophers and theologians of Spain and Portugal failed to grasp the inner secret that had made them so and, careless of it, lost it. For their colonies in the New World as well as for their nations of birth, this failure of Catholic intelligence was a calamity. It is sad to see it being taken up again by a new generation of bishops and theologians, eager once again to prefer state control to liberty, seeking to ally the church with state authority as once their predecessors allied it with the *ancien regime*.

The classical interpretation of Catholic history holds, with Pius XI, that the tragedy of the nineteenth century was the loss of the working class. Trevor-Roper's essay suggests a more radical thesis: the tragedy of the seventeenth century, setting in motion the tragedy of the nineteenth, was the failure of Catholic thinking to grasp the creative potential of democratic capitalism. One result was that many early republicans and liberals, opposed to premodern ways of thought, were confirmed in the practical necessity of being anticlerical and anti-Catholic. The revulsion against religion on the part of liberals and republicans was most pronounced in Latin lands, which to this day still suffer under the legacy of "laicism," as did Pius IX in Italy before he issued his "Syllabus of Errors," and as Mexico has since its anti-clerical revolution. The conflict was not one-sided. Latin Catholic theology bears its due proportion of the blame.

Such theology remains in its premodern phase, as is evident—not only in Latin lands—by such statements as the following, by the Catholic bishops of Peru in 1969:

> Like other nations in the Third World, we are the victims of systems that exploit our natural resources, control our political decisions, and impose on us the cultural domination of their values and consumer civilization. . . . The more we try to change, the stronger the forces of domination become. Foreign interests increase their repressive measures by means of economic sanctions in the international markets and by control of loans and other types of aid. News agencies and the communications media, which are controlled by the powerful, do not express the rights of the weak; they distort reality by filtering information in accord with their vested interests.

"We are the victims," the bishops say. They accept no responsibility for three centuries of hostility to trade, commerce, and industry. They seem to imagine that loans and aid should be tendered them independently of economic laws, and that international markets should operate without economic sanctions. After having opposed modern economics for centuries, they claim to be aggrieved because others, once equally poor, have succeeded as they have not.

Are the bishops really expert in technical matters of international trade? Before pronouncing moral condemnation, do they understand the laws which affect international currencies? Do they wish to enjoy the wealth of our systems without having first learned how wealth may be produced and without changing their economic teachings? The Peruvian aristocracy and military were for three centuries under their tutelage. Did the Peruvian bishops for three centuries teach them that the vocation of the layman lay in producing wealth, economic self-reliance, industry, and commerce, and in being creative stewards thereof?

Yet this intellectual failure appears, as well, among North American bishops. In an unsigned pamphlet, "Development-Dependency: the Role of Multinational Corporations" (1974), the Catholic bishops of the United States say of themselves and their people, "We are a people so deeply committed in theory, if not in practice, to the philosophy or the ideology of free enterprise in the old-fashioned sense of the word . . ." This statement, in form an empirical statement, is not true of the bishops themselves. It is not true of most American economists.

The text and footnotes of the bishops' statement are filled with misinformation and innuendo. The author writes in the name of the bishops:

> In the period between 1950 and 1965, U.S. private corporations invested $3.8 billion in Latin America. Part of the profits were retained in Latin America to increase the total investment of the companies concerned; part of the profits were remitted to the United States. From this investment of $3.8 billion, no less than $11.3 billion in profits were remitted home to the United States, while the profits retained locally increased the investment of $3.8 billion to $10.3 billion.

There are several conflicting statements in this passage, even if we accept its highly problematic figures. First, the total investment made by U.S. corporations between 1950 and 1965, as given, averages out to $253 million per year. This does not seem like sufficient money to make all of Latin America "dependent." Second, the bishops ignore investments made before 1950. As we have seen, these totaled $4.6 billion. This figure must be added to the $3.8 billion invested between 1950-65 in establishing the base on which a return is made. Third, the bishops point out that many profits were reinvested during 1950-65. Presumable the same occurred prior to 1950. The bishops say that with reinvested profits, total investment during 1950-65 reached $10.3 billion. They do not give the cumulative total for the pre-1950 period. Finally, the bishops say that $11.3 billion in profits was remitted to the United States during the fifteen years. There is no way of telling, from their figures, on what base of cumulative investment these returns should be calculated. But perhaps a simple illustration will do. Invested at eight percent interest, money will double in about ten years. In fifteen years, at that rate of return, and investment of $10 billion should have more than doubled, simply if left in a bank. If the bishops intended to shock their readers concerning returns on Latin American investment during 1950-65, they did not make the case.

THE QUESTION OF DEPENDENCY

Consider the assertion of Archbishop Dom Helder Camara of Brazil before the World Council of Churches in 1970: "It is a sad fact that 80 percent of the world's resources are at the disposal of 20 percent of the world's inhabitants."[4] This assertion is not exactly true. Most of the world's oil, for example, appears to be in the hands of nations like Venezuela, Mexico, Nigeria, Saudi Arabia, Kuwait, Libya, and Iran. Such curious expressions as "the third world" and "the South" mask many contradictions. It cannot factually be said that all third world nations are poor. Furthermore, most of the poor in the world—in India and other parts of Asia, for example, including China—are to be found north of the equator. In fact, the word "resources," as used by the archbiship, must also be stripped of ideology. What he describes as "a sad fact" is sad only if looked at from one ideological perspective. It is only a fact, and only a partially true one. Quite diverse cultural histories lie behind it.

The combustion engine was invented under democratic capitalism barely a century ago. The first oil well was dug in Titusville, Pennsylvania, in 1859, and the first oil well in the Middle East was dug only in 1909. If oil is today to be considered a "resource," one must recall how short a time ago the entire human race lay in ignorance of its potential. Most of the materials we today call resources were not known to be such before the invention of a democratic capitalist political economy; many were not known to be such even one hundred years ago. (Presumably, there are others which we do not yet appreciate.) Material remains inert until its secrets are discovered and a technology for bending it to human purposes is invented. The word "resources," therefore, includes within its meaning the factor of culture, of which discovery and invention are expressions. Protestant European culture, in particular, has been exceedingly fertile in the discovery of such resources and in the invention of such technologies. Among Nobel Prize winners in science, Protestants have been conspicuously prominent.

Thus Archbishop Camara might have observed in fairness: "It is a marvelous fact that 80 percent—maybe even 90 percent—of the world's resources have been discovered and put to use during the past century by one of the smaller cultures on the planet. The benefits of such discoveries have been carried to every continent, but more must now be done in this direction." Dom Helder Camara, of course, was trying to make a moral rather than a scientific point. Furthermore, he was trying to make an ideological point. He was trying to suggest that there is something "sad" in the preeminence of a minority culture in the discovery of resources and in the invention of technologies for using them. Some cultures have organized their political economy precisely for this purpose. Others have not.

Nothing prevented Brazilians from inventing the combustion engine, the radio, the airplane, penicillin, and other technologies which give resources their utility. Although Brazil is apparently one of the most richly endowed of all nations in material resources, neither Brazil nor other Latin American nations have so far provided a system favorable to invention and discovery. So, in a sense, the archbishop's observation is merely a truism: Those cultures which value the intelligent and inventive use of God's creation are far better off than those which do not. He cannot mean to imply that intelligence and invention on the part of some obstruct intelligence and invention of the part of others, for that would be absurd. Latin America is responsible for its own condition. It had beginnings very like those of North America. The system established there has not, on the record, been as sucessful as many would now like it to become.

As late as 1850, the difference between the per capita income of Latin America and that of North America was not great. Most of the new technologies the world now knows had not then been invented. Sailing vessels were still of creaking wood and billowing sail. Although steam-powered locomotives were in use, they were still primitive and few. Most agricultural labor was by hand, and such machinery as had been invented—like the reaper and the combine—were pulled by animals. Highways were designed for horseback, carriage, and cart. Wars were fought with muskets and cannon.

In population, Latin America in 1850 numbered 33 million, the United States 23 million (and all North America 26 million). Manufacturing was more highly developed in a few states in North America than anywhere in Latin America, but both continents were largely agricultural. The mining industries of Latin America were far more important than those of North America. The economy of Western Europe was stronger than that of either continent of the New World, and both continents depended upon Europe for most of their manufactures. But in some respects, certain regions of both continents enjoyed a higher standard of living than southern Italy, parts of Spain and Portugal, and other sectors of Western and Eastern Europe, and both, therefore, attracted immigrants.

In 1850, Great Britain was just completing seventy straight years during which, with a dynamism never before matched in history, its gross national product grew every year by an average of nearly two percent a year. This seemingly miraculous achievement introduced into the world the reality of economic development. It also gave material substance to the notion of "progress" which had long fascinated the imagination of the West. The law of patents had greatly stimulated invention, as had the Royal Society. In every decade and in almost every year, new technologies excited the populace.

Why after 1850, then, did the journeys of North America and Latin America dramatically diverge? Why for the next one hundred years did one remain almost static, while the other steadily but ever more rapidly developed? During that century, North America hardly needed Latin America. Latin America hardly needed North America. The volume of trade between them was highest in 1892, when the United States exported goods worth $96 million in Latin America and imported $290 million. Things did not much improve prior to 1950. By the end of 1929, total U.S. investment in Latin America was valued at $3.5 billion, and by the end of 1950 $4.6 billion.

Latin Americans do not value the same moral qualities as North Americans. The two cultures see the world quite differently. Latin Americans seem to feel inferior to North Americans in practical matters, but superior in spiritual ones. In Latin American experience, powerful personages control almost everything. From this experience, it is easy to imagine that the whole world must work this way, and to project such expectations upon North America. It must be said, then, that relations between North and South America are emotional as well as economic. The "Catholic" aristocratic ethic of Latin America places more emphasis on luck, heroism, status, and *figura* than the relatively "Protestant" ethic of North America, which values diligent work, steadfast regularity, and the responsible seizure of opportunity. Between two such different ways of looking at the world, intense love-hate relations are bound to develop. Looking at North America, Latins are likely to attribute its more advanced status to luck—and also to a kind of aristocratic power. In their experience, wealth is relatively static and what is given to one is taken from another.

By contrast, looking at Latin America, a North American is likely to attribute its backwardness to an ethos better suited to aristocrats, monks, and peasants, who lack respect for commerce and industrial life and the moral virtues on which these depend. As Latin Americans do not admire northern virtues, North Americans do not entirely approve of Latin virtues. Thus most North Americans are likely to feel not a shred of guilt for the relative economic position of the two continents.

However, some North Americans are susceptible to the guilt feelings which flow from the reverse side of the "Protestant" ethic: the demand for perfect charity. Some feel unworthy of their own success. Some take many accusations to heart. They are inclined to believe Gustave Gutiérrez's accusation in his bestselling *A Theology of Liberation*:

> The underdeveloped of poor nations, as a global social fact, is then unmasked as the historical sub-product of the development of other countries. In fact, the dynamic of the capitalist system leads to establishment of a center and a periphery, simulaneously generating progress and riches for the few, and social disequilibrium, political tensions and poverty for the majority.[5]

Gutiérrez believes that the decisive liberation for Latin America will be socialism: liberation from private property. This is not a theological interpretation of development, but an economic one. Moreover, his thesis of dependency is only one economic theory among many. It cannot be said to have biblical authority. It does not square with many of the facts. It has many internal problems of its own. Official reports of the UN Economic Commission on Latin America give the most accurate account of the available facts. A brilliant young scholar who works for that commission, Joseph Ramos, an economist for the UN's International Labor Organization and a professor at the Catholic Latin American Institute on Doctrine and Social Studies (ILADES) in Santiago, prepared background papers on economics for the Catholic bishops' meeting at Puebla in 1979, and has elsewhere replied to Gutiérrez courteously and eloquently. In what follows, I draw upon the outline of his assessment of the economics of liberation theology, upon the UN statistical record, and upon U.S. Department of Commerce reports. In particular, I follow his review of Gutiérrez's book.[6]

First, in embracing the dependency theory and the center-periphery theory, Gutiérrez inherits all the factual and theoretical weaknesses of those theories. In an interdependent world, every nation is in some ways dependent upon every other. The most highly developed nations are quite dependent upon the oil-producing nations, for example. If one regards the oil nations as part of the periphery, they are, clearly, able to exploit nations in the center. If they are now to be located in the center—having until recently been on the periphery—then the original theory of center-periphery is a truism: a "center" is any self-reliant, economically active locale.

Moreover, interdependence is seldom symmetrical. The economy of the United States is six times larger than that of Latin America. A recession in the United States may seriously affect Latin America; the reverse may not be true. The dependence of the United States on Latin America is real but different in kind from that of Latin America on the United States.

Secondly, Gutiérrez seems to think that progress and riches in one place must subtract from what is available in another place. In fact, the world economy, since the industrial revolution, has become expansive and dynamic. There is today far more wealth than there was two hundred years ago. Absolutely, the wealth of virtually every nation and region is greater than it was. Average life expectancy is higher. Hygiene and health are better. Some modernization is in place. Yet, relatively, individual nations rise and fall as events, needs, and exertions favor first one, then another. The rise of Japan has been as spectacular as the decline of Great Britain.

Moreover, the mere existence of dependency does not mean that the underdevelopment of Latin America is due to the development of the United States, or vice versa. A battery of facts must be accounted for: (1) Only five percent of total U.S. investment is made abroad, and only seven percent of its production is exported. The United States depends relatively little on foreign trade. (2) About seventy percent of U.S. foreign investments and exports go to developed countries. Fewer than twenty percent of U.S. foreign investments go to Latin America. U.S. investment in Latin America represents less than one percent of the U.S. gross national product. (3) The average rate of return on U.S. investments in Latin America has not been particularly high, either before 1950 or during the years 1950 to 1977. This return has been higher than in Canada but lower than in Europe, Australia, Asia, and Africa. The after-tax return on U.S. capital in Latin America is approximately ten percent. (4) The often-repeated statement that U.S. investors in the third world take out more in profit than they invest is, for all sound investments, a truism. To invest $1,000 in a savings account for ten years is to hope to withdraw significantly more than the original $1,000. These new funds are then available for new investment elsewhere. Without such growth, economies stagnate and investment is futile. One might as well be a miser. (5) To argue that U.S. corporate profits depend to a high degree on investments in the third world is to err. Only about two hundred U.S. firms account for most of U.S. investments overseas. Of these, virtually all make most of their investments in the United States and in the developed world. As a proportion, their investments in Latin America are small. About twenty firms account for half of all U.S. overseas profits. For such U.S. transnationals— General Motors and General Electric, for example—investments and sales within the United States are, year by year, far more significant than those in the third world. In some years, profits made in some operations make up for costs incurred for new investments elsewhere. One must examine investments over time. (6) The United States has for many years suffered a balance-of-payments deficit; the total value of its imports exceeds that of its exports. The net effect is a weakening of the dollar in relation to other currencies.

These six facts oblige Professor Ramos to reject the center-periphery theory of dependence. Belief in such a dubious theory hinges, of course, on other assumptions. Professor Ramos also deals with these. Suppose, he says, exploitation does exist. The exploitation of one people by another has existed since the beginning of history. "However, until the Industrial Revolution, no people, no matter how exploitative or imperialistic they were, could reach a generalized, sustained level of economic development."[7] A few nations first reached this level through science, technology, and economic organization. The "wealth" of the center is due far more to such factors than to its colonies. The contrast between Great Britain and Spain since 1500 permits no other conclusion.

Secondly, Gutiérrez may find it "attractive to place the fundamental blame for our problems on dependency (and by so doing blame others)," Ramos writes, but "might not this dependence rather be a reflection of the internal obstacles which are concentrated within our countries?" Ramos notes that each presently developed country also began in dependency. "The United States broke out of its dependency on what was then the world's greatest power, while Latin America, colonized at the same time, still fails to do so." Since Spain and Portugal are among the most underdeveloped countries of Europe, Ramos suggests that "internal structures common to Latin American and Iberian countries are the fundamental obstacles to overcoming underdevelopment."[8]

In the same vein, Gutiérrez believes (oddly) that underdevelopment in Latin America is due to "private property." But Ramos calls attention to a special characteristic of Latin American property rights: "the initial extreme concentration of economic and political power (since Colonial times) in the hands of a few, and the consequent limitation of opportunities."[9] In the United States, by contrast, property, power, and opportunities were distributed much more equally from the beginning. For Ramos, a narrow concentration of wealth has negative effects quite visible in regional variations both in the United States and in Latin America. In the U.S. South, where power and wealth were concentrated in the landholding system, vigorous development was delayed until after World War II. By contrast, the Midwest and Far West, even though they were also agricultural regions, experienced more rapid development through a system of family property and relative equality. In Latin America, the regions of least economic and political concentration are most developed. Thus private property is not always narrowly concentrated. Development seems to depend on its diffusion.

Thirdly, when Gutiérrez rejects sentimental appeals to brotherhood, which disguise class conflict, Ramos appreciates his desire to abolish the causes of class conflict. But he finds Gutiérrez "ideological and ahistorical" in overlooking "the most significant economic fact of modern times, namely that wealth can be created." All economies prior to the Industrial Revolution were (relatively) static. Under static conditions, the economic improvement of some is necessarily obtained at the cost of others. For this reason, "the central concern of static economies, like the medieval one, has been the fixing of just prices and wages." In the early medieval economy, capital did not produce new wealth. Thus the taking of interest was judged to involve the terrible sin of usury, since through it one took advantage of those in need. But once capital became creative and its utility in economic progress became clear, moral interpretation was obliged to shift its ground. Thus Ramos urges Gutiérrez to shift ground too, by recognizing that relations of mutual advantage and cooperation are essential to dynamic economies, even though relations of conflict never disappear. To emphasize class conflict but not mutual advantage is to ignore real interests.

Ramos does not accept the Marxian theory that classes are rooted in the relation to property. For him the relation to power is more significant, and assumes different forms in different times and places. Relative scarcity yields one common form of economic power. Such scarcity may involve land, water, transport, capital, technology, knowledge, oil, arms, etc. "It does not suffice to have property in order to dominate; domination requires possession of the critical form of power in each historical moment."[10] At different times in history, the military caste, the clergy, the landlords, the industrialists, the bankers, the politicians, the technocrats have been pre-eminent. There is not one class struggle but many; and their root is not property but power. As a result, class struggle will not disappear with the abolition of private property. Struggle over the political allocation of power and goods is historically one of the most bitter forms of struggle. Nationalization of ownership always generates class stuggle, to the extent that the participation of citizens is only a formality, while decision-making power lies in the hands of the party, the bureaucracy, and the police. Private property is a device to limit the power of the state. It undergirds the principle of subsidiarity, by giving citizens rights to make decisions about what each knows best.

Finally, Ramos deplores "the exaggerated tendency of Catholic theology to interpret social relations as though they were interpersonal relations." The error of socialists is to trust the ideals of socialism while disregarding their structural results. Gutiérrez ends his book with a plea for "a definitive stand, and without reservations, on the side of the oppressed classes and dominated peoples."[11] His good motives are clear. But the unintended consequences of his economic theories are not likely to constitute the liberation he desires.

In matters of political economy, much stands or falls on fact. The liberation theologians widely assert that development and reform in Latin America are not working. "Not working" compared to what? It is worth pausing to reflect on the facts, first of success, then of failure.

THE SUCCESS OF LATIN AMERICA

In 1945, the population of Latin America was 140 million. Between 1945 and 1960, the gross national product of Latin America averaged an annual growth rate of 4.9 percent. From 1960 to 1965, the rate was 5.3 percent; from 1965 to 1970, 5.7 percent; and from 1970 to 1974, 6.7 percent. The world recession slowed growth in Latin America in 1975 (2.7 percent); in 1976 the rate was back up to 5 percent.

Thus, for the thirty years from 1945 to 1975, Latin America averaged an annual growth of 5.2 percent. Few regions of the world exhibit such a sustained success. In this century, the wealth of Latin America has doubled, and then doubled again, more than once. Since World War II, manufacturing has grown at a rate of 6.5 percent each year. In addition, agricultural output per worker grew by more than 2 percent a year, and total agricultural output by 3.5 percent each year. Since population growth averaged 2.7 percent a year, agriculture yield has grown faster. This compares favorably with agricultural output in the United States from the end of the Civil War until World War I, when agricultural output grew at 2.1 percent a year and average output per worker at 2.5 percent.

In real terms, wages and salaries in Latin America have grown since World War II at an annual average of two percent a year. This is better than the United States experienced from 1865-1914. Wages and salaries have not grown as fast, however, as returns on capital. In part, this is because large agricultural sectors, with expanding populations, share slowly in the development of commerce and industry which occurs in cities. Rising returns on capital tend to attract new capital. While dynamic growth in some sectors does not automatically flow to other sectors, it does provide new wealth which sound political systems may invest in rural electrification and other institutions.

The rates of growth in real wages, in manufacturing, and in agriculture income and output per worker are all the more remarkable when one recoginzes that during the same 30-year period, 1945 to 1975, Latin America's population grew from 140 million to 324 million. It is a happy thing on every other index to have a living, healthy child; the one index which each new child lowers, however, is per capita income. Yet despite Latin America's immense growth in population, its per capita income has grown at rates seldom equaled on so sustained a basis anywhere in the world. Per capita income in Latin America stood in 1976 at $1,000.

In 30 years, infant mortality was reduced significantly. Life expectancy advanced from approximately 42 years to 62 years. Despite immense population growth, illiteracy has been reduced from 50 percent to 25 percent (absolute numbers, though, remain large: about 80 million persons). In 1945, only 55 percent of primary-school-age children attended school; the figure in 1975 was 90 percent. In high school, the jump was from 10 percent to 35 percent. The percentage of those from 20 to 24 years old attending universities has gone from 2 percent to 9 percent.

Obviously, these figures cry out for improvement. Still, what accounts for the sudden explosion of growth in 1945, after centuries of relative stagnation? Foreign aid and foreign investment cannot account for it, since together these make up less that 4 percent of Latin America's annual internal investment. Favorable terms of foreign trade do not account for it, for these terms have been lower than in the nineteenth century. Structural reforms cannot account for it, for these have been relatively few; there have been few major land reforms, tax reforms, or dramatic institutional reforms.

In the opinion of Ramos, the most satisfactory explanation is that the advantages of being a "late starter" have finally been seized. Latin Americans are closing the technological, organizational and management gaps which once separated them from the developed world. The power of ideals and intelligence, learning and application, is much in evidence. Religion itself is becoming more dynamic. There has been a breakthrough beyond the ranks of the narrow elite at the top. It has not yet reached millions at the bottom, but revolutions in "human capital" have set a great dynamism in motion. Whereas, for example, U.S. AID officers once struck Latin Americans as better prepared than their local counterparts, today Latin American economists and experienced officials possess training and skills superior to those of the average foreign adviser. Finally, late-starting nations may take advantage of already developed technologies and thus deploy relatively less capital in research and development.

THE FAILURE OF LATIN AMERICA

Impressive growth in GNP, in per capita income, in literacy, in education, in health, and in longevity represent human goods of great value to Latin America. But such figures also mask inequalities, uneven distributions, and massive suffering.

Latin economists, Sergio Molina and Sebastian Piñera, have calculated that in 1970 about 40 percent of all Latin Americans (some 115 million persons) received an income below the poverty line of approximately $200 per year. Still lower on the scale of poverty, at the destitution level, about 19 percent (some 56 million persons) received less than the $100 per year required to purchase foodstuffs providing a minimum level of calories and protein for subsistence.[12]

It is clear that the fruits of spectacular economic growth are not reaching all parts of the population. The 56 million destitute need urgent care. The total 115 million poor need rapid improvement of their condition. Between 1960 and 1970, the percentage of the poor fell from 51 percent to 40 percent and of the destitute from 26 percent to 19 percent. But because of population growth, absolute figures were virtually unchanged (down only about 2 million in each category).

What would it take to raise all Latin Americans above the destitution line? Molina, Piñera, and Ramos calculate $100 per year for 56 million persons, or over $5 billion annually. To raise all the destitute and the poor above the poverty line would require another $11 billion per year. Compared to the GNP of Latin America, this $16 billion represents (depending upon its exact calculation) about 5 percent. As a percentage of government spending in 1970 it would have represented 22 percent. As a percentage of the continent's total disposable income in 1970, it represented about 6 percent.

These figures show that Latin America already has at its disposal sufficient annual income and gross national product to raise the level of its 56 million destitute persons almost immediately. The economic capacity is present. The political will and the economic techniques may not yet be present. Techniques which do not discourage greater production are indispensable. On the other hand, the diffusion of purchasing power to the poorest 25 percent of the population is in the interest of domestic manufacturers, farmers, and traders. An additional healthy 56 million persons would provide markets for goods and promote new forms of economic activism. In a dynamic economy, the economic activities and skills of each person offer mutual advantage to all others.

Molina and Piñera observe that income differentials among employees explain only about half the difference in per capita income between poor and nonpoor households. The rest is explained because the non-poor tend to have a higher number of employed adults per household and a lower number of dependent minors. The vast majority of heads of households are employed. A high percentage complains of underemployment (less than thirty-nine hours a week) and desires more. Simultaneously, many large social tasks remain unaccomplished. The economic infrastructure to support future growth will require investment and labor to build roads and bridges, sewage and sanitation, generators and power lines, communications facilities and urban water supplies, rural irrigation and facilities for transport.

The case of Brazil is often cited. Ramos points out that prior to 1964 the nonmilitary governments in Brazil sustained an average annual growth rate of 5.5 percent a year. After the military coup in 1966, the growth rate jumped to 9 percent a year. By 1970, every decile of the population had benefited in real terms. Relatively, however, the poorest deciles were receiving a lesser proportion of national income, the upper deciles a larger proportion. Between 1970 and 1976, the relative position as well as the absolute position of the poorest deciles improved.[13] Still, the contrast between the richest and the poorest is stark. Behind the cold statistics there are families whose children lack sufficient calories and protein for normal activities and normal growth.

Ramos proposes that $5 billion be invested every year for ten years (a total of $50 billion), from funds already internally generated in Latin America, to improve the lot of the destitute. The exact schemes he proposed for this ten-year crash program need not detain us, for they are matters best decided by those closest to them.[14] The central point Ramos makes is that of scale. The problem of reaching the destitute and the poor is not insuperable. Resources are available.

THE CRUX

When they write of institutions, the liberation theologians seem to be in favor of socialism. When they write of individual persons, they seem to be in favor of economic independence, self-reliance, personal creativity, and self-determination. They write of land distribution and of land ownership on the part of peasants. Is it conceivable that by "socialism" many liberation theologians actually intend an ideal compatible with, and more accurately described as, democratic capitalism? They are in favor of self-reliance, the communitarian individual, a sense of providence and serendipity compatible with equal opportunity and self-improvement. They seem to favor an open, mobile, pluralist society. They seem to want private property, independence from the state, institutions of human rights, and full liberties for the moral and cultural system.

On the other hand, they give little encouragement to economic activism, much to political activism. While they do not seem intent upon banning the activities of foreign corporations from Latin America entirely, they do not seem to grasp the role business corporations—especially domestic ones—might play in building up the structures of middle-class democracy. Their rage against the existing order and against foreign multinationals prevents them from thinking institutionally about how to devise checks and balances against corporate power, while using it creatively to check clerical and military power. They have not thought theologically about the vocation of laymen and laywomen in the world, particularly in commerce and industry. They have not discerned the spiritual hunger of the commercial and industrial classes (including white-collar and blue-collar workers) for a theological vision of daily work. They have not seen how the three strongest institutions in Latin America—the clergy, the military, and the traditional landholding class—may be checked by the growth of a new middle class based in commerce and industry. They have not grasped the importance of economic growth to the sense of legitimacy on which democracy depends.

There are many in Latin America who perceive that tyranny necessarily follows from the unitary system of socialism. Many also see that an alliance of the clergy and socialist leaders will result in the same sort of arrangement which has plagued traditional Latin American societies. Many are alarmed at the bleakness and grayness of life in Cuba, at Cuba's total financial dependency on the Soviet Union (funds which may be cut off at any time), and at its subservience to Soviet military and police power. Many are dismayed at Nicaragua's growing army and network of domestic surveillance, its failure to hold elections, its assassinations of dissidents, its economic stagnations, and its international alliances. In Jamaica, enough popular forces were disgusted by the economic shambles to which the socialists had reduced the nation to vote them out on October 30, 1980. Thus support for a democratic capitalist alternative to socialism still exists.

Yet at present there is no intellectual vision of the liberation yet to come through democratic capitalism. There are neither books nor parties, neither leaders nor dedicated followers. This intellectual vacuum is dangerous. But the institutional vacuum is also dangerous. Democratic capitalism depends upon the vigor of many rival institutions. It needs strong, disciplined, intellectually alert unions. It needs churches committed to pluralism, democracy, and the lay vocation. It needs a business community with a vision larger than that of free enterprise alone—a vision of the pluralist system of democratic capitalism—and with a real concern for bringing the entire population into the market system as self-determining agents. It needs a military respectful of legitimacy—the consent of the governed, and constitutional succession in political office. It needs political leaders who can act upon a vision that breaks the traditional oscillation of Latin political cultures between hierarchy and anarchy.

In this respect, liberation theologians have yet to show intellectual mastery of the institutional requirements of a free political economy. Choosing the utopian road, they seem to imitate the Grand Inquisitor, who out of pity for the people promised bread, not liberty.

The continent of Latin America is richly favored in natural resources and immense human vitalities. Its biblical heritage gives it a spiritual basis for that realism which alone leads to political and economic liberation. During this century, its peoples have already experienced a great awakening. Their economic and social achievements are many and more are yet to come.

Yet Latin America does face a crux. Shall the church in Latin America encourage its people along the road of unitary socialism—or along the road of pluralistic democratic capitalism? More than good intentions and high motives are needed. Decisions about the shape of the system qua system, about the political economy qua economy, will have consequences far beyond those willed by individuals. The people desire bread. They also desire liberty. Not only is it possible to have both, the second is a key to the first.

In thinking about political economy, some theologians, myself included, praise the liberation theologians for sustained work that raises important questions. Still, we worry that their path to liberation is ill-defended against state tyranny, is vulnerable to a new union of church and state (this time on the left), and is likely to lead to economic decline. Such results would not be looked upon kindly by future generations.

Liberation Theology

NOTES

1. H. R. Trevor-Roper, "Religion, The Reformation and Social Change," in *The European Witch-Craze of the Sixteenth and Seventeenth Centuries and Other Essays* (New York: Harper & Row, 1969) p. 21.

2. Ibid., p. 28.

3. Ibid., p. 30.

4. Dom Helder Camara, "A Christian Commitment is Needed for Latin America," *Latin America Calls*, March 1970, p. 4.

5. Gustavo Gutiérrez, *A Theology of Liberation*, Trans, Sr. Caridad Inda and John Eagleson (Maryknoll, N.Y.: Orbis Books, 1973) p. 84.

6. See Joseph Ramos, "Reflections on Gustavo Gutiérrez's Theology of Liberation"; "Dependency and Development: An Attempt to Clarify the Issues"; "On the Prospect of Social Market Democrary (or Democratic Capitalism) in Latin America"; and "Latin America: The End of Democratic Reformism?" in Michael Novak, ed., *Liberation North—Liberation South* (Washington, D. C.: American Enterprise Institute, 1981).

7. Ramos, "Reflections on Gustavo Gutiérrez's Theology of Liberation," op. cit., p. 55.

8. Ibid., pp. 55-56.

9. Ibid., p. 56.

10. Ibid., p. 58.

11. Ibid.

12. Sergio Molina and Sebastian Piñera, "Extreme Poverty in Latin America," in *Liberation South—Liberation North*, op. cit., p. 82.

13. Ramos, op. cit., p. 77.

14. Ibid., p. 79.

THE CHRISTIAN CHOICE BETWEEN CAPITALISM AND SOCIALISM

Ronald H. Nash

Ronald H. Nash

Ronald H. Nash is professor of philosophy and head of the department of philosophy and religion at Western Kentucky University. A graduate of Barrington College and Brown University, he received his Ph.D. in philosophy from Syracuse University. Prior to going to Western Kentucky University in 1964, he taught philosophy and religion at Barrington College, Houghton College and Syracuse University. Dr. Nash is the author or editor of twelve books including *Christian Faith and Historical Understanding, The Concept of God, Social Justice and the Christian Church, The Word of God and The Mind of Man, Freedom, Justice and the State, Ideas of History*, and *The Light of the Mind: St. Augustine's Theory of Knowledge*. His articles have appeared in such journals as *The New Scholasticism, The Intercollegiate Review, The Reformed Journal, Christianity Today*, and *Christian Scholar's Review*.

THE CHRISTIAN CHOICE BETWEEN CAPITALISM AND SOCIALISM — Ethics of Capitalism

The foundation of liberation theology is a set of three claims: (1) Christians ought to become politically active on behalf of people who are poor and oppressed; (2) The major cause of poverty, injustice and oppression in the contemporary world is capitalism; (3) Christians should attack capitalism and work to see it replaced by socialism. Although assorted liberation theologians may assert a great deal more than this, it seems fair to say that all liberation theologians agree with these three basic claims.

Like most of the contributors to this book, I happen to believe that Christians ought to be politically active for the poor and oppressed. The purpose of this chapter is to point out the weakness of the liberation theologian's case against capitalism and to suggest that the liberation cause actually needs to be turned rightside up. The poor and oppressed peoples of the world need the help of committed Christians who will become involved in social and political action. But what they really need is a *new* liberation theology that will recognize the irrelevance and falseness of socialist attacks on capitalism, that will unmask the threats that socialism poses to liberty and economic recovery, and that will act to move existing economic institutions and practices closer to the principles of a free market system that alone offers the hope of economic progress.

I have already evaluated critically the fifteen most commonly used arguments against capitalism in two earlier books.[1] Those earlier discussions consider all of the usual Marxist claims that by now are so familiar. This chapter will focus on the kinds of considerations that interest someone who not merely calls himself a Christian, but who sincerely desires his faith and practice to be consistent with the normative documents and teachings of the historic Christian religion.

THE CONTEMPORARY BIAS AGAINST CAPITALISM

It is important to begin by noting that many intellectuals, including a great number of people in so-called capitalist nations, approach any new investigation of the subject with a bias against capitalism. Whatever the reasons, they have already prejudged capitalism to be unjust, evil and irrational.[2] As economist Israel Kirzner points out: "One of the most intriguing paradoxes surrounding modern capitalism is the hate, the fear, and the contempt with which it is commonly regarded. Every ill in contemporary society is invariably blamed on business, on the pursuit of private profit, on the institution of private ownership."[3] Capitalism is blamed for every evil in contemporary society including its greed, materialism and selfishness, the prevalence of fraudulent behavior, the debasement of society's tastes, the pollution of the environment, the alienation and despair within society, and the vast disparities of wealth. Even racism and sexism are treated as effects of capitalism. With such an easily identifiable cause of society's ills, it is little wonder the critic of capitalism has such an easy solution, the replacement of capitalism by a "just economic system," a euphemism for some type of centrally controlled economy.

But when one looks beyond the bias against capitalism for the reasons and arguments that support such strongly negative attitudes, something very surprising emerges. For one thing, what frequently pass as criticisms of capitalism are not arguments but sermons and slogans unsupported by anything remotely resembling reasons or evidence. Moreover, many objections to capitalism result from a simple but clearly fallacious two-step operation. First, some undesirable feature is noted in a society in which a market economy presumably functions. Then it is simply asserted that capitalism is the cause of this problem. Logic texts call this the *fallacy of false cause*. Mere coincidence does not prove a casual connection. Such critics of capitalism conveniently overlook the fact that the features of capitalist societies they find so offensive also exist in socialist societies.

The attempt to produce a fair evaluation of capitalism is complicated further by the fact that the very term *capitalism* has for many people a strongly negative meaning. For most of these people, calling a person a capitalist is tantamount to calling him a fascist or racist. This negative emotive content of *capitalism* is hardly accidental since Karl Marx himself coined the word as a term of reproach.

> As coined and circulated by Marxism, the term has retained up to the present so much of its hate-filled significance and class-struggle overtones that its usefulness for the purposes of scientific discussion has become extremely questionable. In addition, it provides us with only a very vague notion of the real essence of our economic system. Instead of promoting understanding, it merely arouses the emotions and obscures the truth.[4]

Obviously, anyone who sets out to defend capitalism to such an audience already has three strikes against him.

WHAT DOES *CAPITALISM* MEAN?

Liberation theologians seldom if ever tell their audiences what they mean by *capitalism*. Given their failure to define the term, one is forced to read between the lines. Often, it seems, liberation theologians equate capitalism with the economic and political systems of the industrialized Western nations in general and with that of the United States in particular. Even though the present injustices of Latin America may have had their beginning in the exploitative and imperialistic policies of Spain, the major contemporary villain for liberation theologians is the United States. The vagueness and question-begging that characterizes most liberation usage of *capitalism* invites a more careful analysis. This analysis will reveal that socialists often use *capitalism* to refer not to capitalism but to an entirely different economic system known as interventionism that is supposed to mediate between capitalism and socialism. Sometimes, the evidence suggests, people who attack capitalism simply have no idea what they mean by the term.

One step that can help clarify the meaning of both *capitalism* and *socialism* is to see that both words denote not single fixed positions but actually refer to a variety of positions located along a continuum. This continuum should also illustrate the existence of a third economic option known as interventionism.

CAPITALISM	INTERVENTIONISM	SOCIALISM

0   *100*

Capitalism and *socialism* should be thought of as umbrella-like terms that cover a variety of positions. The positions that occupy the range of views along the capitalist side of the continuum have important features in common that set them apart from the options covered by *socialism*. To start with, varieties of capitalism are systems of *voluntary* relationships. To get more specific, they are systems of voluntary relationships which permit people to enter into exchanges.

There are two basic means by which something can be exchanged. The first is what might be termed *the peaceful means of exchange* which can be summed up in the phrase, "If you do something good for me, then I'll do something good for you." But exchange can also take place by means of force and violence. In this *violent means of exchange*, the basic rule of thumb is: "Unless you do something good for me, I'll do something bad to you." While thieves and robbers use the violent means of exchange, it is also extremely useful to some economic and political systems. Of these two basic means of exchange, capitalism clearly exemplifies the peaceful means of exchange. In a truly capitalist system of exchange, the fundamental principle is, "If you do something good for me, then I'll do something good for you." The reason people exchange in a real market is because they believe the exchange is good for them. They take advantage of an opportunity to obtain something they want more in exchange for something they desire less.[5]

I have said that capitalism is a voluntary system of relationships that utilizes the peaceful means of exchange. Building on this, I can go one step further and define capitalism as a system of voluntary relationships within a framework of laws which protect people's rights against force, fraud, theft and violations of contracts. Such a system is designed to serve all human wants with the exception of those that conflict with its framework of laws. The basic function of these laws is to insure the free and voluntary participation of parties in their economic exchanges. An exchange can hardly be voluntary if one participant is coerced, deceived, defrauded or robbed. The rule of law therefore does not really introduce coercion into the exchange process; it is a necessary condition without which free exchange could not exist.

A market economy also begins by assuming a system of human rights, such as the right to make decisions, the right to be free, the right to hold property, and the right to exchange what one owns for something else.

Capitalism also gives people the right to take risks. One reason societies move forward is because of people who are willing to take risks with their time, money, and sometimes their lives. Other people prefer to play it safe and not take such risks. That is their privilege in a free market system. It is interesting to note, however, how often some of the people who are unwilling to take risks feel entitled to rewards from those who gambled and won. Many of these non-risk takers never feel obligated to help out by sharing the losses of those who took some risk and lost. Ownership of capital is normally a result of risk-taking coupled with entrepreneurial ability. Such ability involves the recognition of a hitherto unrecognized opportunity. Obviously, many people who thought they saw such an opportunity were mistaken. They took their chance and lost. Successful entrepreneurs are those who win more often than they lose. But it is a matter of record that most of the people who believe they have spotted an opportunity end up being wrong. Marxists never talk about the vast number of capitalists who lose in a voluntary market system.

Finally, the market has a place for reward. Unless people believe they have something to gain, they will not take risks. But as we all know, the market rewards people in two ways: sometimes they win but often they lose. If someone thinks he sees an opportunity and is willing to take the accompanying risks, he has a right to a return from his investment. What the socialist wants to do is take from the few risk-takers who got lucky and won and give to those unwilling or unable to take the risk. Socialists never talk about sharing the *losses*. Socialists think it is unjust that a few people end up owning land or businesses. But as long as those people or their forebears acquired their holdings honestly, through their risks and ability and effort, condemnation of their good fortune is unjustified, regardless of how much envy we may feel. Liberation theologians are concerned about vast inequities of wealth that have resulted from acts of force, fraud and theft in earlier generations. Their concern is justified. But when their resentment of these injustices leads them to denounce capitalism, they attack the very system that would outlaw the injustices they seek to remedy and they judge unfairly the honest fruits of just and voluntary exchanges in a market system.

A PRELIMINARY OBJECTION

At this point, some will object that the system of voluntary exchange that I have described exists nowhere in the real world. This kind of objection actually supports the position I am advancing, namely, that *capitalism* is an umbrella-term that denotes a variety of options along a continuum. I am happy to concede that the system I have been describing is an ideal that denotes the position at point zero of our continuum. This will help us to see that *capitalism* can be used in two distinct ways. Sometimes the word is used to refer to an ideal market economy in which people exchange goods and services in an environment free from coercion, fraud, monopoly and statist interference with the exchange process.[6] In addition to this abstract and ideal usage of the term, *capitalism* is also used to describe a variety of systems of exchange in the real world that only approximate more or less the freedom of the ideal market. These systems in the real world differ obviously in important ways from the abstract perfection of the ideal market. The relationship between the ideal market system (the position at point zero of the continuum) and real economic exchanges can be compared to that between physiology and pathology. No physician ever expects to find every organ in every body functioning perfectly. His study of physiology provides him with a standard by which he can diagnose pathology. Likewise, the ideal market economy provides standards that can be used to judge the health of economic practices in the real world.

It is important to note that the contemporary usage of *capitalism* is so loose that the word is often used to refer to economic practices and systems that are far removed from the market as I have defined it—so far in fact that the systems and practices ought to forfeit their right to the label. Most of the evils that socialists attribute to capitalism are in fact products of these interventionist systems.

Why do economic practices in the real world deviate from the market ideal? The answer should be obvious. Deviations from the market ideal occur because of defects in human nature. This can hardly come as news to Christians who are supposed to know about sin. Human beings naturally crave security and guaranteed success, values not found readily in a free market. Genuine competition always carries with it the possibility of failure and loss. This human preference for security leads human beings to avoid competition whenever possible, encourages them to operate outside the market, and induces them to subvert the market process through behavior that is often questionable and dishonest. The attempt to gain a monopolistic control through special privilege from government is just one manifestation of the universal propensity to escape the uncertainty and insecurity of the market. Whether Christian socialists who advocate the concentration of economic and political power in the hands of a powerful elite really take the fact of human sin seriously is a question worth pondering.

The most common cause of deviations from the market ideal is governmental interference with the market process. This kind of interference is the major factor in the development of monopolies. The proverbial Marxist charge that monopoly is an unavoidable product of capitalism is false. It is not the market but governments that create monopolies by granting organizations the exclusive privilege of doing business or by establishing *de facto* monopolies through regulatory agencies whose ostensive purpose is the encouragement of competition but whose end result is the restriction of competition. The only monopolies that pose a challenge to market principles are those that result from statist interference with the market.[7] The belief that capitalism breeds monopoly is contradicted by the evidence.[8] But plenty of evidence exists to show how political interference with the market in the form of tariffs, regulations, subsidies, etc. has the effect of offsetting market operations. The only monopolies that have attained lasting immunity from competition achieved that status by governmental fiat, regulation, or support of some other kind. Monopolies could not survive without special protection from government which effectively limits the access of new entrants to the market. The way to terminate monopolies is not to abolish capitalism but to end the economic interventionism that allows governments to give privileged treatment to a small number of businesses or individuals.

THE INFORMATIONAL FUNCTION OF THE MARKET

One of the market's most important roles is its function as an instrument for gathering and transmitting information. Each participant in the market process can receive signs or indicators of what desires other people want satisfied at a particular time and for a particular price. Without these clues, the agent in the market would never know which desires of other people he should attempt to satisfy. The prices at which goods and services are selling is one such indicator which supplies important information telling each person in the market how best to direct his own efforts. The key to market exchange at any given moment is price. When people's wants are matched by a price they are willing and able to pay, they will buy. When a seller can make a profit (or avoid a greater loss) at this price, he will sell. Without the market mechanism, there would be no way to know the wants and desires of more than a few people.

The success of some in the market provides additional indicators that point to directions others should take if they desire similar success. That is, they should provide some service or product at a given price and quality. Of course, when that part of the market becomes too crowded, the signals change and the wise agent will switch his activity in accordance with the new signals. The market offers special rewards to those entrepreneurs who are wise or lucky enough to tap the right market at the right time.

The informational function of the market is negated, however, by governmental interference. Factors such as prices and interest rates which might tell people something in an unhampered market become, following governmental manipulation, distorted and misleading signals that provide no clear message.[9] Statist attempts to circumvent the market process and control an entire economic system from some central agency have been notorious failures, a lesson that liberation theologians have yet to learn. When capitalism is correctly understood, it is incompatible with the economic manipulations of the interventionist. Capitalism opposes statist intervention which subjects the market process to tampering and negates its vital informational function. This results in social costs that far outweigh any anticipated advantage.

THE MEANING OF *SOCIALISM* IN LIBERATION THEOLOGY

Like *capitalism*, *socialism* is an umbrella-term that covers a range of options. What do the options along the socialist range of the continuum have in common? Many times, the common element is simply an opposition to capitalism along with a predilection for centralized economic control. While socialists may not always know what capitalism is, they are certain that it is immoral and irrational. So-called Christian socialists find additional support for their position in the belief that capitalism's stress on the pursuit of profit and its pandering to greed, materialism and selfishness make it an unsuitable choice for any Christian. They find socialism preferable because, they think, it encourages such basic Christian values as community.

The various forms of socialism differ, in one sense, in the degree of centralized control they seek to impose on a nation's life and economy. In the case of the state socialisms of the Soviet Union, China, Cuba, East Germany, and Bulgaria, the centralized control could hardly be more total and ruthless. Such state socialisms are a frequent source of embarassment to some liberation theologians who insist, with few specifics, that the socialism they promote is different. For example, Archbishop Dom Helder Camara of Brazil has stated: "I am a socialist . . . . But I don't see the solution in the socialist governments that exist today . . . . The Marxist record is awful . . . . My socialism is a special one which respects the human person and turns to the gospel. My socialism is justice."[10]

SOCIALISM'S ACHILLES HEEL

The basic flaw in all forms of socialism was noted in 1920 by the Austrian economist, Ludwig Von Mises. Mises objected to socialism on the grounds of its harmful effect on freedom. But his most important contribution was the argument that socialism is hopeless because it makes economic calculation impossible. According to Mises, socialists can never attune production to human wants without free markets to set prices. The impossibility of precise measures of cost accounting under socialism will result in economic disaster. Without markets, economic activity would become chaotic and result in drastic inefficiencies and distortions.[11]

Most socialist countries including the Soviet Union keep the economic chaos at a minimum by imitating the pricing system of free market systems. But the only reason socialist economies can function at all is because their bureaucratic managers carefully monitor the pricing information available from free markets and then apply this information to set their own prices. When this information from free markets is unavailable or ignored, their problems become even more serious.

The great paradox of socialism is the fact that socialists need capitalism in order to survive. Unless socialists make allowance for some free markets which provide the pricing information that alone can make rational economic activity possible, socialist economies would soon collapse. Von Mises' claims were strengthened by the fact that this is exactly what happened in cases where socialist states attempted to abolish all markets.[12] The major consequence of all this is that no socialism in practice can dispense with market exchanges. Consequently, socialism is a gigantic fraud which attacks the market at the same time it is forced to utilize the market process.

ECONOMIC INTERVENTIONISM

Advocates of interventionism (or a mixed economy) believe that governmental intervention in economic matters can successfully achieve desired results while still falling short of the more total controls necessary under socialism. A mixed economy is thought to be a workable third alternative to the freedom of the market and the more total state control of socialism. The state, interventionists claim, only interferes with the market process when necessary to attain some desirable social goal or to avoid some social evil. The interventionist is convinced that many humanitarian goals are unattainable without resorting to occasional and partial statist controls.

Like both *capitalism* and *socialism*, *interventionism* is a word that covers a variety of positions in the middle range of the continuum. To make things even more complicated, both *capitalism* and *socialism* are often used to refer to positions that are more correctly described as interventionist. As so-called capitalist systems allow more and more governmental intervention with the market, there comes a point where capitalism (so-called) and interventionism blend into each other. The economic system of the United States is a good example of this. Hence liberation theologians who attack the United States as the example par excellence of capitalism are flailing away at a straw man. Perhaps the economic practices of the United States deserve condemnation. But if so, we should understand that the disapproval is actually directed against a form of economic interventionism.

Just as there is a point on our continuum where "capitalism" becomes indistinguishable from interventionism, it is also possible to move along the range of socialist positions and reach the point where "socialism" becomes indistinguishable from interventionism. This helps to explain why some interventionists still prefer to use *capitalism* as a name for their position while other interventionists prefer to think of themselves as socialists.

The fundamental weakness of interventionism was also uncovered by Ludwig Von Mises who argued that no logical alternative to a free market and socialism is really possible. According to Mises, there can be no consistent and successful middle ground between capitalism and socialism. Partial government controls, Mises maintained, must inevitably fail and will force any government to choose between two alternatives. Either the state must return to a free market economy and allow the damage resulting from its intervention to ease gradually; or else the state can keep adding more and more controls until all economic freedom ends which, of course, would mean the transformation of interventionism into socialism. Efforts to produce a system of property hampered by government controls will create an inevitable crisis which must lead either to an abandonment of those controls or to a surrender to the total controls of socialism. While partial controls always result in the frustration of the interventionist's goals, the imposition of total controls would mean the end of the experiment in interventionism and a turn toward socialism.[13]

The more freedom a socialist allows, the closer his position is to interventionism. The more freedom an interventionist allows, the closer his position is to capitalism. It is clear that the real issue in the dispute between these three positions is the degree of economic freedom each allows; the crux is the extent to which human beings will be permitted to exercise their own choices in the economic sphere of life. While capitalism is a system of voluntary exchange, socialism is a paradigm of what I earlier called *the violent means of exchange.* The governing principle of socialism is, "Unless you do something good for me, I'll do something bad to you." Socialism means far more than a centralized control of the economic process. It entails the introduction of coercion into economic exchange so as to facilitate the goals of the elite who function as the central planners. Liberation theologians are professing Christians whose entire approach to economics depends upon granting an elite minority the power to deprive the majority of fundamental economic liberties.

IS FREEDOM DIVISIBLE?

As we have seen, a major difference between capitalists and socialists is the former's commitment to defend economic freedom. It is time to notice another, even more fundamental, disagreement. Capitalists recognize that economic freedom and political-spiritual freedom are a whole that cannot be divided. As Wilhelm Röpke saw so clearly, "We are not free to combine just any kind of economic order, say, a collectivist one, with any kind of political and spiritual order."[14] In other words, economics is not simply a matter of expediency in organizing economic life. There is a necessary connection between economic freedom and political-spiritual freedom. Because liberty is an indivisible whole, it is impossible to have political and spiritual liberty without also having economic freedom. Because collectivism in the economic sphere means the end of political and spiritual freedom, economics is the front line in the battle for freedom. Consequently, economists carry the weighty responsibility of directing "their best efforts to the thorny problem of how, in the aggravating circumstances of modern industrial society, an essentially free economic order can nevertheless survive and how it can constantly be protected against the incursions or infiltrations of collectivism.''[15] One part of this task is replying to collectivist attacks against the economic freedom of the market. But another aspect of this chore is taking the offensive and arguing for the moral superiority of capitalism.

THE ETHICAL FOUNDATIONS OF CAPITALISM

The dual truths that capitalism is pragmatically superior to socialism and that economic freedom is a necessary condition for political and spiritual freedom may not be enough to win the day for capitalism in the battle for men's minds. We must also inquire into the ethical foundations of capitalism. Many believe that the fundamental concerns of the market system are part of a sphere that is ethically questionable at best and morally reprehensible at worst. Röpke asks, does capitalism not place us in an acquisitive society

which unleashes naked greed, fosters Machiavellian business methods and, indeed, allows them to become the rule, drowns all higher motives in the "icy water of egotistical calculation" . . . and lets people gain the world but lose their souls? Is there any more certain way of desiccating the soul of man than the habit of constantly thinking about money and what it can buy? Is there a more potent poison than our economic system's all-pervasive commercialism?[16]

It is impossible to take such ethical concerns too seriously. It is important to realize that capitalism does pass the moral test; capitalism is a system that fosters and furthers moral behavior in individuals. This can be seen in several ways.

For one thing, capitalism's stress upon voluntary exchanges and transactions helps to encourage respect for other human beings. Agents in a voluntary system of exchange are forced to be other-directed. A proper understanding of how the market operates will show how the market neutralizes greed. One person may lust after the property of a second person all he wants. As long as the rights of the second party are protected, the greed of the first individual cannot harm him. As long as the first person is prohibited from using force, fraud or theft, his greed for someone else's property must be channeled into the discovery of products or services for which people are willing to exchange their holdings. Greed can never harm another person as long as his rights are protected. If Mr. X is going to satisfy his greed within a market system of rights, he is going to have to offer others something that they want in exchange. His greed must lead him to a product or service for which others are willing to barter. Thus, every person in the market has to be other-directed. Each must ask himself what other people want and how he can best service those wants. Therefore, any greed that might operate in the market involves a paradox. The market is one area of life where concern for the other person is required. The market then does not pander to greed. It is rather a mechanism that allows natural human desires to be satisfied in a nonviolent way. The alternative to the peaceful means of exchange, we repeat, is violence.

Capitalism also encourages moral behavior because private ownership can be a major stimulus to the development of moral behavior. British economist Arthur Shenfield explains:

> Every time we treat property with diligence and care, we learn a lesson in morality. We see this in the behavior of the good husbandman, who has traditionally aroused our admiration. We see it also as we look back on the attitudes of those imbued with what used to be called the Protestant ethic, though in fact it was also to be found in non-Protestant societies where work, saving, and enterprise were admired. The reason for the moral training of private property is that it induces at least some of its owners to treat it as a trust, even if only for their children or children's children; and those who so treat it tend to be best at accumulating it, contrary to popular notions about the conspicuous consumption of the rich, the incidence of luck or of gambling. Contrast our attitudes to private property with our treatment of public property. Every army quartermaster, every state school administrator, every bureaucratic office controller, knows with what carelessness and lack of diligence most of us deal with it. This applies everywhere, but especially in socialist countries where most property is public.[17]

A third moral inducement inherent in capitalism is the sanctity of contract. Shenfield observes that "the thrust of the capitalist system is to favor those who keep their contracts and to hamper those who do not. Sanctity of contract is one of the most important elements in the cement which binds a civilized society together, and it tends to arise naturally in a society where private property is respected. At the same time it has an elevating effect on men's character.''

As a fourth example of how capitalism fosters moral behavior, Shenfield draws attention to the work ethic which he suggests is "a prime agent of moral training and character elevation." Once people realize that few things in life are free, that most things carry a price tag, and that therefore we will have to work for most of the things we want, we are in a position to learn a vital truth about our lot in life. Capitalism helps teach this truth. But, Shenfield warns, "In a world of collectivism everything still has a cost, but everyone is tempted, even urged, to behave as if there is no cost or as if the cost will be borne by somebody else. This is one of the most corrosive effects of collectivism upon the moral character of people."

And so, Shenfield summarizes, "the morality inherent in the institution of private property, and embodied in respect for the sanctity of contract and in the work ethic is cogent evidence for the positively moral effects of capitalism upon the behavior of individuals." But, Shenfield continues, there is something else that is even more basic. How does capitalism stand in regard to what Jesus called the second great commandment, "Thou shalt love thy neighbor as thyself"? Before this question can be answered, we must first determine what it means to love one's neighbor as oneself. Shenfield suggests it means that one desire one's neighbor to have that which we value most. And what is the one thing that we place the highest value upon for ourselves? It is certainly not material gain or the satisfaction we get from material things, both of which can be acquired in ways and circumstances that we find morally repugnant. That thing which we most desire for ourselves—other than loving God with all our hearts and minds and souls (the first great commandment)—is "freedom to pursue our own purposes."

It is only when this is assumed that we talk about the primacy of food, clothing, shelter, and other material benefits. As a corollary to this freedom we want others to respect our individuality, independence, and status as responsible human beings. We do not want to be treated as children or wards of our benefactors, not to mention slaves, serfs, prisoners or conscripts, however generous or indulgent the treatment may be. This is the fundamental morality which capitalism requires and which it nurtures. It alone among economic systems operates on the basis of respect for free, independent, responsible persons. All other systems in varying degrees treat men as less than this. Socialist systems above all treat men as pawns to be moved about by the authorities, or as children to be given what the rulers decide is good for them, or as serfs or slaves. The rulers begin by boasting about their compassion, which in any case is fraudulent, but after a time they drop this pretence which they find unnecessary for the maintenance of power. In all things they act on the presumption that they know best. Therefore they and their systems are morally stunted. Only the free system, the much assailed capitalism, is morally mature.

THE CHRISTIAN CHOICE BETWEEN CAPITALISM AND SOCIALISM

Which choice then should I, as a Christian, make in the selection between capitalism and socialism? The socialist assault against capitalism is one of the most irrelevant, confused and unfair attacks in the history of ideas.[18] There is certainly no compelling reason to believe that capitalism is inherently unjust, immoral or irrational. There are plenty of reasons to question the socialist's claims that his system is more ethical than capitalism. Not only does capitalism deliver the economic goods, it also passes the moral test. Also in its favor is the fact that capitalism takes a realistic (as opposed to a utopian) view of human nature. Wilhelm Röpke comments:

> The market economy has the ability to use the motive power of individual self-interest for turning the turbines of production; but if the collectivist economy is to function, it needs heroes or saints, and since there are none, it leads straight to the police state. Any attempt to base an economic order on a morality considerably higher than the common man's must end up in compulsion and the organized intoxication of the masses through propaganda . . . . This is one of the principal reasons for the fact . . . that a free state and society presupposes a free economy. Collectivist economy, on the other hand, leads to impoverishment and tyranny, and this consequence is obviously the very opposite of "moral". Nothing could more strikingly demonstrate the positive value of self-interested action than that its denial destroys civilization and enslaves men. In "capitalism" we

have a freedom of moral choice, and no one is *forced* to be a scoundrel. But this is precisely what we are forced to be in a collectivist social and economic system. It is tragically paradoxical that this should be so, but it is, because the satanic rationale of the system presses us into the service of the state machine and forces us to act against our consciences.[19]

Röpke ends his discussion with the observation that capitalism needs Christianity. While the market may be one necessary condition for a free society, it is not a sufficient condition. We need something more, namely, the moral and spiritual principles that capitalism presupposes and which all of us must live up to. Capitalists who ignore or violate the moral foundations of the system are in truth as much enemies of the system as those who seek to destroy it from without.

CONCLUSION

Throughout this essay I have argued that the alternative to free exchange is violence. Capitalism is a mechanism that allows natural human desires to be satisfied in a nonviolent way. No one has stated this better than Arthur Shenfield:

Men have always wanted to be rich, whatever the precepts of their religions may have been. Until the rise of capitalism the most effective way to become rich was to seize men's bodies or land. Submission to conquest of territory, enslavement, or reduction to serfdom were the common experience of the greater part of mankind.

But under capitalism, Shenfield explains,

wealth arose not from the seizure of persons or property, but from the enhancement of men's consumption and welfare. However, since envy abides powerfully among most of us, the desire of other men to be rich remains a prominent object of our censure; and since capitalism is the most effective agent for making all men rich, especially the erstwhile poor, its very success makes it the target for hostility, particularly from intellectuals who can see nothing in it but getting and spending.

Little can be done to prevent human beings from wanting to be rich. What capitalism does is channel that desire into peaceful means that benefit many besides those who wish to improve their own situation. To hear Shenfield once more, "The alternative to serving other men's wants is seizing power of them, as it always has been. Hence it is not surprising that wherever the enemies of capitalism have prevailed, the result has been not only the debasement of consumption standards for the masses but also their reduction to serfdom by the new privileged class of socialist rulers."

We began this essay by noting that the *end* liberation theologians seek is to help people who are poor and oppressed. Their selection of socialism as their exclusive *means* for reaching their goal is a mistake that is both tragic and ironic. It is tragic because they have rejected the one system that offers real economic hope for the masses they wish to assist. It is ironic because in promoting the violent means of exchange, they have taken a path that will not only deny their people bread but also deprive them of liberty. That such a movement should call itself *liberation* theology truly is ironic.

NOTES

1. See Ronald Nash, *Social Justice and the Christian Church* (Milford, Michigan: Mott Media, 1983) chapters 10 and 11 and Ronald Nash, *Freedom, Justice and the State* (Lanham, Maryland: University Press of America, 1980) chapter 6.

2. See Ernest van den Haag, ed., *Capitalism: Sources of Hostility* (New Rochelle, New York: Epoch Books, 1979).

3. Israel Kirzner, "The Ugly Market: Why Capitalism is Hated, Feared and Despised," *The Freeman*, Dec. 1974, pp. 724-5.

4. Wilhelm Röpke, *Economics of the Free Society* (Chicago: Henry Regnery Co., 1960) p. 259.

5. Obviously in the real world, assorted pressures may lead people to make exchanges that they find unpleasant. But the absence of coercion in the market process means that when people enter into such exchanges, they still do so freely because they recognize that the other choices open to them are even less desirable.

6. It is a mistake to think of *the market* as a place or thing. As Ludwig Von Mises put it, "The market is not a place, a thing or a collective entity. The market is a process, actuated by the interplay of the actions of the various individuals cooperating under the divisions of labor. . . . The forces determining the-continually-changing-state of the market are the value judgments of those individials and their actions as directed by these value judgments." Ludwig Von Mises, *Human Action* (New Haven: Yale University Press, 1949) pp. 257-8.

7. For more on the indispensable role of the state in monopoly, see Yale Brozen, "Is Government the Source of Monopoly?", *The Intercollegiate Review* 5 (1968-69) and Milton Friedman, *Capitalism and Freedom* (Chicago: University of Chicago Press, 1962) chapters 8-9. Sometimes conditions in a particular region give rise to local monopolies. But if force and fraud are excluded and the situation is lucrative enough, others will quickly seek entry to the market.

8. For a sampling of this evidence, see Donald Devine, *Does Freedom Work?* (Ottawa, Illinois: Caroline House, 1978) pp. 52ff.

9. Governmental intervention that effectively nullified the signals from this mechanical process contributed to many economic crises in America's history.

10. Quoted in Miguez-Bonino's book, *Doing Theology in a Revolutionary Situation* (Philadelphia: Fortress Press, 1975) p. 47.

11. For more on this subject, see Nash, *Social Justice and the Christian Church*, op. cit., chapter 8.

12. See Lancelot Lawton, *Economic History of Soviet Russia* (London, 1922) and Paul Craig Roberts, *Alienation and the Soviet Economy* (Albuquerque: University of New Mexico Press, 1971).

13. For more, see Nash, *Social Justice and the Christian Church*, op. cit., chapter 9.

14. Wilhelm Röpke, *A Humane Economy* (Indianapolis: Liberty Fund, 1971) p. 105.

15. Ibid., p. 105.

16. Ibid., p. 113.

17. Arthur Shenfield, "Capitalism Under the Tests of Ethics," *Imprimis*, Dec. 1981. Other quotes from Shenfield which follow are from the same source.

18. I remind the reader that I have considered the other objections to capitalism not mentioned in this chapter in two earlier books. See the first note to this chapter.

19. Röpke, *A Humane Economy*, op. cit., p. 121.

LIBERATION THEOLOGY IN LATIN AMERICA

James V. Schall, S.J.

JAMES V. SCHALL, S.J.

James V. Schall, S.J. is Associate Professor of Government at Georgetown University. His degrees include the B.A. and M.A. from Gonzaga University, the M.S.T. from Santa Clara University and the Ph.D. from Georgetown University. He formerly taught at the University of San Francisco and the Gregorian University in Rome. His books include *Redeeming the Time* (1968); *Far Too Easily Pleased: A Theology of Play, Contemplation and Festivity* (1976); *The Sixth Paul* (1977); *Christianity and Politics* (1981); *Church, State and Society in the Thought of John Paul II* (1982): *Liberation Theology in Latin America* (1982); and *The Distinctiveness of Christianity* (1983).

LIBERATION THEOLOGY IN LATIN AMERICA — Theology
as Institutionalized Poverty

Rudolf Augstein, the editor of the German Journal *Der Spiegel*,
recently and belatedly discovered that many professedly Christian
theologians and intellectuals do not in fact teach or profess what
the church has traditionally maintained on a number of basic points.
This German innocence and surprise can, doubtless, be excused,
though others besides German journalists wonder about it also.
Nevertheless, "the most rational of the religions" has suddenly
seemed to be overtaken by a kind of bewildering intellectual chaos,
one that cannot but have profound political consequences. The relation between political change and intellectual vision is by no means
a new problem. Professor Hans Schmidt has traced the relation of
political forms and the concept of Christ in various ages to see how
they were related.[1] Indeed, in a broader context, it can be argued
that fundamental changes within the religious concepts and expectations of the great faiths—Hinduism, Confucianism, Judaism,
Islam, Buddhism, and especially Roman Christianity—constitute the
main causes of instability in the public order. This means that judges,
presidents, and prime ministers, as well as dictators, and commissars,
would do well to be briefed daily in theology as in economics and
foreign affairs. Iran, if not Nicaragua and El Salvador, has recently
taught this lesson vividly.

Ever since Ananias and Sapphira dropped dead because they kept
some of the revenue of a dubious land deal in the Acts of the
Apostles, Christians have been bickering and arguing about what
Christianity means. The cynics of history, of course, have claimed
that these controversies were mere abstractions and senseless disputes.
But in truth, they almost invariably touched something basic about
how human life and its destiny ought to be conceived. This is why
we can legitimately wonder why things exist or do not, why they exist
in one way rather than another. And we discover that these reasons
more often than not depend upon a slight nuance or change in

* Reprinted with permission from *Liberation Theology in Latin America*, by James
V. Schall, S. J., copyright 1982 by Ignatius Press, San Francisco, Calif.

Liberation Theology

religious definition. The church, to its credit or infamy, has historically been acutely aware of the narrowness of what separates sanity and insanity, health and moral disease.

The early church, to recall, was full of heresies, such as Gnosticism, Arianism, Monophysitism, Nestorianism, Manicheanism, Donatism, Docetism, Semi-Arianism and Pelagianism to but begin. How the church was none of these very often popular movements is one of the great intellectual dramas of history. In the Middle Ages, there were Begards and Beguines, the Catharists, the Albigensians and the Spiritual Franciscans, whom Chesterton once remarked were not unlike the modern communists. We saw the Quietists and the Diggers, the Levellers and the Jansenists, Febronians, Erastians, and even "Old Catholics" in the more modern period. Thus, it should come as no ultimate shock that today there are Christian Marxists, Christian Maoists, Christian Trotskyites, Christian Socialists, and Christian Castroites. At times, it must seem that Christianity is able to embrace just about anything that comes on the political scene.

Yet, as the German Jesuit theologian, Karl Rahner, said in his essay "On Heresy," Christianity instinctively wants to confront ideas and movements at variance with itself, especially if these have, as does Marxism, some basically Christian overtones in their original mixture. And it would be highly unlikely if some Christians, at least, were not attracted by the most pervasive ideologies of their times.[2] On the other hand, Christianity does have a stable content, serious deviation from which does change how a person or a people may act in the world. And while politics is incompetent in the area of religious truths, still the public order is immediately affected by the status of religion among its professed believers.

Thus, if significant numbers of Christian leaders or peoples can be converted to Marxism or one of its variants, or even if they merely decide it is just another social option, as it is often called, then we are bound to take another look at their politics to see how they decide to act in a socially significant fashion. The consequences and possibility of such a change have been commented upon in the past. John Henry Newman, the great English cardinal and writer of the nineteenth century, in the conclusion to his monumental study, *The Arians of the Fourth Century*, wrote:

And so of the present perils, with which our branch of the Church is beset, as they bear a marked resemblance to those of the fourth century, so are the lessons, which we gain from that ancient time, especially cheery and edifying to Christians of the present day. Then as now, there is the prospect, and partly present in the Church, of an Heretical Power enthralling it, exerting a varied influence and a usurped claim in the appointing of her functionaries, and interfering with the management of her internal affairs . . . .[3]

Newman went on to find comfort in the ability of ecclesiastical authorities to hold their own against deviations in their own ranks.

Nevertheless, as the state influence on episcopal appointments in Eastern Europe and the various radical priests in Latin America suggest, many objective minds are beginning to wonder if this danger of a new heretical power "enthralling" itself into the heart of the church is not becoming a reality. Even some Marxist theoreticians are wondering if their historical opposition to religion might not best be dropped to entice this power to their side. There is no doubt, indeed, that in more and more seminaries, various brands of political and liberation theologies are being taught as quasi-house doctrines. As I have often remarked previously, twenty years ago, young army officers and Roman Catholic seminarians were among the most difficult to convert to a Marxist orientation, while today they are often perhaps the easiest in many parts of the world, ironically in mostly those areas wherein Marxists do *not* officially control the state.

Interestingly too in this regard, since so much liberation thought deals with Christology—that is, who was Christ?—and the civil power, we do well to remember that these same Arians of whom Newman wrote were concerned to demote the divinity of Christ. And they did control many church offices, while supporting the current secular power. Jean Guitton, the French philosopher, made these pertinent remarks in this context:

The Arian crisis is no doubt the most remarkable from both the dogmatic and political point of view. It could be called eminently theologico-political: it introduced an era in which theology and politics will always be more or less closely linked.

Toward the year 380, the Church barely missed turning semi-Arian overnight. The mystery of the Incarnation was being put in question. . . . Christ was merely this superman, this saint, this "chief

of mystics'' who ought to be taken for the ''dim goal of evolution.''
. . . I should add that Arianism, which began as a theological hypothesis and a plausible system, did in the end become established state doctrine. . . . Perhaps it was more liable than other doctrines to lead to Caesaro-Papism, or at least to the confusion of the spiritual and temporal. Reducing Christ to the proportions of man, it was in harmony with the hidden desires of worldly power. And it was easily put to use.[4]

The great danger or temptation of liberation thought, paradoxically, lies apparently along such lines—in its use of Christology—in its being itself used by a certain kind of state

STEPS TOWARD A RADICAL POLITICAL THEOLOGY

Anyone who follows liberation thought realizes that it is directly related to recent more radical theological controversies. However much liberation theology appears to be an indigenous South American product, it is inevitably reflective of the general cultural climate of the West. While the third world may have some cohesion, still the African and Asian do not speak like the Latin American, except, significantly, when each speaks in those terms wherein a common Western ideology is employed. The major intellectual phenomenon after World War II in Europe centered around what is called ''existentialism'' with a kind of revival of humanism in its light. This was a philosophical movement itself reacting against the totalitarianism of the thirties and the consequences of mass armies and societies. Behind it there was also a struggle against the impersonalism of liberalism and the collectivism implicit in the Hegelian tradition.

Existentialism, consequently, deprecated the public order to emphasize personal relationships, doubt, anguish, subjective values and personal commitment. ''I-Thou''—a phrase the Jewish philosopher Martin Buber popularized from Feuerbach, Marx's predecessor—became the catchword of a generation of thinkers who realized the sovereign individual of the classical tradition was nothing without otherness. In large part, the movements that have followed and reacted to this individualist reality—there are atheist and Christian advocates—have tended to stress the corporate and public rather than the private and subjective which latter have often become viewed as inimical to human well-being, whereas they originally were seen in modern thought as its main promoter.

The next pertinent movement was that of the so-called "death of God" theology or "secularization" theology, during the middle fifties and early sixties. Earlier post-war theology, more open perhaps, had tried to stress the positive notion of the "terrestrial realities." Such "death of God" positions, however, became notorious for wondering about such recondite things as "How to be a Christian in a godless world." Nietzsche and modern science were said, almost without argument, to have killed the religious God by defining reality through scientific methodology in such a manner that nothing was left over for God to be or do. For a time, "atheist Christians" were the curious vogue, while secularized Christianity meant transcendence was no longer important because we could supposedly now answer for ourselves all the classic questions thought once to be the exclusive province of religion—even problems of life, death, and human order. The "deification" of man that had been implicit in the modern project at least since the Enlightenment seemed at hand. Vatican II, in a way, was designed to confront and evaluate these theologies which came mainly from the experience of the developed world and the powerful presence of science.

Suddenly, however, another theology was discovered during the late sixties and early seventies that practically inverted the old atheism. There had been a long tradition of "civil religion" since Roman times. But everything in the modern era seemed against this tradition. The "separation of church and state," so much discussed in Vatican II, began to appear obsolete almost immediately after the council. Were not after all the early Christians considered to be "atheists" by the Romans because they doubted all the gods of the Pantheon?

Then, the ecologists came along to discover that Christianity had "secularized" nature, something the Death-of-God school had been pointing to as a virtue. But the Christians cut down the sacred groves and thereby allowed nature to be "exploited." This curious Marxist word came to take on all the pejorative overtones once attributed to original sin. The humanizing of nature was destroying it. As a result, Christianity found itself attacked for being at the origins of science and technology, now seen as the cause of our evils, whereas for the previous three hundred years, religion had been accused of being against science in the rationalist scheme of things. Marxism from this angle often found itself on the side of Christianity in holding for the value of the world found in science and technology.

This controversy, variously described as ecology or the "limits of growth," after a notoriously biased pseudo-study by the Club of Rome, was behind the approaches that came to dominate third world discussions. One maintained that industrial society was at fault, its size, ethos, progress. Mankind could be saved only by austerity and the social reorganization of its wants. This was something to which certain strands of religion seemed to gravitate much too readily. Did not religion preach mortification and were not the rich really the big spenders? When it was discovered by naive statisticians that six percent of the world's population consumed forty percent of its resources, the case seemed open and shut to the unreflective who never understood what "resources" might mean, or whether such "resources" might ever have existed without the productivity of the six percent.

Herman Kahn's *The Next 200 Years* seemed like a voice in the wilderness. Yet such a voice was disturbingly in the air for all who wanted to believe that we were about to disappear tomorrow morning. Moreover, Norman Macrae's sober warning that if this same six percent stopped their producing and consuming, the poor two-thirds of the world would be just that much closer to starvation and destitution, seemed merely incomprehensible. The productivity of the upper one-third of the productive nations alone was what gave hope to the other two-thirds.[5] However, the third world itself suddenly woke up to the fact that they were the first ones proposed to be sacrificed to these same supposed "limits of growth." International congresses soon echoed the charge that the ecological enthusiasm of the rich was but a plot to keep the poor poor.

Thus, in such a context, a third look at a tired old Marxism, whose productivity record was comparatively as miserable as it was, seemed to many to be quite logical. Did it not preach "exploitation" of the poor by the rich as the cause of their ills? Could not its simple and easy to understand theory explain all essential facts? Did it not advocate the strong state everyone in the third world seemed to be looking to justify? What was needed was "redistribution," the old socialist panacea, an idea that even reappeared in a sophisticated form in Harvard Professor John Rawls' *A Theory of Justice*. The normal drives and values of the "people" were not at fault as the ecologists argued but rather political and economic structures conveniently lumped together under the hated "capitalism." Theologians suddenly revived a form of the almost diabolical theory of collective guilt and baptized it as "sinful structures." All the modern economy needed was a proper "reordering," a phrase that always seemed to have overtones of but one specific ideology, the Marxist one, however much some kinds of reordering might prove advisable. The Marxists were already missionaries for their belief and the ecologists were not far behind, making one wonder again about their ultimate and respective theological origins. Everyone apparently wanted to save mankind either from itself or from present exploiting society.

The rise of the self-styled theologies of "hope," "revolution" and "politics" in Europe during the sixties and early seventies was formulated against such a background. For a time, it appeared evident to the West that the way to assist the poor peoples of the world would be for them to imitate, in their own fashion to be sure, the patterns and processes of growth that once took place in Europe, North America and Japan. Indeed, the few countries that actually did this seriously—South Korea, Taiwan, Singapore and Brazil—were among the most rapidly growing in the world. Probably one of the reasons these countries were attacked so strongly was precisely due to their laboratory effect against the worldwide socialist failures and assumptions. In any case, economic development and political modernization theories abounded.

A kind of modernized international Marshall Plan was always in the background; a vast program of self-help was hopefully possible. Yet, the results of the various plans actually tried seemed more and more dubious. Almost inevitably and invariably, socialist economic models were chosen, usually on *a priori* ideological grounds stemming from the European education of many third world leaders. And these plans usually insured, as P.T. Bauer has argued, a failure to develop quickly and normally.[6] Often, the major objective of newly formed third world leadership was in fact merely to retain power, to control people who did not presuppose the values and ideas that motivated most development theories. This demanded evidently another kind of political theory.

The dogmatic theory that prosperity, the product of development, would lead to democracy became questionable. Theories such as those of David Apter in *The Politics of Modernization* , arguing that freedom would itself be the best foundation for prosperity, were rejected. The path to development seemed to require an absolute form of government to discipline the people and direct progress. Mao's China, almost the reverse of every conceivable liberal and humanitarian value, came to be praised by many Christians and liberal people on the grounds that there was order and a better life there. No wonder, then, on the 200th Anniversary of the Declaration of Independence, Daniel Moynihan wrote sadly in *The Public Interest* that only a couple of dozen democracies remained in the world community, even though all nations nominally called themselves by that noble name. Democracy is a thing of the past, not the future. But then, almost as if to grant Moynihan's point, it was possible to mean by democracy a "collective freedom," something to be achieved only after the revolution. And it was possible to think this way in both Marxist and limits-of-growth traditions. Individual freedom became opposed to "public" freedom in these notions.

And so within this context, revolution and politics became popular in Christian circles. This reversed dramatically the previous trend which seemed to want to legitimize politics by withdrawing it from religious organization and practice. The older Christian tradition, particularly the Jesuit one that arose at the beginnings of the modern state in the seventeenth century, did have a theory of the right to change governments in extreme cases of misrule by resort to force. This theory was usually discussed under the heading of tyrannicide. In a sense, modern democratic methods of electing and changing political leaders grew out of a need to eliminate this sort of violent necessity. However, since modern constitutional democracy in a Marxist-type analysis at least could be looked upon as an exploitative superstructure, the old liberal values that guaranteed it were rejected. Thus, "gradualism," "compromise" and "development" became almost dirty words. Nothing could be done until existing structures were radically changed. Since this latter attitude prevented working with any present government, politics often consisted of preventing any governmental success except one with revolutionary control. But such changes to improve things, it was next argued, the capitalists would never allow to happen in any case. Chile became a myth. Fidel Castro's armies roaming Africa "by invitation" were but getting rid of imperialists, aiding the legitimate revolutions. Meanwhile, in South America, revolution was advocated and even joined in by priests like Camilo Torres in Colombia, who was to become something of a martyr of the left. Theologians began to wonder if the machine gun could not somehow be sanctified, or at least justified. A theology of "revolution" had analysts like the Belgian priest Joseph Comblin who was for a long time stationed in Latin America. This was not the main line of the Latin American church, of course, but such ideas gained respectability as a direct result of the supposed necessity to embrace socialism and reject developmentalism.

THE GERMAN CONNECTION

Meantime, in Germany, where many Latin American theologians had studied, a formal "political theology" was itself evolving with both Protestant and Catholic versions. Indeed, in this area, old-fashioned denominational lines are no longer as pertinent as the degree to which one accepts the new social theories about poverty. J. B. Metz, Jürgen Möltmann, Dorothy Sölle, among others, became prominant figures. "Political theology," as it was called, was by no means a new term. It was directly related to the Roman notion of civil religion, to "Christendom," to Rousseau's remarks on civil religion in the *Social Contract*, to Saint-Simon's "Essay on New Christianity," to the political theologies of the Catholic Restoration in the nineteenth century responding to the French Revolution, to Carlo Schmitt's efforts during Hitler's time to establish a public religious justification.

In the current German context, political theology is a reaction against humanism and existentialism, against what is called the "privatization" of faith and religion that leads men to be excessively concerned about salvation and personal holiness. This is argued against the background of modern industrial society and modern German metaphysics. In this view, no Christian society has existed or can exist. On the other hand, formal religion should have an effect in the world. This must logically be a political one since that is what the world is about. And as values in religion are real and meant to affect men where they are, religion must free itself from every particular political form to be able to "criticize" what goes on in politics in the light of religion's objectives. This view, in theory at least, acknowledged the autonomy of politics. As Johannes Metz put it:

> In a pluralistic society, it cannot be the socio-critical attitide of the Church to proclaim one positive societal order as an absolute norm. It can only consist in effecting within the society a critical, liberating freedom. The Christian task here is not the elaboration of a system of social doctrine, but of social criticism. The Church is a particular institution in society, yet presents a universal claim; if this claim is not to be an ideology, it can only be formulated and urged as criticism.[7]

Such political theology tends to stress not how difficult it is to live in and support any existing society, but concentrates on all the defects and imperfections in the light of some utopian or future norm.

In more classical Christian theories, by comparison, there was not too much expectation that politics would yield overly much. Christians were given spiritual reserves and resources to suffer and endure what "had to be." Aquinas always advised law not to expect men to be perfect. The political theologies, on the other hand, arose out of a fear of compromising themselves with the realities and necessities of any *de facto* worldly order, so their critical force came down upon what was yet left to be done. In the older structure, bishops and popes were expected to realize the difficulties of political orders in particular and the human condition in general. Now, the political theologies were set apart from any more conservative appreciation of the difficulty of doing anything positive at all in this world. The older view expected a kind of practical paralysis when nothing but the perfect critical position was taken by religion.

Political theology, however, is not exactly identical with the Latin American intellectual movements. The background and thought patterns diverge. Germany is a most developed country. In a sense, it is a model of development, both in its own first industrial revolution under Bismarck when it imitated the British, in its World War I state-organized economy, with which Lenin was so impressed, and finally in its remarkable record after World War II. The German model has always tended to stress the use of the state combined with individual initiative and social security in a mutually supportive fashion. The Nazi experience, however, must always condition German thought about the dangers of the omnipotent state. This latter strain of thought especially seems lacking in Latin American revolutionary Christian thought.[8]

Political theology in a way rejected a compromise political philosophy or practice, one based on a more realistic view of what was possible. And it did this in the name of a future that would presumably come to be. Thomas Aquinas' view of politics—that we cannot expect too high a level of virtue from most ordinary men in politics—seemed to be strangely forgotten. The focal point became not so much the present but the on-going history of men who are not seeking a private salvation for themselves—the only possible one for an Augustine—but something more, something in the nature of a public order that would justify and mediate their salvation. The notion of a "holy" society was to be rejected verbally, yet the idea seemed implicit.

One of the major tasks of political theology, then, was not to allow Marxism the public world to itself. This meant, paradoxically, that the denial of a specifically Christian politics tended to result in reuniting religion and politics in a new fashion, whereby their real objects involve the same processes and ultimate goals. To be orthodox, of course, political theology usually maintained the gratuity of the Kingdom of God in an ultimate sense. This German-oriented background served as a kind of justification and position against which liberation theology found its intellectual content.

The Latin American versions of political theology were deliberately called "liberation theologies." While the two ideas are obviously similar, they are not exactly the same in origin or emphasis. Alfredo Fierro's remarks are worth citing in this context:

> A similar [to Germany] turn toward politics soon appeared in Latin America. Its peculiar situation was a general one of inequality within a country and dependence vis-á-vis the outside world. This fostered

a new kind of theological reflection cut off from the earlier dogmatics and essentially found in the process of liberation in connection with exploited peoples. This new theology was usually presented as a "theology of liberation." It was rooted in the social context of Latin American Christians and their public *praxis* and embodied as critical awareness of their faith. As such it was fully autonomous and autochthonous, not merely a reflection of European theology.[9]

The distinctiveness and general importance of this Latin American social thought are, in its own terms, to be measured by its practical effects. This would logically have a criterion of its success from within history as well as a judgment of religion about its performance.

Yet, as Fierro also noted, this newer theology does not appear as original and as independent as it likes to pretend:

Historical materialism has been the overt or covert interlocutor of the most recent theology—that is to say, of the theologies . . . which, by virtue of their clear involvement in the realm of the *polis*, can be described as political theologies. In some authors, however, acceptance of the historical-materialist analysis of socio-economic relationships has moved to the forefront and decisively shaped their theological position. That is the case of those theologies that accept the fact of class conflict and the consequent need to opt for some class.[10]

In this light, then, it is possible to judge the comparative performance of this Latin American movement. The arguments for this newer system, its roots, and its ambitions seem rather clear enough at this stage. Of course, it has not really produced as yet, if it ever will, a viable political power on the basis of which we can actually judge performance. However, there is perhaps another way to ascertain its value and validity. This would not only be to question the degree in which the classical doctrines and practices of Christianity remain themselves, but also to wonder if the analyses used actually conform to the professed goals better than other systems. In this sense, liberation thought seems strangely distant from the actual ambitions and dreams of the poor themselves, this in spite of its repeated insistence that the poor are the origins of its enthusiasm and analysis.

AN EVALUATION OF LIBERATION THEOLOGY

How ought liberation theology to be judged then? Fundamentally, I think, the only just evaluation is that we have here a worldview with much heart and very little real hardheadedness about the world. Not only is the road to hell paved with good intentions, but even more so is the road to utopia. Undoubtedly, the most difficult thing about the human condition is the agonizing dichotomy between the dreams of betterment which we can earnestly conceive and the actual programs to achieve them, with the empirical results we achieve when we finally have the power to do what we conceive. This is so because there is a structure to life, laws of the human being that remain even in their breach. Experience itself limits our visions, and this is the best thing that can happen to many of our visions. Aquinas' instinct from Aristotle that a small error in the beginning would lead to a huge error in the end was meant to teach us that we cannot afford to neglect the import of ideas, no matter how small or unimportant they might seem initially.

Many American and European intellectuals and clerics have decided—and it is that, a "choice," not a necessity—that this seemingly novel liberation critique of the ills of the third world, even though there are others perhaps more cogent, is basically valid. Thus, these, along with various token Marxist professors now featured regularly in American university faculties—these latter are not yet in full control as they are in too many western European faculties—conceive it their sacred mission to advocate that no more missionaries should be sent south until they are first converted to this new ethic. Better yet, they are often advised to stay at home and preach in their own houses. The structural analysis of liberation thought, as we have suggested, puts most of the faults and sins in the First World, especially in the United States. Logically, this means that there is really no drama in the confrontation of "good" and "evil" in Latin America anyhow, since the causes of both lie elsewhere. Paradoxically, liberation thought again makes South America theoretically insignificant since it claims that the real fault is in the North. This is happening at a very time when so-called neocapitalism makes the Southern Hemisphere more and more important.

There are many sources for a "liberation" analysis of American and South American society.[11] Here, an attempt is made to inflict the so-called "third world guilt" on the consciences of the developed countries. This is seen as a methodology to change their structures; it is argued in the name of a kind of social science. The Latin American hierarchy in general, evidently, has not accepted the ideological background of this sort of analysis. Rather it has taken a more pragmatic, human-rights, common-good position that is free to criticize, while recognizing the dangers of greater evils and the difficulties of doing anything at all.[12]

Furthermore, the vast intellectual effort to come to terms with Marxism as the main way to help the poor is not wholly unexpected.[13] There is probably no task so crucial for the world's well-being than the slow or, preferably, rapid evolution within Marxism to something with which we can live more comfortably and humanely. The hostility towards, or at least avoidance by liberation theology, of the kind of thought represented by Alexander Solzhenitsyn and the Russian and East European dissidents over the precise Christian evaluation of Marxism is probably the most important controversy in this area. In so many words, if a Solzhenitsyn is right, liberation theology is disastrously wrong in many of its premises and perspectives. Undoubtedly the arrival of a Polish pope in the Vatican has had a welcome and powerful effect on many of the extremes of liberation thought in regard to its Marxist and socialist orientations. What the liberation school and a Solzhenitsyn do share, however, and this is important, is a strong critique of the West for many of its moral failures and positions. Yet, the main failure that Solzhenitsyn sees in the West seems to be precisely the toleration of those views most advocated as the solution for South American ills by the liberation schools.

Writing in 1971, Edward J. Williams at the University of Arizona argued that the effects of the changes in the Latin American Church to that time, and hence their significance for policy, had to do with the strengthening of the secular nation-state:

> The most salient characteristic of the present polity-religion equation in Latin America highlights the increasing cogency of Latin American Catholicism's role as legitimizing nation-builder. As the religion has updated and redefined itself, it has emphasized elements that contribute to the emergence of the secular nation-state. . . . Secular

reforms issuing from secularizing national governments elicit the blessing of Church and religion as both necessary and legitimate. . . . Latin American Catholicism legitimizes the secular nation-state by repudiating its traditional totalistic orientations. By redefining itself as a minority creed and positing the essential secularity of contemporary society, Latin American enthusiasm propels the secular nation-state into a position of primacy.[14]

Such an analysis strikes one today as almost totally missing the point of the direction of liberation theology in Latin America, which is totalistic and tending to transform rather the secular into a quasi-religious element of sacral history, a trend probably not so clear in 1971. The liberal, secular nation-state, in a sense, hardly exists for liberation theology, as it did not for classical socialism. The secular state seen in terms of the national security state is, indeed, seen as the main thing to be eliminated.

However, if we are to estimate the main origins of the intellectual confusions that ground and presumptively justify liberation thought, insofar as it is not merely a growth of the central line of Catholic social doctrine, which it does not claim to be, we shall have to look at what it means by a growing "gap" between rich and poor, at its analysis of profit and incentive, at its empirical perception of modern economic institutions, and most importantly at its use of the idea of the poor. The basic view that shall be argued here is that liberation theology is, in its essential outlines, itself a cause of continued underdevelopment, that its eventual growth and success would institutionalize in Latin America a life of low-level socialist poverty enforced by a rigid party-military discipline in control of economic enterprise and the movement of peoples.

The danger for the Catholic church resulting from this kind of thought is, moreover, very great, as it risks being identified again with an authoritarian or totalitarian movement. No one argues that the present authoritarian regimes are paragons of virtue or justice. But there are degrees of evil and corruption which any realistic politics or religion must keep in mind. It is clear that the present situation has elements that need changing. But it is dubious whether the models and notions proposed in liberation thought are at all better in the long run. And to maintain that something is not better than the present is not necessarily to say that the present situation is ideal.

This is why classical political philosophy insisted on treating all forms of possible government, arranging them in an order of hierarchical principle and practical performance.

Perhaps some indication of the validity of these hesitations about the potential efficacy of the socialist-orientated liberation approaches can be seen if we refer to a recent essay in *The Economist* of London:

> In 1972-78 the 240 million people of the five ASEAN countries (Thailand, Malaysia, Singapore, Indonesia and the Philippines) plus the 60 million people of three neighbours (Taiwan, Hongkong, South Korea) have achieved between 6 percent and 11 percent average annual growth in national GNP; this is now the only group of countries in the world in which real GNP is doubling every seven to twelve years. It is nonsense to say the benefits are going only to the rich. In all these eight countries life expectancy is lengthening dramatically, in most of them mugging rates and drug-trafficking have been cut, in each the sense of national and regional self-confidence is growing. . . . In the genuinely free elections which none of these eight peoples is allowed to have, the proportion who would freely vote communist is probably not much more than it is in Glasgow, certainly much less than it is in Milan. . . . The purely economic burdens on the ordinary man from corruption in these governments is less than the burden on him from bureaucracy in countries which take much more from him than the 15 percent of national income in taxes, and then do not get the economic growth.
>
> . . . If ASEAN continues to double its grip each decade, the rich capitalist one-quarter of the world will soon center on three groups with 200-250 million people each (the United States, EEC, ASEAN) plus one group (Japan) with half that number. Of the coming world's big four, ASEAN has the most valuable recent experience in achieving economic policies that work together with political set-ups that are just tolerable, in the mine-strewn ideological background over which the poor three-quarters of the world are soon to advance.[15]

With even China recently tending to wonder if some imitation of the Japanese model is not a better way for it to go, this kind of an analysis becomes even more striking.

In the context of Latin America, moreover, it is most important to come to terms with this more progressive kind of development, for it belies graphically the seemingly ironclad argument that poor nations cannot become rapidly richer. Furthermore, it argues against the idea that socialism is the best method for the poor countries to use. The one Latin American nation that has been developing as rapidly as the ASEAN ones is probably the most important one, Brazil. And it is interesting to note the double standard applied to it in liberation literature about its successes and failures as compared to those of socialist systems.[16] In a real sense, the Latin American Left has a vested interest in seeing to it that Brazil fails to become the world power it seems to have every potential of becoming.

Actually, the total number of liberation theologians is not particularly large. The strength of the liberation system seems to be overly argued in terms drawn largely from European Marxist sources. An example of this is perhaps the use of the so-called "gap" theory, one popular in many even nonsocialist sources, one with a definite historical origin. Again, the argument ought not to be conceived as being over which group has greater sympathy for the poor. Rather it is over what kind of analysis really applies to the situation.[17]

THE GAP BETWEEN RICH AND POOR

Is the gap between rich and poor growing every day? And if it is, does that mean the poor are getting " poorer?" This thesis is an old one. Reaction to it goes back to Edouard Bernstein and the revisionists, who found that European workers in the nineteenth century were not in fact getting poorer, but richer. Lenin's *Imperialism*, whose inspiration comes largely from an English economist on this point, sought to save the theory by arguing that the "workers" in the colonies were getting poorer instead of the workers in Europe. However, the idea that an increasing gap means that the poor are actually getting poorer is, of course, quite unclear and illogical. Growth proceeds at different rates at different times. The idea of linear growth that so often dominates population and development studies needs greater circumspection. If the poor are getting poorer, we have some explaining to do in the light of a statement such as this:

Latin America's growth rate in 1973 was 7.4 percent, thus giving an average of 6.8 percent for the period of the present decade which has so far elapsed. The rise in per capita income in the same year was 4.5 percent, which is quite a high figure considering the big population increases recorded for the region as a whole.[18]

We could say, to be sure, that the rich are getting all of this so it is a structural problem. But there is no real evidence that the poor are themselves getting objectively poorer in any place on earth except in societies with seriously mismanaged or overly ideological institutions. Usually a resort to a "gap" explanation is necessary to uphold the thesis that the poor are getting poorer, an *a priori* thesis that arises from other sources than evidence. Furthermore, the gap thesis does not even begin to approach the problem of whether an egalitarian and controlled distribution system can provide motives for any growth at all.

For the most part, then, everyone is getting richer, even the so-called fourth world, but at widely differing rates. And these rates usually follow a pattern such that a country basing itself on work and enterprise usually achieves a higher growth rate. The ASEAN example clearly suggests that the poor can become richer and relatively quickly, something that Japan and Germany proved twice each in modern times, but only if they imitate the proper way and adapt to their own situation the ideas and institutions that cause growth. Furthermore, as Herman Kahn argued in his *The Next 200 Years*,

... by the year 2000 perhaps a quarter of mankind will live in emerging post-industrial societies and more than two-thirds will have passed the levels of $1000 per capita. By the end of the twenty-first century almost all societies should have a GNP per capita greater than $2000 and be entering some form of post-industrial culture. The task is not to see that these societies proceed along the same path as Europe, North America and Japan, but rather that each should find its own way. However, even in the year 2100 there may be large income gaps. Today per capita GNP ranges from about $100 to $10,000, and it would not surprise us if the range at the end of the twenty-first century were still rather large, perhaps from a basic minimum of a few thousand dollars to a maximum of ten to twenty times greater.

As far as we can tell, arithmetic differences (as opposed to ratios) in per capita product will generally increase for the next 100 years, with of course many exceptions. But this should not be disastrous either morally or politically since there are very few peasants, workers, or even businessmen in developing countries who care much about gaps (whether arithmetic or geometric), no matter how much intellectuals, academics, and some businessmen profess to. The major objective of most people is to increase their own safety and improve their own standard of living and their own capabilities. When they make comparisons, it is usually with others at their socioeconomic level or with those who have recently been at their own or a lower level.[19]

The "growing gap" theory and its implications, then, must be mostly rejected as a hypothesis, if it implies that the poor are getting poorer by some absolute standard. This is why the theory must present itself as psychological, that someone feels himself getting comparatively poorer. But this is clearly a spiritual and not a factual problem, clearly at the roots of why Plato and Aristotle were so concerned with envy as a factor in politics.[20]

WESTERN RESPONSIBILITY FOR THIRD WORLD POVERTY

The next essential element of liberation thought holds that the rich are rich *because* they are exploiting the poorer nations. Again, this is a fundamental tenet of liberation thought, usually accepted as methodologically and empirically true. The recent remarks of Philip Scharper, editor of Orbis Books, prime publisher of liberation theology in English, a noted lay commentator, serve to illustrate how this notion is used.

> Gunnar Myrdal has estimated, for example, that United States corporations, directly or indirectly, control or decisively influence between 70 and 90 per cent of the raw materials of Latin America, and probably more than half of its industry, banking, commerce, and foreign trade. . . . [Development failed so that] the developed nations continued to grow at the expense of the underdeveloped. . . . The "have" nations are not about to change patterns of trade in order to benefit the "have-nots". . . . History seems to show. . . . that effective altruism is seldom found in nations or groups possessing wealth and power.[21]

This latter idea of altruism would also be Augustine's and Reinhold Niebuhr's political realism. But in that case, all groups would have to be included, including socialist and radical ones, so that it is unfair to imply that only American corporations have this tendency. However, this is an interesting example of a tendency found in much liberation thinking to apply an essential spiritual category (effective altruism) to particular institutions under fire for political purposes.

The core of the issue here, however, has to do with the idea that business and commerce necessarily "exploit" when they operate for a profit to do large-scale, worldwide business which would not exist without the profit incentive. This is the other side of the question of the nature of profits and incentives themselves, something many modern clerics and intellectuals are reluctant to understand. The following example might, perhaps, be illustrative of this point:

> "Every time the word 'profit' comes up in that room, you can feel it," the Rev. William J. Inderstrodt said. . . . slowly clenching his fists as he stood outside the Economic Education Conference for Clergy. . . . "You can feel the tension."
>
> . . . "If you look at the preparation they get in the seminaries," said Edward L. Hamblin . . . "they don't have much insight on the economic sources which move society, if they are called upon to interpret these forces from the pulpit. The very basic elements we're talking about are how the market functions, and what the payoffs are, like the creation of wealth. This group is particularly sensitive to equity factor. . . ."
>
> "How are you going to deliver food to these people when agriculture is run on a profit basis?" [the Rev. John B. Ferra] asked.
>
> "To say food is for people and not for profit, would eventually preclude all of you from having food," countered Luther E. Stearns of the American Farm Bureau Federation. . . .
>
> "We never talk in the churches about incentives." [Mr. Inderstrodt] said. . . . "Most business executives look at the clergy as softheaded, and most clergy look at business executives as less than used-car salesmen."[22]

The claim is often made, moreover, that business operates differently in Latin America. But again the question must be posed against the culture that accepts and limits its operations. Business has probably recognized long before the moralist or politician the complexity of dealing with governments or unions that demand bribes to continue any sort of operation at all. Furthermore, the failure of Marxist-socialist analysis to grasp the meaning of the profit incentive and its relation to freedom has long been noted.

Catholic social thought has traditionally articulated the danger of abuse of profits, beginning with Leo XIII. But it has always recognized their meaning and legitimacy, as well as the close relationship they bear to incentive and the capacity of the free person to act on the world. The essential point, then, is that profits do not represent automatically "exploitation." That is, they do not take away from someone what is his. Rather they create something that is new, that would never otherwise have existed. When they fail to do this there are, properly speaking, abuses. Professor P. T. Bauer put this issue well:

> Many of the assertions concerning Western responsibility for poverty in the third world express or reflect the belief that the prosperity of relatively well-to-do persons, groups, and societies is always achieved at the expense of the less well-off, i.e., that incomes are not generated by those who earn them, but are somehow extracted from others, so that economic activity is akin to a zero-sum game, in which the gains of some are always balanced by the loss of others. In fact, incomes (other than subsidies) are earned by the recipients for resources and services supplied, and are not acquired by depriving others of what they had.[23]

If this be basically true, as it seems to be, the whole basis of the exploitation analysis is undermined, and a truer picture of the world is open for consideration. This newer one would have a more proper place for incentive, abundance, growth, and alleviation of poverty in a system that demands not the struggle of class against class, as liberation thought insists, but rather the operative competition and intelligence of all, for an objective good, one called by the central line of Catholic social thought "the common good."

MULTI-NATIONAL CORPORATIONS

Norman Macrae has often and forcefully argued that one of the best institutions for the rapid transferal of skills, capital, and production to the third world is the much criticized multi-national corporation.[24] Almost by instinct, liberation theology, which on this score betrays little of the famous sixteenth and seventeenth century Spanish Jesuit moral pragmatism at the advent of capitalism over the question of usury, has zeroed in on this so-called sinful structure of the corporation as its main target. This had entailed a rejection of the famous and still worthy thesis of Jacques Maritain in his *Reflections on America* about how such economic institutions, imperfect as they might be, really work, guided by law and custom and public opinion.

John Kenneth Galbraith, never a full fan, has even found it necessary to say a few kind words of the multi-national corporation:

> If to be a part of the Third World is to be a hewer of wood and a supplier of food and natural produce, the United States and Canada are, by a wide margin, the first of the Third World countries and should vote accordingly in the United Nations.
>
> International trade always had to be defended against those who saw only its costs, never its advantages; who saw only the intrusions of foreign competition, never the resulting efficiency in supply or products or the reciprocal gains from greater exports. The multi-national corporation comes into existence when international trade consists of modern, technical, specialized or uniquely styled manufactured products. Accordingly, it should be defended as international trade was defended, for its contribution to efficiency in production and marketing, to living standards, and to reciprocal opportunities in other lands for the enterprises of the host country. . . .
>
> . . . Critics allege that multi-national corporations export jobs, capital, and technology. This is one of the few matters on which the multi-national enterprise has developed a defense. It holds that, in one way or another, it cares most about the home country and its labor force—these are its primary interests. It should hold more often than it does that, as it goes abroad, others from abroad should come in. The aggregate result is a more rapid spread of technology, a better international division of labor, greater productivity, greater aggregate employment.[25]

Again, such observations serve as a corrective for the implicit theory which holds that because business in a foreign country produces and makes a profit, it only "takes" from that country and that the same or better level of development would be possible without it and its innovations.

ECONOMIC AND THEOLOGICAL DUALISM

The final and perhaps most serious defect of formal liberation thought is what is called its "manichean" tendency. This is a temptation to divide good and evil according to rich and poor. The whole exploitation analysis is open to this danger. The Brazilian-based Dominican François Lepargneur pointed out the problem:

> One can beautifully reinterpret the gospel as he wishes, but if he will remain honest, he will recognize that the construction of the Kingdom of God is founded essentially on personal conversion and not on an intellectual dialectics of force. And ideology, even if it present itself under the title of theology, which rests essentially on the accusation of someone else as the author of all evil, is not to be confounded with a viable interpretation of Christianity which is, in its very principle, an appeal to the conversion of him who receives the call of grace, of salvation. Otherwise, one does not speak of the same salvation, of the same God, of the same religion.[26]

And this thesis of liberation theology, that it speaks for the poor who are implicitly the "good" against the rich who are "bad," this endeavor to see all through the eyes of the poor, needs further attention.

Fortunately, both Jacques Ellul and Hannah Arendt have called our attention to the erroneous and one-sided way "the poor" are used in modern thought. Ellul, the French Protestant sociologist-theologian, sharply pointed out in his *The Betrayal of the West*, how selective the precise denomination of the poor really has been. The poor become much too often, and in an unacknowledged way, those who conform to the theoretical exigencies of ideological demands, not those who really suffer for justice or poverty. This is usually seen in the selective way the poor are denominated in a given system. Poverty is used surprisingly often as a tool and ideological weapon for achieving a certain kind of society and that alone.[27]

Hannah Arendt, in her *On Revolution*, has reminded us of the curious connection between the radically different notions of the poor in the American and French Revolution. The intellectual significance of this is very important.[28] Essentially, she argued that the "passion for compassion" which dominates the discussion comes from the French Revolution, wherein essentially political and social questions were confused. The notion of poverty was transformed into part of a necessitarian program in the Hegelian tradition so that all revolutions were supposed necessarily to follow the path of the French Revolution. This path had to be built into any revolutionary project. Thus, the terror and poverty were logically joined together through an idea or tradition; they do not imply one another. "The poor" again became signs in such an analysis, tools for a societal process.

Hannah Arendt's observations are remarkable in the light of liberation theology's self-proclaimed priorities and values which place the poor at such a central point:

> In this stream of the poor, the element of irresistibility, which we found so intimately connected with the original meaning of the word "revolution," was embodied. . . . All rulership has its original and its most legitimate source in man's wish to emancipate himself from life's necessity, and men achieved such liberation by means of violence, by forcing others to bear the burdens of life for them. This was the core of slavery, and it is only the rise of technology, and not the rise of modern political ideas as such, which has refuted the old and terrible truth that only violence and rule over others could make some free.
>
> *Nothing we might say today could be more obsolete than to attempt to liberate mankind from poverty by political means; nothing could be more futile and more dangerous.* For the violence which occurs between men who are emancipated from necessity is different from, less terrifying, though often not less cruel, than the primordial violence with which man pits himself against necessity, and which appeared in the full daylight of political, historically recorded events for the first time in the modern age. The result was that necessity invaded the political realm, the only realm that can be truly free.
>
> The masses of the poor, this overwhelming majority of all men, whom the French Revolution called *les malheureux*, whom it transformed into *les enragés*, only to desert them and let them fall back into the state of *les misérables*, as the nineteenth century called them, carried with them necessity, to which they had been subject as long as memory reaches, together with the violence that had always been used to overcome necessity. Both together, necessity and violence, made them appear irresistible. . . . [29]

What can be stressed from these remarks of Ellul and Arendt, then, is that the peculiar force and manner in which "the poor" are reiterated and used in most liberation theology have an intellectual structure closer to this French Revolutionary kind of analysis than to anything in Scripture or classic Catholic social thought. This is the ultimate root, too, of the otherwise inexplicable anti-Americanism in most liberation approaches. This is something, as Arendt suggested, that must go back to the basic differences between the French and American revolutions.[30] In this light, consequently, the theses on the growing "gap," on the necessity of violence, on profit, on the poor all flow from this intellectual background and explain why it is not able to take the more pragmatic—and more philosophical—avenues found in the American tradition, in much papal analysis, in Maritain, Kahn, Macrae, Bauer, and others who are looking also at real poverty and what relieves it.

Hans Urs von Balthasar, the noted Swiss theologian, suggested that this would be an appropriate attitude to take to liberation theology:

> I feel that the combined efforts of theology in the United States and Europe should also be directed toward helping the Latin American theology of liberation, which often becomes self-seeking and confused. I mean helping to clarify it with a sympathetic understanding of its genuine claims. Teilhard de Chardin (the French Jesuit philosopher) saw the future of theology as supranational, global, but he did not recognize the concerns of liberation theology. We must include them in our theological thinking, but in doing so, we must show greater discernment than our South American brothers do. Usually, their analysis of the social situation is based impulsively on Marxist categories of "exploiting" and "exploited" countries. . . . The tragic situation is more complex and we must show them that.
>
> . . . The exponents of this third (liberation) direction must learn— with all due regard to their justified claims—that the Kingdom of God cannot be coerced into existence by any amount of social or political effort. It remains the gift of God and of the returning Lord to a world that cannot perfect itself by its own efforts.[31]

These words of von Balthasar suggest why the movement of Christians Arising in Latin America is mostly an "impractical *praxis.*" For it seems constantly to confuse the goal for a mere aid and means, while ignoring the real means available for the goal it does profess, the elimination of poverty. The ironies of the situation, of course, are many; but Latin America is now thinking of the United States and Europe, and these countries are thinking of it. How each thinks of the other remains the vital question for both. For it is still mostly what men think that determines what they shall endeavor to put into effect.

Liberation Theology

NOTES

1. Hans Schmidt, "Politics and Christology: Historical Background", *Concilium*, no. 36 (New York: Paulist Press, 1968) pp. 72-84.
2. Karl Rahner, *On Heresy* (Montreal: Palm Publishers, 1964).
3. John Henry Newman, *The Arians of the Fourth Century* (London: Longmans, 1908, 1st ed. 1833) pp. 393-94.
4. Jean Guitton, *Great Heresies and Church Councils* (New York: Harper, 1965) pp. 21, 95.
5. Compare N. Macrae, "America's Third Century", *The Economist*, London (October 25, 1975); Michael Novak, *The American Vision* (Washington: American Enterprise Institute, 1978); and Michael Novak, *The Spirit of Democratic Capitalism* (New York: Simon & Schuster, 1982); see also Roger Heckel, *The Theme of Liberation* (Rome: Pontifical Commission on Justice and Peace, 1980) pp. 21-24.
6. P. T. Bauer, "Western Guilt and Third World Poverty", *Commentary* (January, 1976); T. W. Schultz, "The Economics of Being Poor", *Journal of Political Economy*, no. 4 (1980) pp. 639-51; P. T. Bauer, "Breaking the Grip of Poverty". *Wall Street Journal* (April 18, 1979).
7. J. D. Metz, "The Church and the World in the Light of a 'Political Theology' ", *The Theology of the World* (New York: Herder, 1969) pp. 122-23. See the author's *Christianity and Politics* (Boston: St. Paul Editions, 1981).
8. Compare F. L. Fiorenza, "Political Theology: An Historical Analysis", *Theology Digest* (Winter, 1977) pp. 317-334; Jeane Kirkpatrick, "Dictatorships and Double Standards", in Schall's *Liberation Theology in Latin America* (San Francisco: Ignatius Press, 1982) pp. 162-190; M. Dodson, "Prophetic Theory and Political Theory in Latin America", *Polity* (Spring, 1980) pp. 358-408.
9. A. Fierro, *The Militant Gospel* (Maryknoll: Orbis, 1975) p. 15.
10. Ibid., p. 16.
11. Cf. J. Holland, "Marxian Class Analysis in American Society Today", *Theology in America* (Maryknoll; Orbis, 1976) pp. 317-28; Fathers E. Toland, M.M., T. Fenton, M.M., and L. McCulloch , M.M. "World Justice and Peace: A Radical Analysis for American Christians", *IDOC—North America* (Summer, 1973) 1-8; in Europe, Father Giulio Girardi serves a similar function, cf. his "Christianity and the Class Struggle", *IDOC—North America* (November 14, 1970) 5-18, and his *Christianesimo, Liberazione Umana, Lotta di Classe* (Assisi: Citadella, 1972); A. F. McGovern, *Marxism: An American Christian Perspective* (Maryknoll: Orbis, 1980); P. Lernoux, *Cry of the People* (New York: Doubleday, 1980).
12. Cf. Bishops of Argentina, "National Security vs. Individual Rights", *Origins* (June 2, 1977); the results of the III Episcopal Conference of the Latin American Bishops in Puebla, Mexico, in 1979 also are a basic source to see where the bishops stand on most of these questions. See document no. 2, below.
13. Cf. R. Coste, *Analyse marxiste et foi chrétien* (Paris, 1976).
14. Edward J. Williams, *The Emergence of the Secular Nation-State and Latin American Catholicism*, Tucson, Arizona, University of Arizona, Research Paper no. 7 (1971) pp. 21-22.

15. See *The Economist*, London (May 13, 1978); N. Macrae, "Must Japan Slow", *The Economist*, Survey (February 23, 1980).

16. Cf. D. Moynihan, "The United States in Opposition", *Commentary* (March, 1975) pp. 31-44.

17. Cf. "The Moving Frontier", *The Economist*, London, Survey (September 2, 1972); "On, Brazil", *The Economist*, Survey (August 4, 1979).

18. Enrique V. Iglesias, "Latin America and the Creation of the New World Order", *Economic Bulletin for Latin America*, U.N., no 1 and no. 2 (1974) p. 1.

19. Herman Kahn, *The Next 200 Years* (New York: Morrow, 1976) pp. 48-49. Ben Wattenberg makes this same kind of point in *The Real America* (New York: Capricorn, 1976); H Kahn, *World Economic Development* (New York: Morrow, 1979).

20. Cf. D. Vree, *On Synthesizing Marxism and Christianity* (New York: Wiley, 1976); cf. *Solzhenitsyn at Harvard* (Washington: Ethics and Public Policy Center, 1980).

21. Philip Scharper, "Toward a Politicized Christianity", *The Commonweal* (June 16, 1978) p. 395. Cf. in this context, Irving Kristol's "Human Nature and Social Reform", *The Wall Street Journal* (September 18, 1978); N. Macrae, "The Brusque Recessional", *The Economist*, London, Survey (December 28, 1979).

22. M. L. Wald, "Clergymen Get Short Courses in Economics", *The New York Times* (June 21, 1978); cf. P. Johnson, "Capitalism's Futures", *Wall Street Journal* (January 22, 1981).

23. P.T. Bauer, "Western Guilt and Third World Poverty", *Commentary* (January, 1976) p. 36.

24. Cf. Norman Macrae, "The Future of International Business", *The Economist*, Survey (January 20, 1972); "America's Third Century", *The Economist*, Survey (October 25, 1975). Cf. also Michael Novak's *The American Vision: An Essay on the Future of Democratic Capitalism* (Washington: American Enterprise Institute, 1978); I. Kristol, "No Cheers for the Profit Motive", *Wall Street Journal* (February 20, 1979).

25. John Kenneth Galbraith, "The Defence of the Multinational Company", *The Harvard Business Review* (March-April, 1978) pp. 85, 88, 89; cf. also S. Brennan and E. Molander, "Is the Ethics of Business Changing?". *The Harvard Business Review* (January-February, 1977) pp. 57-71; T. J. Purcell, "Management and the 'Ethical' Investors", *Harvard Business Review* (September-October, 1979).

26. François Lepargneur, *"Theologies de la liberation et théologie tout court"*, *Nouvelle Revue Théologique*, Louvain (February, 1976) pp. 167-68.

27. Jacques Ellul, *The Betrayal of the West* (New York: Seabury, 1978) Chapter II, "The Truly Poor and the End of the Left", pp. 87-146; cf. M. Krauss, "Social Democracies and Foreign Aid", *Wall Street Journal* (September 12, 1979).

28. Hannah Arendt, "The Social Question", in her *On Revolution* (New York: Viking, 1965) pp. 53-110.

29. Ibid., p. 110. Italics added.

30. Cf. ibid., pp. 62-68.

31. Hans Urs von Balthasar, "Current Trends in Catholic Theology", *Communio* (Sprint, 1978) pp. 84-85.

A PILGRIMAGE IN POLITICAL THEOLOGY

Clark H. Pinnock

Clark H. Pinnock

Clark H. Pinnock is presently professor of theology at McMaster Divinity College in Hamilton, Ontario. Prior to this he taught at Regent College, Trinity Evangelical Divinity School, New Orleans Baptist Theological Seminary, and the University of Manchester (England) from which he gained his doctorate in New Testament. He is the author of *Reason Enough*, *Biblical Revelation*, and *Set Forth Your Case* and has two new books in the press on biblical inspiration and contemporary theology. He has been contributing editor of *Christianity Today* and *Sojourners* in recent years.

A PILGRIMAGE IN POLITICAL THEOLOGY — A Personal Witness

While evangelical Christians agree about the central doctrines of the Christian faith, their thinking about social and political issues evidences increasing division and disagreement. Evangelical reflection about social and political issues is like a turbulent river which turns this way and that, and contains several strong currents. Persons who lack strong convictions in such matters can easily find themselves tossed about with uncertainty. To some extent, this has happened to me. Since I believe that this record of my own pilgrimage may help explain how committed Christian leaders can be misled into thinking that the Bible requires a rejection of political conservatism and an acceptance of leftist convictions, I have decided to tell my story. I hope it will help others who are struggling in this difficult and confusing area.[1]

Many evangelicals in our day realize that privatism in faith is wrong. The gospel speaks to the whole of life; its social implications are inescapable. The "great reversal" of which Timothy Smith speaks has in large measure itself been reversed. Many contemporary believers are eager to apply their faith to the issues of life in society. The issue today therefore is what *kind* of involvement and what *sort* of action is required by the Bible. We agree that God's will ought to be done on earth as it is in heaven. But what is His will? The poor ought to be helped. But what specific actions will help them? Unlike the social apathy that often existed a generation ago, we all believe now in the social implications of the gospel. But what program shall we follow and on what platform shall we stand? To which evangelical thinker shall we turn for leadership? What policies and actions will bring liberty and justice in their wake? Finding the correct answers to these questions constitutes the agenda for the 1980s.

My own pilgrimage has been a struggle to gain a degree of clarity in this area. My path over the years has turned out to be a fairly straight line with the exception of one enormous zigzag in the middle. My own quest went through three major phases. Until I began experimenting with political radicalism in 1970, I had moved quite generally in the mainstream of North American evangelical political thinking. My theological conservatism was coupled with leanings in the direction of political conservatism. Because my eschatology during those earlier years was amillenial, I really did not place much emphasis upon political affairs. I valued democracy, our historical Christian roots, and capitalist institutions. But in 1970 my political thinking underwent a paradigm shift—a total transformation. Living in the United States at the time, I began to read the Bible from an anabaptist perspective and soon found myself looking at society through the eyes of the new left. Things formerly valued in American society became targets of my disapproval as I became more conscious of the effects of materialism, racism, injustice and the Viet Nam war. The radical edge of Scripture had caught my attention and I could not ignore the evils of democratic capitalism. It was a new political-theological world to move in and it produced a heady experience which intoxicated me and many others. It led my personally to sympathy and support for the Marxist movements of the world. By 1974, having returned to my native Canada, I even voted for communist candidates in the Vancouver civic elections. Looking back on this radical period now, it seems incredible that I could have accepted so many implausible things and I am reminded forcefully of my human condition. It is now easier for me to understand how people can be swept along in their support of strange causes like the German people in the 1930s. The real excitement that can be created by a new ideology can sweep away a good deal of critical sense.

The third phase in my political pilgrimage began after I had spent some eight years in the radical movement. This new conversion followed much the same course as my earlier conversion to radicalism. Gradually, I began to reassess my position and my alienation from North America began to fade, replaced by a certain critical appreciation of democratic capitalism that I had had before 1970. At the same time, I was becoming more conscious of the reasonableness of Reformed hermeneutics over against the anabaptist approach. The urgency I had acquired from the radical evangelicals has, with regard to political action, been internalized and applied to my new political orientation. I have not returned to the relative indifference I felt toward politics in my first phase but have picked up some enthusiasm for what I would term neo-Puritan politics. With this brief outline of my sojourn now drawn, let me turn to a more detailed account of my search.

PHASE ONE: IN THE MAINSTREAM, 1953 - 1969

I was born and raised in a middle class southern Ontario home and a socially respectable progressive Baptist church. I was converted through the witness of evangelical believers and organizations like Youth for Christ. While for a time my theology could be described as fundamentalist, I came increasingly under the influence of the kind of mainstream evangelical theology associated with the old Princeton Seminary. During the years following my conversion, I was introduced to all the major lines of evangelical social thought. I admired Billy Graham and accepted his approach to social change through evangelism. While he taught us to love America, he also helped us recognize her sins. While spending some time at L'Abri in the ealry 1960s, I came under the influence of Francis Schaeffer. Through him, I learned to emphasize theological over political issues. While Schaeffer sometimes spoke in support of the Viet Nam war, he also spoke out against the rise of secularism in America and showed sympathy for the flower children who needed Christ. What seeds of radicalism I may have picked up from Schaeffer came not so much because he broke with democratic capitalism (he didn't), but because he identified with alienated youth in a way that appeared to support some of their concerns. Carl Henry also influenced me (in the direction of a cautious reformism) through two books on ethics and his writings in *Christianity Today*. I also have to admit a fascination and respect for Bill Buckley and the feisty way in which he defended the capitalist way against its critics. (I still do today.)

During phase one of my sojourn, I was far more concerned with the problem of biblical inerrancy than the issue of racism. I was fairly skeptical of the effectiveness of governmental intervention in economic matters and in the case of social welfare. I viewed the "Great Society" as a bit of a farce. I thought that society's greatest need was the conversion of its people. I saw democratic capitalism in a good light and strongly disapproved of atheistic communism. As far as Viet Nam was concerned, I was a Canadian who felt it was an unpleasant American duty to defend freedom in Southeast Asia; I wished them well.

In addition to the possibility that Schaeffer may have quickened the radical impulse in me, my conversion to premillennialism in the late 1960s through influences at Dallas Theological Seminary could be seen as another radical seed. Although it is true that dispensational premillennialists are notoriously passive politically, it is also true that such an eschatology puts one in radical opposition to the powers that be and makes one a potential radical.

PHASE TWO: OUT ON THE EDGES, 1970-1978

A contagion was in the air for young people in the 1960s and influenced many of our generation. It happened late for me. At Trinity Evangelical Divinity School Jim Wallis gathered a small group of people deeply critical of America and supportive of radical politics and anabaptist hermeneutics. Out of this circle came first the *Post American* and then its successor, the widely influential *Sojourners*. In sympathy with these young people, I too began to be turned off by what we saw as plastic culture, the violence in Viet Nam, and America's unacknowledged racism. Without my conscious awareness, I bought into a fusion or synthesis of the new left and anabaptist thought.[2] At that time I perceived the union as enjoying God's favour.

I can best explain my new standpoint by referring to three corners of a triad. First, there was a deep alienation from North American culture. Some of the mainstream evangelicals like Carl Henry, Francis Schaeffer, and Billy Graham had emphasized the point that America was corrupting herself and selling her birthright, but they had something different in mind. They did not mean that the whole system was evil or that the church had betrayed the gospel. They wanted reform of a basically good culture, not a complete overthrow. But we saw North America as the polar opposite of the gospel. We saw practically nothing to celebrate in it. Our rhetoric knew no bounds. We applauded William Stringfellow when he identified America with the great whore of Babylon of Revelation 17-19.[3] To be fair, we believed in the great American revolutionary heritage as we understood it, but saw no evidence of that tradition at work in the present. In our ideology, America was wholly given over to the Babylon pattern and was a worthy successor to Nazi Germany. Now it is also true that we viewed *all* earthly systems as evil in line with our anabaptist exegesis, and if pressed would insist that we disliked the Marxist societies just as much. But it is doubtful if this really was the case. I at least looked wistfully at those 'revolutionary' societies which seemed to embody the communitarian ideal more perfectly than my own.

But our concentration was not on political solutions. We tended to be skeptical of those. As evangelicals and anabaptists we tended toward a new community where Christians would give up their privileges in the middle class, share their possessions and assets, and embody the new humanity beside the poor. That was the solution we were committed to, God's 'original revolution'.[4] In our minds, it was God's wise social strategy, and it mattered not if the world complained it was not enough. As radicals, we did not accept the ideals of our fellow evangelicals such as individualism, patriotism, and capitalism, but bought into the denunciation of the Western democracies as a zone of oppression and injustice. It was doomed, and we planned to sing the Hallelujah Chorus when it fell. We were convinced by the crisis mentality of the Club of Rome and found ourselves out of line with almost every policy and behavior we saw our culture pursuing. It was a revolt of the advantaged. We hated those who were successful in the system, and therefore ourselves who had tasted all of its benefits. For me, radicalism served to take away the guilt I felt for being born into an advantaged situation. I do not fully understand the dynamics at work here, and leave the matter to a psychologist.[5]

Second, about the same time there was a resurgence of anabaptist theology and it facilitated the radicalizing process by providing theological foundations. When it dawned upon us, we had the feeling of a second conversion. It was Christ-centered and biblicist and so appealed to our evangelical instincts, but it was radical and subversive of every status quo and so confirmed the cultural alienation we felt.[6] It taught us a way to go back to our conservative churches and preach the new gospel of Christian radicalism in an evangelical modality. The Bible teaches a radical message, we said, and that was that. Anabaptist theology was made to order for our situation. It told us that North America, like all cultures, was a fallen order with which the Christian could not compromise. Jesus Christ had come to smash all such systems, not by violence, but by speaking of a new order in which all systems of domination in regard to money, rank, and hierarchy will be overthrown, and those who are first in this world will be last in that one. The great mistake of the church, committed first by Constantine, was the decision to ally herself with satanic power and betray her radical identity. The call was for the faithful to come out from Babylon, including the apostate evangelical churches, and form radical communities which would take their courageous stand against the materialism and violence of our culture. Simple lifestyle, nonviolence, economic sharing, equality, communitarianism—these were the signs of the authentic church today. By this means perhaps the world could be changed through the effect of a light that cannot be hid. Anabaptist theology supported our alienation admirably. To be a Christian was to be a radical and a subversive! We exist as sojourners to call the establishment into question, and to live our lives for others. It was also a hermeneutic which interpreted the New Testament, and particularly the Sermon on the Mount in a radical way. Historically it led believers to avoid the use of oaths, personal or military force, legal justice, and at times even the possession of private property. It also tended to cause them to withdraw from political and social life and to a strict separation of church and state. As radical evangelicals, we did not withdraw from public life, but our involvement in it was always counter-cultural and never culture-reclaiming. There was a dualism between the pure community and the evil social order and a situation of constant tension.

Third, the political context of the radical movement of which we were a Christian segment was the new left. It was alienated from America and could say why in non-theological terms. Corporate capitalism was the root of America's degeneracy and the source of its injustice, violence, and racism. It was a system which raped the enviroment and ruled the world on behalf of the wealthy minority. It was a corrupt system and had to be overthrown. Without being ideologically left myself, I was in considerable agreement with what the new left said both by way of criticism and suggestion. I remember being asked if I realized the Marxist content of what we were saying in the *Post American* and being puzzled by the question. I was a babe in political thinking and was saying things based on what I thought were exegetical grounds, the importance of which I did not fully understand. I felt that the poor were poor because the rich were rich, and what was needed was state intervention and voluntary poverty on the part of Christians. It seemed reasonable to think of the rich as oppressors, and the poor as their victims. The Bible often seemed to do the same thing. It was obvious to me that the welfare state needed to be extended, that wealth ought to be forcibly redistributed through taxation, that the third world deserved reparations from us, that our defense spending was in order to protect our privilege, and the like. I did not require proof of such propositions— they all seemed obvious and self-evident. The excitement of the change of thinking suppressed even the small amount of critical judgment I had acquired before 1970.

Socialist ideals also provided allurement. Was socialism not a grand vision of a just and humane order which distributed its resources fairly and equitably among all its people according to their need? Was it not true democracy where decisions were made not by the wealthy elite but by the people? Without equating the two, it was so easy for me to associate in my mind the socialist utopia and the promised kingdom of God. There was a high-mindedness to the vision which made it compelling. It was this attraction which had drawn churchmen in the ecumenical movement to the left for decades prior to our conversion. We admired what we thought was happening in the new China under Mao, and we hoped that the Viet Cong would win out against American forces. Our radicalism was a fusion of anabaptist hermeneutics and new left political orientation.[7]

PHASE THREE: RETURN TO THE CENTER, 1978-1984

Late in the 1970s each of the three points of the radical triad began to lose their power over me. First, I began to awaken out of my radical dream, and to see once again the positive tendencies of democratic capitalism which had been eclipsed. I began to view such things as free speech, limited government, an independent judiciary, genuine pluralism, and a concern for human rights to be evidence of the promise of America in a world so largely lacking these privileges. It now struck me as somewhat ridiculous to overlook those positive features of North American life which had incidentally made it possible for radicals like me to express and live out our concerns. How could I have had such deep contempt for a culture which surely stands as a beacon of hope in this suffering world? How ironic to call for 'liberation' in the very place there is probably more of it than anywhere else in the world, and to be sympathetic toward those societies where neither liberty nor justice is in good supply. It began to dawn on me that if one was looking for Babylon in this present world, one might rather look toward the threat of totalitarian government which seeks to usurp all sovereignty in a culture. What really endangers liberty and justice in our world is not a flawed America, but that political monism, whether of the facist right or the communist left, which declares itself to be absolute and answers to no transcendent value. How ironic that the *Reader's Digest*, which we refused to read in the 1960s, should now seem to have grasped the truth about the world, and *Ramparts*, which we read avidly, should have been so blind. But it is so. We radicals thought we loved peace and justice, but we simply did not grasp the nature of tyranny in the modern world. We thought Stalin was an aberration in the history of socialism rather than its symbol. We refused to see that communism was facist and spelled the destruction of the human spirit, as Solzhenitsyn put it, 'a levelling unto death'.[8]

Once freed from the hold of the radical perspective, many of the old issues took on a different aspect. For example, I used to find discrimination everywhere, whereas now I do not. What impresses me now is the degree we have been able to overcome racism and the fact that our society in North America is remarkable for its open pluralism. On the ecological side, the old crisis mentality seems quaint. We are not running out of energy or natural resources, but are finding abundant new ones. We are not running out of land or food—production outstrips demand. Pollution is not insoluble, but decreases as soon as we take the problem seriously.[9] Even the Viet Nam war looks quite different now. Although the peace movement meant well, it addressed itself to the wrong powers and as a result led to the enslavement of large parts of Southeast Asia. Solzhenitsyn does not exaggerate when he says that we radicals were accomplices in the betrayal of those nations. Christians must be peacemakers, but surely that does not mean we have to assist totalitarian powers gain still more slaves. Will we never learn the lesson of Neville Chamberlain?

In one respect, though, my politics continues to be radical. Not radical in the directions I now disavow, but in the direction of a neo-Puritan vision. Still a millennialist, I now see a greater realization of the kingdom in society before the eschaton. I anticipate Christ's enemies being put beneath his feet and his rule extending to all nations in history. He commanded us to disciple all nations, to bring them under his sway, and now I have a stronger faith this will actually be done. Like the post-millennialists of an earlier era, I look forward to the day when Jesus shall reign wherever the sun, as Watts puts it, and the knowledge of the Lord will cover the earth. This is, of course, the old Puritan eschatology and vision, and we see it undergoing a resurgence on many sides, in the recent work of Schaeffer, in the ministry of the New Right, and in the Chalcedon movement for Christian reconstruction.

Although I do not believe the program we should follow is yet complete or beyond criticism, I do think it is a positive direction and constitutes a major new form of evangelical social theology. One of the implications is that the church need not find itself perpetually in a countercultural posture. In cultures like our own where the gospel has taken deep root and penetrated many areas, the task of the church can be to encourage the christianization of the culture and call the nation to the will of God, and to assure people that God will surely bless the nation whose God is the Lord. Christians should be busy calling for fiscal responsibility, effective law enforcement, limited government, the right to life, the stability of the family, adequate defense, the needs of the poor, the problem of pornography, and the like. I agree with the radicals that the gospel is meant to have far-reaching social implications, and look for the coming of God's kingdom and a society governed according to his law.

Second, just as the cultural alienation of the second phase required an anabaptist hermeneutic to sustain it, so this phase is in keeping with a Reformed one. To effect the shift from one to the other all one needs to do is recover the Old Testament as the foundation of

New Testament politics. The anabaptist reading of the Bible pits the Old Testament against the New at many crucial points. It turns away from its emphasis on the legitimacy of earthly powers and the responsibility believers have to exercise them in a godly manner. It finds virtue instead in a repudiation of such power and delights in powerlessness as the mark of the Christian. The true believer is supposed to refuse to try to manage society even if he has the opportunity and to avoid all coercive activities. But this makes no sense in the context of the Old Testament, where blessing is pronounced upon the godly rulers. It seems to me now that it is unnatural to read the New Testament as if it rejects the Old Testament framework in these areas. We are told to pray for the governing authorities because they are ordained by God. The gospel affirms the abiding validity of God's law, including such things as the proper responsibility of civil magistrates and their duty to resist evildoers. While it is possible to read the Sermon on the Mount differently, it is not necessary to do so. I have returned to the view that evangelical political work ought to have an institutional as well as intentional component. It is not just a question of building new community, but also of bringing society under God's law. Human societies need not be under Satan's sway and the goal of political theology ought to be to conform to God's scriptural will. In the case of our Western democracies, it seems plain to me now that the Christian heritage operating in them is profound and precious, and renders them worthy of critical support and reforming efforts, The future is open. It belongs to the Lord of history who intends to reclaim the whole creation. Therefore, we ought to be hopeful and energetic in pressing the crown rights of the Redeemer.[10]

Third, there is an ideological component in all this too. I have changed my mind about democratic capitalism. Like Peter Berger and many others, I have come to see it in a very different light. Far from being the enemy of the poor, it now seems to me to offer both liberty and prosperity in abundance and to deserve our cautious support. Socialism, on the other hand, has a dismal record of providing neither.

I am not an expert in economics, far from it, but I can now see why North America is rich and many other nations are not. It is not because we have exploited the third world and robbed them of their wealth. Quite the contrary, the world is poorest precisely where there has been no contact with the West. What prosperity there is in the third world has often been the result of contact with it.[11] No, the rapid economic growth we have experienced is largely the result of a set of factors including the rise of industrial capitalism. In Britain alone in the nineteenth century there was a 1600 percent rise in goods and wages.[12] It was as if the human race had at last hit upon an effective formula for raising whole populations from poverty to unheard of standards of wealth. The capacity of capitalism to generate wealth is unparalleled in history, and quite possibly one of the greatest single blessings bestowed on humanity. No system has been so helpful to the poor and provided such opportunity to rise out of suffering. It has done so chiefly by reason of the fact it allows wealth to be diversely controlled and be freely invested in new causes. Real wealth is not the possession of natural resources. It is human creativity and ingenuity and that is what democratic capitalism releases in good measure. Any system will prosper which gives liberty to this ultimate resource. It is irresponsible for me as a theologian to be ignorant of what will help the poor while claiming piously to be in solidarity with them. We have to say what is needed if the standard of living of the poor is to rise; namely, a commitment to economic growth and liberty for economic agents to undertake the kind of risks and investments which will lead to an accumulation of wealth for the people. Democratic capitalism has a proven record in the area of wealth production; if we care for the poor, we ought to promote it rather than condemn it. In addition to providing material prosperity, the system also produces liberty, since it is an economics in which individuals can operate at will and the state does not take charge. Political freedom is consonant with a free market. As Milton Friedman has said, "I know of no example in time or place of a society that has been marked by a large measure of political freedom, and that has not also used something comparable to a free market to organize the bulk of economic activity."[13]

Should we go so far as to say that the Bible supports this economic policy? I think we should be cautious in this area. If the Bible does teach this policy, it is strange why we did not discover it earlier. It is also risky to tie the Scriptures to any such system, thus repeating the radical mistake of regularly linking it to socialism. Nevertheless, the Bible offers many insights which bear upon economics and are at least consistent with market practices. It calls upon all of us to be stewards of resources and to have dominion of the earth. It implies that it is a moral activity which we choose or refuse to do. It praises diligent and honest labor. It prohibits theft of property and promises wealth to the godly. It insists upon stable currency, just weights and measures. It does not see the role of the state to be active in this area except to ensure justice. Scripture teaches us that long term economic growth flows from obedience to God and that stubborn poverty is the result of disobedience. It defends the rights of the disadvantaged and calls upon the godly to help them get on their feet by means of the Lord's tithe. God is not on the side of the poor in some abstract general sense, but he is moved in mercy toward the oppressed and commands his people to show mercy in speaking on their behalf and extending favor to them. Often when we hear talk about Christian economics, it is actually secular economics imported into theological ethics. What we need to do is study and utilize the biblical materials on this subject more fully.

Although I do see democratic capitalism as a resource of relative good and hope in this fallen world, I do not think its future is necessarily bright. We have become secular and materialistic and risk losing all we have been given. We have succumbed to the very materialism which has produced the communist tyranny. We no longer stand tall for the great values that lie beneath our feet. There is nothing to prevent our civilization from ending up on the scrapheap of history. God's law makes it plain that while he will bless the faithful, he will not hesitate to judge the unfaithful. Consider the enormous deficits we have amassed which rob future generations, inflate the currency, and slow the engine of growth. Think of the irresponsibility of our banks which have lent out vast quantities of our resources to unworthy debtors, thus placing our own economy in jeopardy. In many ways we are drifting and deserve ruin and judgment. We have a great opportunity to exercise leadership in the world, but it is not certain that we have the ability and maturity to do so. Instead of presenting a spiritual alternative to the Soviet barrenness, we have ourselves fallen into self-centered materialism which reduces everything to a monetary value. The same God who promises to bless his faithful people and those who respect his law also threatens to curse those who refuse to follow his statutes (Deut. 28:1-68).

Aligned to this reawakened belief in the promise of democratic capitalism came a corresponding disillusionment with the socialist ideal. I have come to feel with so many others that socialism represents false prophecy and a cruel delusion. It is an enemy of the poor because it destroys prosperity. By uniting economic and political power in one center, it produces tyranny. Marxism promised to explain and then change the world, but it has done neither. It exists as an orthodoxy to justify and legitimate total power. As Kolakowski puts it, "Marxism has been the greatest fantasy of our century . . . (it) neither interprets the world nor changes it: it is merely a repertoire of slogans serving to organize various interests."[14] Worst of all it has led to a nightmare of oppression and totalitarian control.

Even in its democratic form as in Sweden and North America, it threatens our liberties and bankrupts our economies.[15] Even the welfare state which seems to be such a genuine response to the plight of poor people and which as a radical I thought ought to be expanded is no solution. Its general effect on the poor is to destroy their families (because the payments are better if the husband has left the family) and lock them into their sorry condition (because its payments make the unattractive entry-level job seem even less appealing and encourage permanent joblessness). Welfare is an enemy of the poor and friend of the vast and expensive bureaucracies which it creates. It prevents poor people from taking the only road that leads out of poverty: development through hard work and accumulation. It is important to be truthful when it comes to poverty and not perpetuate myths regarding the morality of the rich and duties of the poor.[16]

Living in Canada has afforded me daily examples of how to destroy the private sector and prosperity and how to expand government so that it gains control in every possible area of life. Pierre Trudeau has led what amounts to a socialist government for a dozen years and has brought Canada to its knees economically by eating up about forty percent of the GNP and introducing government regulation into every sector.[17] The budget is out of control. The state owns 175 (at last count) "crown corporations" whose financial affairs are not under close parliamentary scrutiny. It has a national energy policy which has devastated the petroleum industry and

diverted huge funds into the state treasury instead of fresh exploration and development. We have a huge bureaucracy, a million officials for only twenty-five million Canadians. Although the country is rich in space and resources, it is in pathetic shape because of
socialist policies on every hand. Ironically, the Catholic bishops are
calling for more government intervention and handouts. They do
not explain how one can redistribute wealth not available or how
one creates jobs if industry has been brought to its knees. But it is
quite typical for theologians to dogmatize political matters in which
they have no expertise.

In Conclusion

This has been my pilgrimage to date in political theology. I hope
I have been making progress. Certainly I am learning from the struggle to achieve clarity. The process has not been painless. One does
not embrace and then break with a radical movement without being
viewed with suspicion and resentment. I feel badly that some who
appreciated my writing during the radical period now find me some
distance from those ideals. I realize that our idea was to convert
mainline evangelicals to the radical vision and not the other way
around. But this is what happened to me and I set it forth as a possible lesson to all. The zigzag experience in and out of radicalism confirmed for me the considerable truth of the hermeneutical circle. We
are deeply affected in our reading of the Bible by our circumstances.
It is virtually impossible to disentangle the threads of biblical teaching
and cultural experience. In particular it compels me to ask at this
time in my life whether my present position is really scriptural or
reflects my own class setting. At least one valuable remnant of my
earlier radicalism is the fact I have to ask such questions of myself.
In the late 1960s evangelical social thought jumped forward in a pas-
sionate radical expression which continues to impress itself upon an
important minority of our movement. Now in the 1980s we see the
rise of a liberal (people call it neo-conservative) neo-Puritan cultural
vision which is sweeping large numbers into its program. Though
viciously criticized from the left and often shallow in its thinking,
this democratically-oriented social movement is the new liberation

theology of our time, and in the days to come a great debate will take place around the issues it raises. Given my meandering, I have to wonder where it will lead.

NOTES

1. For helpful clarification of the spectrum of opinion, see Robert B. Fowler, *A New Engagement, Evangelical Political Thought 1966-1976* (Grand Rapids: Eerdmans, 1982).

2. Arthur Gish saw it in these terms and communicated that to me at least: *The New Left and Christian Radicalism* (Grand Rapids: Eerdmans, 1970).

3. William Stringfellow, *An Ethic for Christians and Other Aliens in a Strange Land* (Waco: Word, 1973).

4. John H. Yoder was the thinker behind the change in our social and political thought. See his *The Original Revolution* (Scottdale, Pa: Herald Press, 1971).

5. Norman Podhoretz refers to this dynamic in his own biographical memoir covering this period: *Breaking Ranks* (San Francisco: Harper & Row, 1979), pp. 361-65.

6. Not all radical evangelicals bought the whole anabaptist package, however. In Toronto there was a group at the Institute for Christian Studies which shared the cultural alienation within the Reformed context. They published a *Survival (!) Handbook for Radical Christians Today* in 1971.

7. I would have agreed with Orlando Costas when he says that the poor can only receive justice "in a socialistically organized society." *Christ Outside the Gate* (Maryknoll, N.Y.: Orbis Books, 1982), p.95. See also Rael and Erich Isaac, *Sanctifying Revolution* (Washington, D.C.: Ethics and Public Policy Center, 1981).

8. *Solzhenitsyn at Harvard*, edited by Ronald Berman (Washington: Ethics and Public Policy Center, 1980), p.12.

9. Julian L. Simon, *The Ultimate Resource* (Oxford: Robertson, 1981).

10. Rousas J. Rushdoony, *God's Plan for Victory* (Fairfax, Va: Thoburn Press, 1980). On the anabaptist hermeneutic, see Willem Balke, *Calvin and the Anabaptist Radicals* (Grand Rapids: Eerdmans, 1981), ch. 10,12.

11. P. T. Bauer, *Dissent on Development* (Cambridge, Mass: Harvard University Press, 1976) and Karl Brunner, editor, *The First World and the Third World* (Rochester: University of Rochester, 1978).

12. Paul Johnson in *Will Capitalism Survive?* Ernest W. Lefever, editor (Washington: Ethics and Public Policy Center, 1979), p.4.

13. Friedman, *Capitalism and Freedom* (Chicago: University of Chicago Press, 1962), p.9.

14. Leszek Kolakowski, *Main Currents of Marxism* (Oxford: Clarendon, 1978), p. 523

15. On Swedish socialism see Roland Huntford, *The New Totalitarians* (New York: Stein and Day, 1980).

16. George Gilder has a lot of insight in such matters in *Wealth and Poverty* (New York: Basic Books, 1981).

17. *The Economist*, August 7, 1982, "The Crumpled Maple Leaf".

THE IMPERIALISM
OF POLITICAL RELIGION

Edward Norman

Edward Norman

Dr. Edward Norman, an Anglican priest, has been Dean of Peterhouse in Cambridge, England since 1971. Holder of the M.A., Ph.D. and D.D. degrees from Selwyn College, Cambridge, Dr. Norman has served as Fellow of Selwyn College, Cambridge (1962-64) and fellow of Jesus College, Cambridge (1964-1971). His books include *The Catholic Church and Ireland*, *The Conscience of the State in North America*, *Anti-Catholicism in Victorian England*, *The Early Development of Irish Society*, *A History of Modern Ireland*, *Church and Society in Modern England*, *Christianity and the World Order*, and *Christianity in the Southern Hemisphere*.

THE IMPERIALISM OF POLITICAL RELIGION* — Jesus as Subversio de Nazaret

"Christ was a great revolutionary." So Fidel Castro declared during his visit to Jamaica in 1977, adding that he saw no incompatibility between Christianity and Cuban socialism.[1] In 1970, just after his election as president of Chile, another Marxist, Salvador Allende, observed that the Catholic Church had "changed fundamentally." In fact he saw it now as being, as he put it, "in our favour." And of his Marxist alliance he said: "We are going to try to make a reality out of Christian thought."[2]

These extraordinary remarks testify to the very considerable shifts of emphasis that have occurred within South American Christianity in the last two decades; they point to changes which are only imperfectly appreciated in western society. This lack of understanding in part derives from the greater preparedness of western Christians to listen to the views of Latin American ecclesiastical progressives than to the opinions of the more typical, institutionalized religious leadership. Christians of the developed world regard the Latin American radicals as authentically speaking for the oppressed and exploited of the third world. But are they? It is indeed the case that South America is the only wholly Christian continent of the developing world. Yet despite some obviously unique features in recent Latin American religious history, there is a lot that is extremely familiar about the politicization of the progressive element in the church— the part which has acquired so much influence both inside and outside South America. Much of their thinking, however, as elsewhere in politicized Christian circles, depends upon ideological presuppositions that are neither distinctively Christian nor Latin American. It may be none the worse for that. But Latin American Christianity does provide a very clear example of what happens when Christians accommodate the political values of surrounding opinion. In the 1930s and '40s, the church leadership adopted the ideals of the European corporate state; in the 1950s they were attracted to "Developments" social reform; in the 1960s they reflected the radical critique of capitalist society then common within the Western intelligentsia; in the 1970s they moved on to identify Christianity with the ideology of human rights.

*This chapter is reprinted from *Christianity and the World Order* by Edward Norman. © E. R. Norman 1979. Reprinted by permission of Oxford University Press.

There is, however, one feature which is peculiarly South American, and which explains many aspects of change in the church quite independently of political activism. There is in the hemisphere, as everyone will tell you, a "crisis of the church." So there is in the western developed nations. But here it is produced by the failure of the churches to retain the support of the populations, by the impact of secularization, by the loss, among Christians themselves, of any distinct sense of the historical claims of Christianity. In Latin America, the "crisis of the church" is not caused by lack of faith— that is a phenomenon still restricted to sections of the intelligentsia.[3] There the crisis reflects the *confidence* of the church, with its energetic adjustment to social transformations, and especially to its attempts to meet the chronic manpower shortage in its ministry. This is often lost on western Christian observers of the Latin American scene, who speak, in consequence, as if what South Americans themselves call *socialcristianismo*—the social and political interpretation of Christianity—was the decisive element in contemporary religious history. The really dramatic changes of the present "crisis," however, are not produced by radical social theorizing but by flexible response to the changed social context in which the church operates.

The most basic consideration here is the twentieth century population explosion and the rapidly increasing mobility of people, the drift of the rural workers into the cities—creating the *barrio* or *poblaciones*, the shantytowns of the poor, which are found around almost every large center of population. The ecclesiastical parish has more or less broken down as an effective pastoral unit in very many places. It no longer corresponds to manageable, or even definable, social groups. Parishes in the northeast of Brazil—still one of the least developed areas in the continent—sometimes contain 40,000 to 50,000 souls; and in other places there may be as many as three parishes in the care of a single priest.[4] Vocations to the priesthood are fewer than you would expect in what is still a broadly Catholic culture, and foreign priests, from Europe and North America, are brought in on a large scale. In countries like Bolivia and Brazil, a third of the clergy are from overseas. Not surprisingly, this situation has led to extensive questioning of ecclesiastical structures and great readiness to experiment with new patterns of ministry. With the addition of some social theorizing, often imported by the foreign priests, this has now become the attempt to create what church leaders call *Iglesia del pueblo*—the "people's church."[5] Emphasis is placed on simplicity and austerity in clerical lifestyles and dress.[6] The atmosphere generated throughout the entire Catholic church by the Second Vatican Council acts as a supplementary incentive to change. There are, as elsewhere in the world, radical liturgical experiments. Combined with the wish to create a "people's church," this has in South America resulted in amused newspaper references to the mass as "misa a Gó Gó" and "misa a la Gaucho." The bishops of South America are now firmly committed to structural changes. Through the Council of Latin American bishops (CELAM), set up in 1955, with a permanent secretariat and a series of specialized commissions, the leadership of the church has fashioned a unifying ecclesiastical organization, with markedly progressive sympathies.[7] Again, many of the staff priests working within this bureaucracy are foreigners.

There are, of course, considerable variations within the degree both of structural reform and of politicization within the church: Chile has always been particularly advanced, and Colombia notably conservative, for example.[8] And, as elsewhere in the Christian world, the leadership tends to be considerably more progressive than the laity. But it is the foreign clergy who are everywhere noted for their radical politics and who are most forthright in expressing them. Indeed, much of what is taken by Western Christians as characteristically "Latin American" Catholic thought turns out to be the influence of European and North American mission and staff priests.[9] The same is true of Protestantism—which suffers, in fact, from its association with North Americanism. It is a gringo religion.

The development of radical politics by the foreign clergy is well illustrated in the career of "Paul Gallet," the pen name of a French priest working in northeast Brazil from 1962. By March 1964, just before the right-wing military coup, he had come to hope for what he called "a revolution like Cuba."[10] Another, Protestant example is provided by the Lutheran Bishop Helmut Frenz, banned from Chile by the military government in 1975. "I became a highly politicized Christian," he later admitted; and added, "class struggle is no Marxist propaganda; it is a reality."[11] Bishop Frenz had been one of the presidents of the "Committee for Cooperation for Peace"—the Chilean Human Rights agency—and an observer for the World Council of Churches. Apart from the foreign clergy themselves, the others most noticeable for their political radicalism are Latin Americans who have trained for the priesthood, or studied abroad—especially at the European universities, and particularly at Louvain, in Belgium. There they picked up versions of Marxism from the bourgeois radical circles in which they mixed. Thus Camilo Torres, the Colombian priest who gave up the priesthood in order to work for the poor, as he put it, had studied social sciences at Louvain. There he met the Peruvian priest, Gustavo Gutiérrez, later to become the most distinguished of the Marxist theologians in South America.

But not all the foreign clergy, or those who have studied abroad, become left wing by any means; it is simply that those who do get themselves listened to. Earlier, in 1978, I visited the working class *poblaciones* around Santiago, in Chile, and met some Italian priests, who run a home for deaf and mute children in the district of Lampa. Neither they, nor any other priests working among the poor I heard about during the visit, were in any way politicized. But their love of the poor for whom they worked was among the most impressive things I have ever seen.

Social concern is not a new development within the leadership of South American Catholicism. In the 1930s and '40s it took the form of seeking to embody Papal teachings on social questions in the structure of the corporate state. The influence of Franco's Spain, Salazar's Portugal, and Mussolini's Italy were important in this. There has been some enduring influence, too. For much of the contemporary Christian criticism of liberal capitalism in Latin America—now rendered in Marxist language[12]—is a familiar echo from the rejection of capitalism made in the thirties by fascism. The transition may be traced in the life of Dom Helder Camara, Archbishop of Recife in Brazil, and known, because of his small size and enormous energy, as "the electric mosquito." Camera is the only South American Catholic leader known to most western Christians. He is a highly politicized man—and always has been. He was a convinced Fascist as a young priest.[13] Now he is a convinced Socialist.

In the later 1950s and '60s, the church leaders moved on to Christian democracy. This corresponded to the "Developmentist" stage of Latin American politics: the conviction that underdevelopment could be overcome within existing but reformed social and political structures by capitalist economics and external aid. Yet within Christian Democracy—just as within the thinking of western bourgeois radicalism in the 1960s—there grew up a sharp rejection of capitalist society. This is especially associated with Eduardo Frei, both during and after his term as Christian Democrat President of Chile. It could, indeed, be fairly remarked that in the now celebrated election of 1970 the social program of the Christian Democrats was scarcely distinguishable from that of the successful Marxist candidate, Salvador Allende.[14] The transition to increasingly radical social teachings can be seen in the Pastoral Letters of the bishops of all the Latin American republics during the 1960s, their opinions more or less exactly corresponding to the adoption of social radicalism within the western intelligentsia in general. Extensive reforms in living conditions were more and more frequently linked to calls for structural political change. In some measure this was inspired by fear of Communism—buying off the revolution with reforms. But the main motive was a genuine shift to more radical ideology.[15] Even the evangelical Pentecostal churches have come to acquire a radical political position; an unusual illustration of the movement from "sect" to "church" type of religion, since their new radicalism is the characteristic not of the poor but of the affluent intelligentsia.

Both the development of radical social criticism, and the renewed conflicts of church and state that this inaugurated in some Latin American countries in the present decade, have signaled a further development. This is the adoption by the church of the pervasive enthusiasm for Human Rights which has grown within western liberal opinion during the 1970s. Conservative governments have attacked the church for meddling in politics:[16] again, a classic sign of the politicization of religion. The church has replied by insisting that its concern is not political but moral—and has spoken of Human Rights as something superior to the authority of the state. Christians have also argued that the clergy have been drawn into politics by the need to defend social justice in countries where the church is the only free institution, the only independent voice.[17] Thus in Guatemala—a country with a long, nineteenth-century history of church and state conflict—the clash between the bishops and the government over Human Rights in 1976 prompted the vice-president to accuse the church of political interference.[18] A similar pattern has recently appeared in Argentina, Bolivia, Paraguay, Nicaragua, El Salvador, and, above all, in Chile since the military coup in 1973. In Chile, Christian work for *Derechos Humanos*—Human Rights— has been deeply mixed up with political criticism of the government, leading to the detention or exile of many priests.[19] The ecumenical Committee of Cooperation for Peace, which was unambiguous in its condemnation of what it called "the situation of oppression" in Chile,[20] was closed down by Cardinal Silva, Archbishop of Santiago, in 1975, after representatives from General Pinochet, President of Chile. He accused it of having become infiltrated by Marxists.[21] In 1976, the progressive attitudes of the Chilean bishops earned the approval of Moscow Radio:[22] a tribute, perhaps, of doubtful utility to their cause. The church's voice remains something to be reckoned with. And when, in June last year, the Chilean Minister for Justice called the bishops "stupid Marxists," he had to resign.[23]

In contrast to the progressive elite who dominate the thinking of South American Catholicism are the conservative majority. As in Europe and North America their ideas have failed to achieve respectable articulation; in fact they have often shown themselves to be lamentably ignorant of the subtleties in their opponents' positions. At that level, fear of Communism really *is* often advanced in opposition to all reform. Right-wing Catholic groups, like the Society for the Defence of Tradition, Family and Property, in Chile and Brazil, tend to reject even the most necessary alterations of the church's pastoral function. And the promotion of politics for what are thought of as distinctly *Christian* reasons is not a monopoly of the left. The conservative military regimes that now govern so much of South America see themselves as the guardians of traditional Christian values and of Christian civilization. These claims often correspond to deeply felt and popular instincts, expressed in nationalism.[24] Traditionalist Christians accuse the bishops of being too far ahead of public opinion, of listening to the intellectual left with too much respect.[25] In 1974 the Protestant Churches in Chile articulated opinions of the silent majority, when they publicly thanked the military for having saved the country from Marxism; and Bishop Helmut Frenz, the exiled Lutheran leader, is said to have lost the support of three-quarters of his church membership as a result of his work for the Peace Committee.[26]

At the other end of the political spectrum is the small group of actively Marxist priests. Some of these, again, like the North American Maryknoll fathers who joined guerrilla forces in Central America, are foreigners.[27] The revolutionary priests have attracted a lot of overseas attention. Camilo Torres was "better known in Paris than in Bogota," his home town, according to the Colombian press.[28] Torres called for the formation of *Ejército de Liberación Nacional*— a national army of liberation—to start a "people's war" for the overthrow of the bourgeois state.[29] Departing to the Colombian countryside to join a guerrilla band, he was shot to death during an ambush at El Carmen in 1966, and has since become something of a cult figure, a sort of ecclesiastical Che Guevara. It is sometimes thought that one of the reasons why young Latin Americans do not offer themselves for ordination is that the image of the priesthood lacks masculinity—that religion is something for women. If that is so, at least Camilo Torres has put *machismo* back into Christianity. Other Marxist clergy have been rather more economical with their lives. The most organized were the 450 who gathered at Santiago in 1972—while Allende was President of Chile—and founded the "Christians for Socialism" movement. Their object—in the words used in one of the later publications—was "the rise of a Christianity with a proletarian character capable of being freed from the dominant bourgeois ideology."[30] Since the gathering was itself almost exclusively bourgeois in composition—as is inevitably the way with South American Marxist Christians—the task was clearly a formidable one. There was to be "participation in the struggle which opposes the exploiting class," as they said in their declaration.[31] Individual Marxist priests have also been active within many of the official church agencies. The Latin American Institute for Doctrine and Social Studies (ILADES), opened in 1966 under episcopal authority, rapidly advanced to a rigorous Marxism under the inspiration of Fr. Gonzalo Arroyo[32]—a Chilean Jesuit who later campaigned for Allende.[33] Similarly, a Protestant agency called Church and Society in Latin America (ISAL), started in 1960 in Peru, adopted Marxism in 1968 and aimed henceforth at what it described as "the mobilization of the people."[34] Marxist influence has also been evident in religious journalism. The Jesuit magazine *Mensaje*, published in Chile, is perhaps the most well-known. In the later 1960s it attacked Frei and Christian Democracy for their moderation, and supported Che Guevara and the student political left. Even after the coup in Chile, it has continued to raise a critical voice against the suppression of Marxism.[35]

The high-water mark of the official, respectable progressivism of the Catholic church was reached in 1968, at the Second General Conference of Latin American bishops, held at Medellín in Colombia. Pope Paul, in Bogota for the Eucharistic Congress, opened the conference himself. The preparatory papers which were the most radical documents ever produced by the Catholic hierarchy of Latin America, were drawn up by the Brazilian bishops under the guidance of French and Dutch priests.[36] Using distinctly revolutionary rather than reformist language,[37] and luxuriant in Marxist rhetoric, they condemned the "imperialism" of multinational corporations and the "institutionalized violence" of capitalist society. Intended as an answer to what Mgr. Eduardo Pironio has called "the profound and legitimate aspirations of the Latin American peoples,"[38] the bishops affirmed their belief that radical change had to come by political means.[39] The church, they said, had to show its solidarity with the poor and marginated and must do this concretely by "criticism of injustice and oppression."[40] Since 1968, many bishops have gradually withdrawn from the advanced positions taken up at Medellín. It is now to be seen in the context of 1968: the year of the Paris student riots, the anti-Vietnam demonstrations, of the pervasive, and heady radicalism of the bourgeois intelligentsia of the western world. The uneasy balance between those loyal to the Medellín outlook, and those seeking to moderate the politicization of the church, became evident during the preparations for the third conference of Latin-American bishops, due to be held at Puebla, Mexico in October 1978. Compromise documents had to be drafted at the last minute in order to avoid a major disruption. As it happened, the conference had to be postponed because of the death of Pope John Paul I. But divisions had clearly become very serious.

Now between the radicalism of the South American bishops and the Marxist activist priests there lies the academic expression of *Socialcristianismo*—though I must use the word "academic" with caution, because the exponents of the Theology of Liberation argue that their ideas are decidedly *not* academic. They believe they are derived, unlike traditional theology, from social reality. "We, then, in Latin America," as Juan Luis Segundo has said, "began to think about liberation before thinking about a theology of liberation."[41] The influence, as Gustavo Gutiérrez has written, was "to a large extent due to Marx."[42] The content of the new theology does not come from received spiritual knowledge but from the Marxian concept of *praxis*:[43] of the involvement of the oppressed in the historical process of change. The theologian will be engaged—another quotation from Gutiérrez—"where nations, social classes, people struggle to free themselves from domination and oppression."[44] The church must be involved in making people aware of the "institutionalized violence" of bourgeois society, for this justifies the use of revolutionary violence for political change.[45] Salvation is not some "other-worldly" condition: it is the practical construction of social justice in the existing world.[46] The biblical exegesis of the liberation theologians is in fact very conservative. With the exception of the Protestant writers, like Ruben Alves, the Brazilian scholar, they have not proclaimed the "death of God," or questioned the divinity of Christ, as western theologians have done in recent years. It is just that they believe the scriptural texts contain a political message. Christ himself is understood as a political liberator,[47] the *Subversio de Nazaret*—a sort of urban guerilla.[48] As Maurice Clavel has remarked, "Christ has been converted into the John the Baptist of Marx."[49] Not surprisingly, perhaps, President Molina of El Salvador has publicly described the Theology of Liberation as "the ideology of the subversives."[50] The liberation theologians would be quite happy to accept the description.

They all contend for a sort of South American version of "Eurocommunism"—a socialist order untainted by Soviet authoritarianism and shorn of atheism. As Archbishop Helder Camara has said: "The great mass of Communists will give to religion their attention and sympathy when they see it resolved never to give cover to absurd injustices committed in the name of the right to property and private enterprise."[51] This utopianism is, of course, repudiated by orthodox Communists, as incompatible with historical materialism. The collapse of Allende's Chile, which Marxists attribute precisely to his reverence for bourgeois legalism, and his failure to dismantle the bourgeois state structure, seems a clear enough indication that a peculiar brand of Latin American Communism, or a peaceful transition to socialism, are unlikely.[52] Dr. David Owen, the British Foreign Secretary, has made the same point, adding that the Communist leaders in Eastern Europe made similar commitments to pluralist democracy in the later 1940s, none of which were honored.[53] One of the main political objectives of the liberation theologians was therefore overtaken by events—in the Chilean coup of 1973. In the less euphoric atmosphere of the middle 1970s, Latin American radical theologians have come to place more emphasis on the spiritual dimensions of human emancipation,[54] and on the value of folk religion, despite its conservatism.[55]

Liberation Theology also stresses the importance of education in generating social awareness among the masses. But it is to be very ideological education—intended to make the workers and peasants conscious of just how oppressed they actually are. The process reminds one of the candidate in the Irish election of 1826 who promised the voters that he would tell them about five hundred grievances "which they had previously known nothing about."[56] This education is known as *conscientization*, and its apostle is the Brazilian educationalist, Paulo Freire, who has worked for the World Council of Churches. At its center is a distinction between education for "domestication," as Freire calls conventional learning, and education for "liberation," that the masses might create, not an "armchair revolution" but a real one.[57] Freire's writings and methods—according to the "Conscientization Kit," a packet of literature on the subject put out by the World Council of Churches—are "pregnant with revolutionary intention." The document continues: "Conscientization is never seen as having strictly educational objectives. It is always seen as enabling people to take political charge of their own history."[58] The oppressed are to teach *themselves* about their own oppression. Like the slave in *Meno*, the dialogue of Plato, who solves mathematical problems, though ignorant of mathematics, assisted by the directive questioning of Socrates, the workers subjected to conscientization are in fact victims (or beneficiaries) of external suggestion. To put it bluntly, despite the heavy use of technical language to describe conscientization, it is ordinary political indoctrination. As such, it has been employed by radical priests in many parts of South America. Yet it is also ostensibly encouraged by liberal churchmen, anxious to be in with the educational trends. For them it implies no more than a generally progressive attitude to education, and perhaps to the addition of social studies to the curriculum. It is in this manner, surely, that we are to interpret the endorsement of Freire's ideas by the Church of England's Board of Education in 1973, and by the Anglican Consultative Council in the same year.[59]

In some areas, the Liberation theologians have performed a very useful task. In unmasking the bourgeois values and assumptions hidden behind western Church thinking, they have provided a critique of liberalism which Church leaders in the developed countries would do well to take seriously. They have pointed to the social class references implicit in much of the self-conscious reformism of the western churches—as well as in their own. But the lessons are unlikely to be taken to heart. For liberal churchmen have themselves adopted the vocabulary and style of Liberation Theology, and in the process have diluted the strength of its social critique. As Juan Luis Segundo has noticed: "Everyone mouths the words, only to go on as before."[60]

Latin America, then, illustrates the politicization of Christianity in a way which is very characteristic of the Church everywhere. To the Church's real and important concern with the conditions in which people live has been added a succession of ideological superstructures whose content has been acquired, not from a distinctively Christian or religious source, or from a particularly Christian understanding of the nature of man and his social state, but from ideas current within the educated classes of the western world in general. There are, of course, some local features about *Socialcristianismo*, but both its inspiration and its politics are familiar enough expressions of western thought. Western Christians who listen in to the Latin American church, in the belief that this is the authentic word of the Third World, hear only the echoes of their own voice.

Liberation Theology

NOTES

1. Reported on B.B.C. Radio 4, "Sunday," 6 November 1977.
2. Quoted in Frederick C. Turner, *Catholicism and Political Development in Latin America* (Chapel Hill: University of North Carolina Press, 1971) p. 156.
3. Fr. Renate Poblete S.J., "The Church in Latin America: A Historical Survey," in *The Church and Social Change in Latin America*, ed. Henry A. Landesberger (Notre Dame: Notre Dame University Press, 1970) p.47.
4. Abbé François Houtart, "The Roman Catholic Church and Social Change in Latin America," in Landsberger, op. cit., p. 120.
5. See, for example, S. Galilea, *El Evangelico, Mensaje de liberacion* (Santiago de Chile, 1976) p. 40.
6. *Segunda Conferencia General Del Episcopado Latinamericano, Medellin, Setiembre de 1968, Documentos Finales* (Buenos Aires: Ediciones Paulinas, 1972) p. 192.
7. Juan Rosales, *Los Christianos, Los Marxistas, y la Revolucion* (Buenos Aires, 1970, p. 43.
8. See Joseph Fichter, *Cambio social en Chile: un estudio de actitudes* (Santiago, 1962) and David E. Mutchler, *The Church as a Political Factor in Latin America, with Particular Reference to Colombia and Chile* (New York, 1971).
9. Turner, op. cit., p. 46.
10. Paul Gallet, *Freedom to Starve* (London, 1972) p. 97.
11. Quoted in Derek Winter, *Hope in Captivity, The Prophetic Church in Latin America* (London, 1977) p. 59.
12. See, for example, *Segunda Conferencia General del Episcopado*, p.31, on "sistema liberal capitalista"; and p.45, on "monopolios internacionales."
13. Turner, op.cit., p. 150; Jóse Míquez Bonino, *Revolutionary Theology Comes of Age* (London, 1975) p. 45.
14. Ian Roxborough, Philip O'Brien, and Jackie Roddick, *Chile: The State and Revolution* (London, 1977) p. 75.
15. Assisted by Papal teaching: the influential encyclical *Populorum Progressio* (1967) is widely quoted throughout Latin America as evidence of authority for extensive social change. See especially the critique of capitalism, p. 15 of the English edition (Catholic Truth Society, 1970) and of unjust world trade terms, p. 28.
16. Jóse Miguez Bonino, *Ama y haz lo que quieras, Una etica para al hombre nuevo* (Buenos Aires, 1973) p.83.
17. *Violence and Fraud in El Salvador* (London: Latin America Bureau, 1977) p. 27.
18. Roger Plant, *Guatemala, Unnatural Disaster* (London: Latin America Bureau, 1977) p. 27.
19. Bernardino Piñera C., and P. Fernando Montes M., *La Iglesia en Chile Hoy* (Santiago, 1977) p. 27.
20. *Elementos De Reflexion Sobre El Comite De Cooperacion Para La Paz En Chile Y El Caracter De La Continuacion De La Tarea*, p.1. A copy of this paper may be found in the Latin American Archive, Regents Park, London, in a folder marked "Committee for Peace" in the Chile section.

The Imperialism of Political Religion

21. The Cardinal, in his letter of 14 November 1975, to the President, admitted that "the purity of the service might occasionally have been clouded over by the intervention of elements foreign to its original nature," but saw this as "a risk inherent to every good work and of which no institution can be infallibly exonerated" (Copy: Latin American Archive).

22. Moscow Radio, "Escucha Chile", broadcasts on 23 and 24 February, 1976.

23. Council on Hermispheric Affairs (Washington, D.C.), Press Release of 9th June 1977: "Pinochet Campaign Against Catholic Church Revealed."

24. Florencia Infante Diaz, *Iglesia, Gobierno, Principios* (Santiago, 1975) p. 23.

25. See *La Iglesia del Silencio en Chile* (Santiago, 1976), published by the "Sociedad Chilena de Defensa de la Tradicion, Familia y Propiedad".

26. Winter, op. cit., pp. 87-88.

27. Bonino, *Revolutionary Theology*, p.49. See also, J. Lloyd Mecham, *Church and State in Latin America. A History of Politico-Ecclesiastical Relations*, revised ed., (Chapel Hill: University of North Carolina Press, 1966) p. 158.

28. Alain Gheerbrant, *The Rebel in Latin American* (London, 1974) p. 27.

29. Camilo Torres, *Christanismo y revolución*, second ed. (Mexico City, 1972) p. 556.

30. *Christians for Socialism*, published by the World Student Christian Federation (Geneva, 1975) p. 4.

31. Fernando Morena Valencia, *Christianismo y Marxismo* (Santiago, 1977) p. 16; ("Documento Final" of the "Primer Encuentro Latinamericano de Christianos por el Sociolismo", April 1972). For episcopal criticism of the movement, see *Documentos el Episcopado*, Chile, 1970-1973 (Santiago, 1974) p. 183, "Fe Bristiana y Actuación Política" (Aug. 1973).

32. Sergio Torres and John Eagleson, eds., *Theology in the Americas* (Maryknoll, New York: Orbis, 1976) p. 32.

33. Mutchler, op. cit., p. 388.

34. Bonino, *Revolutionary Theology*, pp. 54-55.

35. *Mensaje*, No. 265, Dec. 1977, p. 716; "Chile: sa Future Democracia."

36. Mutchler, op. cit., p. 101.

37. *Theology in the Americas*, p. 23.

38. Eduardo F. Pironia, *En El Espirita de Medellin. Escritas. Pastorales Marplatenses II* (Buenos Aires, 1976) p. 52.

39. *Segunda Conferencia General Del Episcopado Latinamericano*, p.35.

40. Ibid., p. 190.

41. *Theology in the Americas*, p. 280.

42. Gustavo Gutiérrez, *A Theology of Liberation. History, Politics and Salvation* (London, 1974) p. 9. This, the most important text of the Liberation theologians, was originally published in Lima, in 1971.

43. Ibid., p. 13; *Theology in the Americas*, p. 407; Moreno, op. cit., p. 24.

44. Gutiérrez, op. cit., p. 13.

45. Ibid., p. 103.

46. Ibid., p. 151.

47. Ibid., p. 175.

137

48. Moreno, op. cit., p. 85.
49. Ibid., p. 102. See Clavel's *Dieu est Dieu, nom de Dieu!* (Paris, 1976).
50. *Violence and Fraud in El Salvador* (London, 1977) p. 19.
51. Helder Camara, *Church and Colonialism* (London, 1969) p. 59.
52. Roxborough, O'Brien and Roddick, *Child, the State and Revolution*, p. 264.
53. David Owen, *"Communism, Socialism and Democracy"*, by David Owen, *NATO Review*, vol. 26, No. 1, February 1978, pp. 8-9.
54. *Ministry with the Poor. A World Consultation in Latin America* (Geneva: World Council of Churches, 1977) p. 19.
55. *Historia y Mision* (Santiago, 1977) p. 10: "La Religiosidad Popular" by Jorge Medina Estevez.
56. Edward Norman, *A History of Modern Ireland* (London: Penquin Books, 1971) p. 18.
57. Paulo Freire, *Pedagogy of the Oppressed* (London, 1972) p. 41.
58. *Conscientization Kit.* A dossier published by the World Council of Churches, May, 1975: "The Pedagogical Debate", a document of the Institute of Cultural Action, Geneva.
59. *Annual Report of the Board of Education (1972-3)*, G.S. 152 (London, 1973) p. 25; "Education: A Process of Liberation for Social Justice" in *Partners in Mission. Anglican Consultative Council, Second Meeting. Dublin. July, 1973* (London, 1973) p. 20.
60. Juan Luis Segundo, *Liberation of Theology* (London, 1977) p. 4.

JÜRGEN MOLTMANN'S THEOLOGY OF HOPE

Robert C. Walton

Robert C. Walton

Dr. Robert C. Walton is Professor and Director, Seminar Library for Modern Church History and History of Doctrine, the Protestant Faculty, University of Munster/Westphalia, West Germany. He holds degrees from Swarthmore College (B.A.), Harvard Divinity School (B.D.), and Yale University (M.A., Ph.D.). He has done foreign study at the universities of Marburg, Göttingen and Zurich. His previous publications include *Zwingli's Theocracy, Over There: European View of the Americans 1914-1918*, and soon to be published articles on Zwingli. He has served as President of the American Society for Reformation Research and as co-editor of *Archiv Für Reformationsgeschichte*.

JÜRGEN MOLTMANN'S THEOLOGY OF HOPE — European Roots of Liberation Theology

"Do you want to join my sect? I can give you hope. Let me be your Fuhrer!"

Jürgen Moltmann's political theology, the Theology of Hope, is seminal for the development of the Theology of Liberation. Moltmann has done a great deal to make the Theology of Liberation acceptable among theologians in Europe and North America. His theology and its very great success[1] raises several very central issues which go to the heart of the problems which face the Protestant churches throughout the world and in particular the American Protestant churches. It is quite natural that the work of Professor Moltmann would raise some very acute problems in the United States because the U.S. is as G. K. Chesterton has asserted and as Sydney Meade affirmed, the "nation with the soul of a church."[2] It is practically impossible to deal with the entire literature produced by Moltmann himself and the theological world's response to it. Special attention will be paid in this essay to Moltmann's three major works: *The Theology of Hope* which first appeared in Germany with the title *Theologie der Hoffnung* in 1964 (the English version was published in 1967); *The Crucified God* went to press under the title *Der gekreuzigte Gott* with the Christian Kaiser Publishing Company in 1973 and appeared in English in 1974. The Christian Kaiser Press printed *Die Kirche in der Kraft des Geistes* in 1975 and it appeared in English in 1977. These three form the heart of Moltmann's theological system. *Das Experiment Hoffnung Einführung* appeared in Germany in 1974 and was translated into English as *Theology and Joy*. Moltmann's collection of essays bearing the German title *Zuknunft der Shopfüng* (1977) and the English title *The Future of Creation* (1979) is also important for any consideration of his theology. His recent book, *Trinitat und Reich Gottes* (1980), i.e. *The Trinity and the Kingdom of God* which appeared in 1981 is also of significance. It has the added advantage that its style is not nearly as complex as that of Moltmann's earlier works. The main focus of this paper will be upon the significance of Moltmann's doctrine of the church for modern society.

To deal with Moltmann requires that he and his theology be put in what the form critics would call its proper *Sitz im Leben* and we might prefer to call its proper context. To assess his impact in North America the same technique should be applied. It is necessary to understand the *Sitz im Leben* in which Moltmann's theology was received and interpreted. Only then is it possible to settle down to a careful examination of this theology, especially its ecclesiological significance.

Jürgen Moltmann's *Sitz im Leben*:

(1) The position of the German Professor:

Although the church and the state in Germany were separated after the collapse of the Hehenzollern dynasty's rule in 1918, the state continues to collect the church taxes for the *Volkskirchen* (people's churches) in the various German states (*Länder*).[3] The churches to which a citizen may pay his taxes are the: Lutheran, The Reformed (Calvinist), and the United Church, an administrative union of Reformed and Lutheran Churches which was imposed by the government of King William III of Prussia in 1817. Most Germans are not active church attenders but the majority are content to pay taxes to the established church for which they receive the services of a clergyman at funerals, marriages and baptisms.

The state renders one other service to the churches. The ministries of education in the various states of the Federal Republic pay for the basic theological education of candidates for the ministry by supporting theological faculties at virtually every German university with the exception of Bremen. Professors of theology are appointed by the state government with the approval of the Territorial Church (*Landeskirche*). Once appointed, the professor becomes a civil servant (*Beamter*) who can be fired only in very rare instances, and receives a salary from the state government until he dies. The case of the Catholic professor at Tübingen, Hans Küng, illustrates the extent to which the professor enjoys the security of a civil servant. Küng was forced to leave the Catholic faculty at Tübingen, because what he taught was declared contrary to the teachings of the Catholic church. However, he remained a civil servant and the ministry of education, in Baden Wurttemberg, gave him a special chair, so that he could continue to teach outside the Catholic faculty, because as a civil servant he had done nothing to merit dismissal.

Suffice it to say that the professor, especially the theology professor, enjoys the freedom which only the security of being a civil servant in the German system can bestow. Theology professors are also free from any subservience to their church. They can say what they like without fear of dismissal and they can have as much or as little to do with their church as they wish. In fact they are left with only one acute problem, that of relevance, as Germany finally develops a fully urbanized, industrial society with its accompanying social mobility and egalitarianism. Indeed since the beginning of the student difficulties in the late 1960s, various German public opinion polls indicate that the respect and position which professors in general, not just theology professors, enjoyed during the Second Empire, The Weimar Republic, the Hitler period, and in the years just after the end of World War II is rapidly eroding. Nevertheless the professor remains free from the consequences of most of his acts and all of his ideas. Even a very radical shift to the left or the right in German politics would hardly affect the financial security of the professor. It would, in fact, take a general collapse of the German economy or a devastating war ending with the occupation of Germany by a third world power to achieve this.

(2) The intellectual foundation for the professor's position:

The position which the professor enjoys is a product of the Prussian tradition and can be viewed as the natural result of what many historians call the Prussian "welfare" or "regulative state." Otto Hintze asserts that the appointment of a civil servant is an act of state which makes the position of the civil servant unique. And he also reminds us that legal conditions governing the appointment of civil servants are derived from the Prussian civil service law (*Beamtenrecht*) and still reflect much of the spirit of the old absolutist princely bureaucracy.[4] Hintze made these remarks in 1911 but, despite two military defeats and radical changes in the German constitution, what Hintze describes is still largely true.

The fact that it is factual affects how all Germans think about the state and its servants. For many the state is an abstraction of higher value which must be served and is surely greater than the sum of its parts. Civil servants of all kinds serve "The State," not those who come to their offices for help or advice. The Prussian school of historians in the nineteenth century did a great deal to prepare the way for German unification under the Prussian leadership by praising the Prussian state and its bureaucracy as the model for a unified German state. The best known spokesman of this school, Heinrich von Treitschke, admired the concept of the state in its Prussian garb with uncritical enthusiasm.[5] The Prussian school was of course influenced by the philosopher George Wilhelm Friedrich Hegel.[6]

Hegel's life spanned the period from 1770-1831. During these brief sixty-one years he experienced the apparent success of absolutism under Frederick the Great, the failure of absolutism when confronted with the ideology of the French Revolution and the military might of the French army led by Napoleon, and finally the period of restoration which began after Napoleon's defeat in 1815. Hegel could not remain unmoved by these events and their impact led him to assert the value of the consciousness of freedom which he felt had been made possible by the Protestant Reformation. Once the Reformation had freed men from external authority and made them conscious of their freedom, it became possible to construct the modern "rational state." Of necessity this state had to be Christian and Protestant.[7] As the reader will see, Hegel's concept of Protestantism and progress and his definition of the consciousness of freedom which Protestantism engenders is basic to Moltmann's theology.

Hegel also championed the new theory of economic liberty which had emerged from the reaction to absolutism; he believed firmly in the equality of every man before the law and, most important for this essay, he advocated the creation of an aristocracy of ability rather than birth to govern society.[8] Even today this concept forms the self image of all the more senior German civil servants and especially that of the professors. This fact also has an important bearing upon Moltmann's concept of himself as a theologian.

Other elements of Hegel's thought are equally important for the task of understanding Moltmann in his *Sitz im Leben*. Moltmann's function as a social critic and an advocate of radical reform, and even revolution also has its roots in Hegel's concept of the state and those who have the right to govern it. All these seemingly liberal elements which Hegel championed had to be developed within the context of the most perfect form of state which could be imagined, the rational state, which in Hegel's eyes was best exemplified in the Prussian bureaucratic state (*Beamtenstaat*). As it should be, this state was bound together by a constitution that left the King of Prussia the freedom to exercise sovereignty. Hegel did not believe in democratic government. Every person should, he thought, enjoy personal freedom and equality before the law but that did not mean to him that every person should have the right to deliberate upon matters of importance to the public interest. Each person should have his place in an heirarchical society in which representation was achieved through three major classes or estates (*Staende*) whose functions determined the amount of influence which they enjoyed: the agricultural class, the industrial class, and the class of civil servants which Hegel termed the universal class and to which he looked for leadership. The universal class was to be and Hegal believed that in Prussia it already was, an elite based on education and ability rather than birth.[9] According to Hegel, the ideal state, governed by the elite found its final unity and significance in war. He believed that wars preserve the "moral health of peoples" and perform a historic mission, because they are instruments of the "eternal spirit."[10] In Moltmann's theology the theologian as a member of the elite leads the congregation to revolutionary war against an exploitive society.

There is another group in Hegel's scheme of society which requires our attention. At least in part, Moltmann's dislike of this group to the point of excluding its members from all possibility of being part of the elect, God's chosen people, is derived from the function which Hegel assigned to this element in society. In so doing Hegel reflected an aristocratic contempt for the middle or commercial classes which was widespread in conservative circles and is equally widespread among twentieth century socialists and many American liberals. In their dislike and prejudice they are the true heirs of the restoration conservatives and England's ultra-Tories who hid their colors later in the century behind the thin facade of Tory democracy.

Hegel's view of the intermediary or industrial class, while positive, left them in a position of lesser importance than that of the civil servants. Hegel identified the basic function of the agricultural class and the role of the civil servants in general with the pursuit of ideas and solutions to problems which compelled them to transcend the confines of mere subjectivity (i.e. their own self-centeredness) and to reach the realm of the objective (i.e. the universal plain on which institutions in which reason embodies itself can be developed for the whole society). The industrial class had far greater difficulty in doing this, because they dealt with only "particular problems," or as Hegel would have it "the particular;" thus they were not compelled to transcend their own subjectivity. Hegel believed that the very nature of their commercial life made it necessary for the state to intervene in their activities. But in the last analysis he was convinced that with the proper leadership the industrial class would direct itself towards the universal.[11]

Despite these qualifications, the innate foundation for a prejudice against the industrial class is present in Hegel's conception of the ideal state and its social structure. The praise lavished upon the Prussian state both by Hegel and the historians of the Prussian school has outlasted not only the Prussian school itself, but also the old Prussian state and the Second German Empire (1871-1918). The Constitution of the empire gave the German emperor just that independent authority which Hegel said the monarch of an ideal state should have and this was one of the things which brought the Second Empire to ruin and defeat. The civil service developed by the Prussian state was passed on to the empire and survived it largely intact with its prestige virtually unquestioned. The civil servants, especially the intellectual elite among them, remained untarnished by the mundane concerns of the marketplace; they were well paid and even better respected, because they continued to pursue the best solution to the problems which beset society. Their function was far nobler than that of the industrial class.

This conception of the role of the intellectual elite in state service helped create an anti-capitalist attitude among influential segments of the German civil service after the creation of the Second Empire. It also contributed to a tradition of cultural pessimism and a sense of impending doom in German intellectual life as the Second Empire became ever more industrialized. The very success of the industrial society awakened ever greater pessimism in conservative and progressive circles alike. The First World War and its disastrous end did not improve things. The consequences of the leveling and naturally democratic creation of an industrial society became fully obvious during the brief years of the Weimar Republic; that very fact was repugnant to the majority of Protestant clergymen, many intellectuals, and not a few civil servants, though their expression of this repugnance found its focus on the right rather than the left.

All the dissidents found solace in the cultural pessimism manifested in the writings of Oswald Spengler whose monumental work, *The Decline of the West*, did a great deal to destroy confidence in the young republic and prepare the way for the seizure of power by the Nazis under Adolf Hitler (*Die Machtergreifung*). Central to Spengler's critique of society was the assertion that "mammoth technology, like all gigantism, was a symbol of the decline of civilization."[12] The pessimism generated by Spengler and his followers made the promise of the Nazis that they would purify Germany, abolish capitalist abuses, and create a new racial ideology which would effectively counter Bolshevism, i.e. Soviet Communism, seem valid and desirable. Spengler's dire view of the emergence of a complex industrial society lived on even in the world of the post-1945 era. Freudian Marxist social critics like Herbert Marcuse were much influenced by Spengler, though Marcuse eventually became enamored with the possibility of modern technology and spent his declining years championing a "realistic" idea of utopia based upon the "actual productive capacities of advanced technology." In his opinion the proper application of this technology required only the "correct rational-organizational system" to achieve a true utopia here and now. When Marcuse elaborated these views at a colloqium entitled "The End of Utopia" (*Das Ende der Utopie*) held at the Free University of Berlin in 1967, he really abandoned his earlier utopianism which fitted the standard definition of utopianism: "the leap into a new state of being in which contemporary values in at least one area—the critical one for the utopian—are totally transformed or turned upside down."[13]

In this neither Moltmann nor most of Germany's present day Greens have followed Marcuse. There are too many advantages to be gained from an older tradition of cultural pessimism which always was and still is highly respectable in Germany. The great change which has occurred since 1945 is that the focus of discontent with the consequences of the creation of an unbelievably prosperous, egalitarian Germany is now on the left rather than the right as it was in the Weimar period. Moltmann's theology is in fact very much the continuation of an aristocratic, bureaucratic, anti-capitalist tradition. Like so many of the protests which come from the ranks of those who belonged to the bureaucratic elite of the German civil service, there is a nostalgia about their complaints. Whether consciously or unconsciously they look back to a Prussian tradition truly unsullied by industrial capitalism in which the elite of intellect and their ally the Prussian king transcended themselves and attained the univeral plain. This nostalgia which is shared by many West German intellectuals reveals how deep-seated an unconscious allegiance to the Prussian tradition is in today's Germany.

The very fact that nostalgic protest is an important component of the modern German scene, as can be observed in the contradicting program of the Greens, demonstrates what Barrington Moore terms a "Catonism" which Moore asserts is most likely to occur in reaction to a rapid period of social and economic change,[14] and represents an attempt on the part of the established or old upper classes to retain control of the masses, and, if possible, to exploit them. The fact that the old Prussian state was a "regulative or welfare state" which practiced mercantilistic forms of state capitalism means that "Catonism" in Germany inevitably has to take an anticapitalist form. Moltmann's theology is a continuation of the Catonic tradition in German theology begun by Karl Barth and it also serves the social interests of a traditionally privileged class. It is a late form of Catonism which differs markedly from the early Catonism of Barth's theology which was certainly anticapitalistic. His theology also paralleled and was in dialogue with the first wave of twentieth century nihilistic anticapitalism which took the form of national socialism. Moltmann's theology is in dialogue with and parallels the neo-Marxist repudiation of industrial society which itself was deeply influenced by Hegel.

Moltmann's theology accepts Marcuse's idea that it is necessary to free society from economic repression in its most subtle forms, so that man's alienation can finally be ended. Both in the instance of the early and later Catonists, the villain has remained the success of industrial capitalism in providing an unprecedented standard of living for the common man. That is in achieving what both Marxism and Nazism failed to do without the militarization of society through "a war socialism" and then finally the resort to war. Moltmann's theology, especially his ecclesiology, provides the blueprint for the creation of what can be termed "hunter killer" congregations who follow the God of Exodus, the God who demanded the sacrifices of whole cities to satisfy his honor, out into the "desert" of modern society.[15] In a modern context the cities to be sacrificed as an offering to the desert God are the middle classes and their churches.

There is a reason for Moltmann's theology to take this turn. It is part of his *Sitz im Leben* and can probably best be explained in terms of the Jungian idea that the individual and collective life of a people "can be taken over by an archetype," in this case Wotan, "the god of frenzy and violence." Jung asserts that this possibility grows as Christianity declines and the welfare state turns the people into "sheep" and their leaders into "wolves."[16] Moltmann was born in 1926 and his youth was dominated by the experience of National Socialism which has rightly been called "The Revolution of Nihilism." It ended in death and destruction for millions and the reduction of Germany itself to a heap of rubble. Moltmann was given an emergency high school diploma (*Notabitur*) in 1944 and hurried off to a military career which ended in a British prison camp. Moltmann experienced the frenzy of the final effort to defend the borders of the Reich.[17] After the war he shared with his fellow countrymen the shame of the exposure of the extent of German war crimes. He then also experienced the remarkable reconstruction of West German society after 1948. The economic miracle did not convince Moltmann of the value of the "social free market economy" (*sozialer Marktwirtschaft*) championed by Finance Minister Ludwig Earhardt, and economic theorists, such as Friedrich von Hayek. He became an even more ardent socialist and his devotion to the cause of socialism became a key component in his theology of hope. Today he views Germany's new industrial society as corrupt and exploitive.

His theology speaks very clearly to a restless younger generation in Germany, who have found a place either in the militant left wing of the Social Democratic Party or with the Greens. The Greens are environmentalist radicals who now sit in Parliament. Their aims are neither clear nor consistent, but their goals appear to reflect a new wave of anti-industrialism and Luddite destructiveness in German society. The romantic longing for a more simple and more peaceful world is manifest. To achieve this end, many young people advocate the forcible destruction of the present industrial structure. As Jung suggested it would as the welfare state grew, the spector of violence once again stalks the land.[18] Moltmann speaks to and from the frenzied violence which often characterizes youth protest in today's Germany.

General Principles of Moltmann's Theology

Several general factors require consideration. The reader should not forget that in every generation theology borrows from the scientific paradigms which are current and usually makes good use of the philosophy which is then dominant. Thus in the past medieval and later Protestant scholasticism looked to Aristotle's logic and his physics to find the proper framework for theological discussion. Protestant scholasticism had the advantage of drawing on the improved Aristotelianism of the University of Padua and the Italian Renaissance in general, as well as the theological genius of Thomas of Aquinas and the Jesuit theologian, Suarez.[19] In the course of the seventeenth century the scientific and philosophical paradigms changed and the physics of Sir Isaac Newton replaced that of Aristotle and the philosophy of the moderate English and Scottish Enlightenment, especially the Scottish Common Sense Philosophy, provided Protestants in England and North America with a new framework which helped to make possible both the theology of New England Unitarianism and the Princeton Orthodoxy of Samuel Miller, Archibald Alexander, and Charles Hodge.

As a theologian, Jürgen Moltmann is no exception to this general rule. His theology draws upon the philosophical paradigms but not the scientific paradigms of our own day. One might claim that his theology derives a certain justification from Heisenberg's principle, but in the main it is clearly post-Kantian and draws heavily upon the tradition of German idealism embodied in Hegel and Schleiermacher and the modern Marxist school of philosophy represented by Ernst Bloch and the Freudian-Marxist interpretations of Herbert

Marcuse. What is new about Moltmann is his use of Marxist philosophy and its corollary, Marxist theories of economics, and in particular the economic theory of imperialism as a framework for his theology. This is, in fact, the basis of his new conception of election: his doctrine of God and his belief that only the poor and oppressed can be God's people.

His doctrine of God continues a liberal tradition in German theology which has its origins in the claim of the church historian. Adolf von Harnack, a member of the school of Albert Ritchl, the Greek philosophy that had been used to overlay and blunt the originally simple message of the gospel as it is found in the New Testament. The first great Christian heresy, that of the gnostic Marcion, sought to free Christianity from the contamination of the God of the Old Testament. Moltmann's theology seeks to free Christianity once and for all of the Hellenistic overlay which blunted its cutting edge and allowed it to become the religion of the Roman state. Moltmann wishes to call men back to the image of the Old Testament God of Israel, the nomad God who led his people out of the land of Egypt.

The Golden Age of the Church and Reformation Reductionism:

The Reformation emerged from the humanist movement which began during the Renaissance. Humanism was a largely non-philosophical trend dedicated to the revival of the knowledge of classical languages and literature. Some of the students of the new philology applied their knowledge of the ancient languages to the sources of Western theology: the church fathers and the Scriptures. Through the study of the sources they hoped to find a more accurate knowledge of what they termed the "philosophy or wisdom of Christ." The Roman world which they looked back to in their study of the sources was the empire after the conversion of the Emperor Constantine to Christianity. In this period Christianity was the religion of state and adherence to the correct form of Christianity was very much a matter of public truth.[20]

The most enthusiastic and typical of the humanists was Erasmus of Rotterdam (1466 - 1536). He was firmly convinced that there had been a golden age of Christianity which could be recovered through the proper study of the sources. The model of the golden age served him as a means to criticize the church of his own day which was undergoing a severe crisis of leadership. Erasmus' model of a purer and more simple Christianity called for a simplification of the theology, worship, and structure of the Christian church.[21]

Though Luther was certainly not a humanist, his original message was understood by more educated people as a statement which could only be understood in terms of Erasmus' call for a return to the golden age of the church.[22] All branches of Protestantism and also the Catholic reform movement reflected this basic impulse. Not everyone agreed when the golden age had ended, but all sought to restore it. The differences between the churches which emerged from the Reformation era were largely the result of differing interpretations about the time when the golden age of the church ended. Luther and his followers thought in terms of the fall of the church, i.e. that the church became corrupt in the course of the seventh century. The Reformed, better but improperly known as the Calvinists, argued that the golden age ended with the pontificate of Gregory I who died in 604 A.D. The Anabaptists, or *Taeufer* true to an even more Erasmian impulse, believed that the church became corrupt with the conversion of the Emperor Constantine who made Christianity the religion of the state.[23] From its very beginnings Protestantism was dedicated to the assumption that the reform of the church required that the golden age of the church be clearly identified, that the norms of the golden age be applied to the church of the present day to end the corruption, or fallen state, into which the church had degenerated. Protestantism was essentially a reductionist movement; the institutional and theological accumulations which were the product of historical development had to be cleared away, to enable the church to return to its pure and unblemished state. The idea of a golden age is the classical example of that utopianism which has played such an important role in Western thought through the centuries.[24]

Moltmann stands squarely in the tradition of reductionism so basic to Protestantism. For him the church became corrupt with the emergence of the office of monarchical episcopacy at some time in the latter part of the first century of our era. In effect, he rejects all that happened in the years after this dreadful catastrophe occurred because the development of the bishop's office made it possible for Christianity to become a religion of society. This included the entire development of Western theology including that of Augustine of Hippo whose theology was so central to the Reformation. Moltmann calls today's Christians back to the organizational forms of the primitive church, indeed to those of the Jewish Christians who originally dominated the young movement at Jerusalem and expected the Lord to return to them very soon. In many ways his program resembles that attributed to the Montanists of the second century A.D. who longed for the eschatological enthusiasm and security of the first century church.[25]

What is striking about Moltmann's reductionism is that he constantly asserts that since and because of the Enlightenment, thinking Christians have ceased to look back to a golden age and, indeed, can only look forward to God's future.[26] He does not seem to see anything contradictory in talking about the fall of the church in the first century and looking to the model of the primitive church; and then at the same time claiming that Christians must escape the past so that they can look forward to the future. As long as one talks of the fall of the church and advocates the model of the primitive church and its eschatology as the key to the future, one can hardly claim to be advancing into the future unhindered by the past. All that Moltmann is in fact doing is reasserting a basic motif in Protestant ecclesiology in a modern and for him "progressive" setting.

Moltmann is not alone in his future orientation and his reductionism. He belongs to a group of theologians who are generally referred to as the theologians of hope. The names most commonly associated with this group are those of Moltmann and Pannenberg, and the Catholic theologian, Johannes Metz. Other figures, such as Carl E. Braaten and Gabriel Vahanian, are also of importance for this movement which had its origins in the early sixties. All of them seek in one way or another to expose the true meaning of Christian hope. They do so by rejecting "Orthodoxy's otherworldly and neo-orthodoxy's this worldly interpretations of eschatology," i.e. the doctrine of the last things.[27] They all desire to free the church from the past and in general see the fall of the church in terms of its Hellenization. In stressing eschatology the theologians of hope attempt "to recover the primitive faith of both the Jewish and the Christian communities" by reconstructing "biblical eschatology in the modern context."[28] Vahanian probably expresses their aim best when he claims that mankind and the world are "in transition from a mythic to a technological civilization."[29] Moltmann would probably reject this assertion, for there are strong elements of Luddite romanticism in his view of technological civilization which he would reject if possible.

Moltmann's reductionism is typically utopian and draws on the strain of Marxist utopianism which is best represented by Ernst Block who provides the essential "this wordly" definition for Moltmann's conception of hope. Until his death at ninety, Bloch never abandoned the belief that the pursuit of utopia permitted the constant exploration of new possibilities for modern man. Utopianism in general was for Bloch, as it is for Moltmann, a critical vehicle which, "made men aware of the imperfections of the present and spurred them to transform it in the light of the utopian revelations."[30]

Bloch also believed to the end that the masses could be aroused in support of "the revolution." In this respect Moltmann is perhaps not totally a true follower of Bloch, though he could be understood as one. He is a Blochian in terms of the constant hope of Bloch's followers that they could link up the West's utopian past with "the future of new hope."[31] As the Manuels in their study of utopianism have observed: "Recent German Protestant theologians have achieved marvels of syncretism, as theoretical strands of utopia and theology are woven together."[32] Moltmann's synthesis is one of the most important.

Moltmann's interest in eschatology reflects in part Bloch's fascination with the millenarian heritage of Christianity. Bloch frequently referred to the God of Exodus and the messianic Jesus and paid special attention to Joachim of Fiore's concept of the ages of the Father, the Son, and the coming age of the Spirit, because he believed that Joachim had put the idea of the kingdom of God back into history. This fitted Bloch's purpose which was to put the eschatological perspective in "world historical terms."[33] As Bloch so often asserted: "The forward look has replaced the upward look."[34] When this takes place, then the oppressive status quo should be set aside by means of the work of reaching out to the realization of what Bloch called "practical utopias." For Moltmann, Bloch's conception of hope put him in a unique category of a philosopher who spoke in terms of hope within "the world process" in what Moltmann termed "practical categories."[35]

What Moltmann prizes most in Bloch is derived from Bloch's anthropology which sees the primal element in man as his anticipatory consciousness. For Bloch, man's identity and consciousness are derived from his awareness of the future;[36] by the fact that he is always seeking the new. In Bloch's thought the end and not the beginning was genesis; here Moltmann and others follow Bloch to talk of such things as "world openness," "tendencies and latencies," etc.[37] Morse adds that these elements in Bloch's philosophy, which are indeed crucial to Moltmann's theology, were complemented by the twentieth century's future mindedness and the fact that some theologians see this future mindedness as the basis for a possible link with biblical theology.[38] Bloch's belief that Christianity's "principle of hope" is its great contribution to humanity when understood in terms of this world but not the next is central to Moltmann's theology.[39]

The philosophical principles which Moltmann derived from Ernst Bloch are probably more important to his theology than are its biblical sources. However, Moltmann would certainly claim that he works in a consistently Reformation tradition which places the Bible at the center of his systematic theology. Like the theology of all modern systematic theologians, Moltmann's theology is only biblically based in a secondary sense. His biblical orientation is largely dependent upon the latest development in New Testament criticism. His eschatological approach to the doctrine of the church is derived largely from the critical scholarship of Ernst Käsemann. Though he also draws a good many of his ideas from Rudolf Bultmann, he remains critical of many of the major names in Bultmann's theology.[40] Ultimately, his biblicism is as reliable and relevant as is most of the critics whom he chooses to follow. This may well be the only possible approach for a systematic theologian to follow in the present day.

The use of the latest interpretations of biblical scholars to develop a systematic theology gives Protestant theology a great degree of flexibility. For Catholics the teaching authority said to be vested in the church performs the same function, but the new interpretations are accepted somewhat more slowly in Catholicism. The tempo of change in Protestant theology is often bafflingly rapid. And the ongoing problem of authority and coherence in Protestant theology remains largely unsolved in its modern context. This fact makes it extremely difficult for any Protestant theologian to attempt a critique of Moltmann's theology, for there are hardly any widely accepted stands left in Protestantism on which such a judgment can be based.

This problem is not merely the result of biblical criticism's impact upon the Protestant conception of authority. Almost two hundred years have passed since Kant's critique of pure and practical reason denied our ability to obtain any rational knowledge of God or his revelation, except in the moral sphere of practical reason. Indeed the subject of this essay, Moltmann, sees Kant's critique and the "transcendental subjectivity" which emerged from it as a major problem for modern theology and has developed his theology of hope with its emphasis upon eschatology to meet Kant's challenge, without abandoning Kant's categories.[41] Whatever the reader's opinion of Moltmann's theology may be, he should realize that at this point Moltmann has put his finger upon a major problem for all modern theologians and theologies. There is no space to deal with this problem in this essay but it is high time that the result of Kant's critique be re-examined in terms of modern knowledge and the possibilities which it offers to theology. All modern German theology is post-Kantian; gradually all American theology with a few exceptions has also become post-Kantian theology. James Gustafson sums up the results for the sphere of ethics: "Most modern Protestant ethical thought is inexplicible without recourse to the impact of Kant and various post-Kantian developments in philosophy." Gustafson goes on to say that the consequences of Kant's critique make it difficult for anyone working in this philosophical tradition to believe in "universally applicable principles of morality" and in "the possibility of rational knowledge of a universal moral order."[42] We, like Moltmann, live in a post-Kantian world and must face the consequences.

Moltmann, Ernest Troeltsch and the "Sect" type:

The criterion which I have chosen to employ in considering Moltmann's theology, in particular his ecclesiology is derived from Ernst Troeltsch's typology of the church-type and the sect-type. In developing his ecclesiology, Moltmann is consciously or unconsciously in dialogue with Ernst Troeltsch. A very brief summary of Troeltsch's definitions of the term "sect" and "church" should aid the reader in understanding Moltmann's ecclesiology.

(1) The "church type"

He defined the church-type as overwhelmingly conservative. It accepts the social order and is indeed an integral part of it. Consequently, the church-type seeks to dominate and to direct the whole life of the masses. Hence it "stabilizes" and "determines" the social order. Its weakness is that the church-type tends to become dependent upon the upper classes. The church-type also views the whole social order as a preparation for a supernational aim. Asceticism is for the church-type merely a subordinated element in the pursuit of this aim.[43] The church-type, as well as the sect-type, looks to the primitive church and claims a direct relationship to it. Troeltsch sees the early development of the Christian church as a series of fluctuations between the sect-type and the church-type.

Paul opened the way for the universalism of the church-type by accepting the function of the state as ordained by God; the opposition between the sacramental-hierarchical church defended by St. Augustine against the Donatists is typical of the way in which both types developed. For Troeltsch, Augustine, like Paul before him, defends universalism. The church-type which Augustine defended had already made the basic compromise with the state for which Paul had prepared the way. In Troeltsch's words: the church-type meant: ". . . the eternal existence of the God-man; it (the church-type) is the extension of the incarnation, the objective organization of miraculous power, from which by means of the divine providential government of the world, subjective results will appear quite naturally.[44] The church-type institution must remain "holy and divine." If one sought a corrective to Moltmann's theology which is a theology of the sect-type, perhaps it can best be found in Troeltsch's assertion that both types are a result of the gospel. He saw the church-type as the natural continuation and transformation of the gospel and not a deviation from it. The point which Troeltsch wanted to stress here was that: the starting point of the church is the apostolic message of the exalted church, and faith in Christ the

Redeemer: this constitutes its objective treasure. The church-type becomes still more objective in its sacramental—sacerdotal institution. Troeltsch saw the church-type as the conveyer of the gospel message to the world and believed that the sect had emerged as a reaction to the objectification of the gospel. The last important aspect of the church-type which is relative to this essay is that the church-type's conception of natural law is a compromise which makes relative divine law, (i.e. the moral law of nature) on the grounds that in a fallen world the absolute standards of the divine law could not be realized.[45] This is, of course, the position taken by Thomas Aquinas and the later Swiss Reformer, Zwingli. Natural Law in the world tends thus to support the state and society as they are. The church-type which Troeltsch defined is the church-type which Moltmann rejects.

(2) The sect-type is Troeltsch:

Troeltsch's concept of the "sect-type" was simple. A sect consists of a small group which seeks personal, onward perfection, and direct personal fellowship. Each sect has a different attitude towards the state; some are indifferent, others hostile, but every sect seeks to avoid being controlled by the state.[46] Probably quite incorrectly, Troeltsch claimed that the sect was recruited from the lower class and those who are opposed to the state and society.[47] Its members, he said, "look up from below." The sects, Troeltsch reminded his readers, exist in opposition to the world and the established church. They take the Sermon on the Mount seriously and their stress upon individual and collective asceticism is central to the opposition to the world, as well as their belief that the church has fallen away from the true norms of the "primitive church."[48] Troeltsch saw in the sect a true attempt to radicalize the "fellowship of love" and "heroic" indifference to the world, the state, and civilization which was generally manifested in a general mistrust of possessions.[49]

In such a group the emphasis upon the importance of the layman in the religious life of the community is quite natural as is the stress upon religious equality among the members. Both are rationalized by an appeal to the norms of the New Testament and those of the "primitive church."[50] The sect, Troeltsch observes, is a voluntary organization and an independent sociological type, and cannot ever develop into a church dedicated to universalism. The tension between the universalism of the church and the appeal of the sect to select groups drives the sect to revive what Troeltsch calls the "eschatology of the Bible."[51] Symptomatic of the tension which impels the sect to revive eschatology is its appeal to the teaching of Jesus while the church looks to the writings of Paul. The sects appeal to natural law to give their biblicism a deeper emphasis, so that they are able to oppose existing conditions and apply absolute norms to demand, if not achieve, either a reform of the church or an ecclesiastical revolution.[52] To this assertion Troeltsch adds the observation: "Where, however, the idea (the Law of Nature) is also directed against the unnatural and ungodly conditions within the state and society, it then develops into a democratic socialistic revolution, which does not shrink from violence, but justifies it by appealing to the Old Testament and to the Apocalypse."[53] The sect becomes revolutionary in part because it substitutes the idea of the law of God for the church as an organ of grace and redemption.[54]

Another element in Troeltsch's analysis is of particular importance for our consideration of Moltmann's theology. Troeltsch believed that at the end of the Middle Ages, the "radical individualism" and the "radical ethic of love" which combined in the sect-type smashed the church-type of that era. The sect-type was more "mobile and flexible" and also more "subjective." It was "truer" and was more "inward and consequently more exclusive and powerful." The sect-type was firmly based upon the literal interpretation of the gospel and therefore could prevail. But Troeltsch added that, despite the success of the sects in the late Middle Ages, it was the church-type, not the sect-type, which survived in Protestantism. Though he admitted that the Protestant churches were more "voluntary and subjective" than the medieval church, he added that they "still cannot tolerate the radical lack of culture, the 'conventicle-like' narrowness which is bound up with the social form of the sect, and its literal interpretation of the Gospel."[55] Using Ernst Käsemann, Moltmann evolves "a literal interpretation" which may well cause his new sect-type to prevail against the church-type.

The eschatological norm:
In an article written for *Theology Today* in 1971 Moltmann

defined the function of "political theology" very simply: ". . . political theology designates the field, the milieu, the environment, and the medium in which Christian theology should be articulated today."[56] As far as the structure of the church is concerned, i.e. as far as political theology refers to ecclesiology, its aim is to free Christianity from what Moltmann terms, "the anachronistic symbiosis of church, society, and state, which today is euphemistically termed Christendom."[57] Though, as Moltmann laments, the process had begun far earlier, the conversion of the emperor Constantine finally opened the way for the establishment of Christianity as the "public religion of the state" by the Emperors Theodosius I and Justianian. Christianity became part of the "political order." The acceptance of Christianity as the state religion completely eclipsed that voluntary community, the church congregation, which had been the central institution of Christendom in its formative centuries.[58] By the end of the fourth century, the church congregation and the civil assembly of the citizens were one. The church gained enormous influence through this development but in Moltmann's eyes lost the one institution which was the true key to its dynamic appeal to the common people.

In the Middle Ages the earlier tradition of the voluntary organization was able to live on only in the monastic orders. Though the Reformation again placed the congregation in the center of its ecclesiology, it stopped short of re-establishing the voluntary congregation and developed instead its own form of what Moltmann terms "Protestant Constantinianism."[59] As this system matured, European Christians were freed from the obligation to attend church but they were not permitted, as are Americans, to attend the church of their choice. Their religion was not truly voluntary: tradition, public opinion, and the custom of infant baptism bound them to the established form of Christianity which Moltmann believes was the direct cause of the rise of altuism. The reason for this development was clear enough. Though one spoke of a *Volkskirche*, a people's church, it was really only a church for the people.[60] The church did not belong to them.

If Moltmann's entire theology has one ecclesiastical purpose it is to return the churches to the control of the people and to end the Constantinian era for all time. The church-type so carefully described by Troeltsch and designated by him as the dominant ecclesiastical type must, at least in Moltmann's homeland, by replaced by an American style voluntary religion and polity. Conventicles of believers who freely join together are the only possible structure for the future church.[61] What is striking about Moltmann's argument is his obvious misunderstanding of American denominationalism and the religious "folkways" which it has created.[62] Moltmann has spelled out this belief in his more recent works such as *The Open Church* and *The Trinity and The Kingdom of God*.[63]

The Trinity and The Kingdom of God presents a new definition of the doctrine of the Trinity which Moltmann believes will make it possible for the congregation to develop a "true doctrine of freedom." This doctrine will "point towards a community of men and women without supremacy and without subjection."[64] To achieve this end, Moltmann rejects the traditional Western Augustinian emphasis upon the persons of the Trinity and advocates the Eastern Orthodox communitarian or social understanding of the Trinity. A social understanding of the Trinity prevents the development of an idea of God who is an "omnipotent, universal monarch" and is reflected in earthly rulers," especially absolutist rulers. Unlike Eusebius, Moltmann refuses to accept a doctrine of the Trinity which makes God, "the archetype of the mighty ones of this world."[65]

Traditional Western Trinitarianism has two other deep flaws which Moltmann feels justifies its rejection. The first great fault permits the doctrine to aid in developing and accepting a "monarchical monotheism" which "justifies the church as hierarchy, as sacred dominion." Moltmann wishes to put an end to such a justification and observes that, "the universal and infallible authority of the pope represents God as almighty" which is simply wrong.[66] In the "community of believers" God is represented "as love" and He is experienced as the members of the congregation accept each other. Proper Trinitarianism sets the "principle of power" aside and replaces it with "the principle of concord." When this happens, "authority and obedience are replaced by dialogue, consensus and harmony." And faith in the individuals' "insight into the truth of revelation" takes the center of the ecclesiastical stage.[67] Moltmann's "social Trinitarianism" permits him to develop an idea of "grass roots" democracy within the church, which he feels will generate a sense of "brotherhood" and "sisterhood" in the church. The pursuit of grass roots democracy, or as the new German party, the Greens, call it *"Basisdemokratie,"* leads Moltmann to assert that the best way to realize democratic community in the church and to set aside a "hierarchy which enforces unity" is to accept: "the presbyterial and synodical church order and leadership based upon brotherly advice," because this polity best expresses the "doctrine of the social Trinity."[68] As an American Presbyterian who has also experienced the function of a German style "Presbyterial-Synodical" polity, it is difficult for the author to suppress a wearied smile at these assertions. Just as it is hard for him to believe that Eastern style social Trinitarianism can serve anything but the Caesaro-Papalism with which it has lived in peace and harmony for more than fifteen hundred years.

These reservations will never daunt Moltmann who goes on to bolster his argument in favor of social Trinitarianism with the help of Ernest Bloch and Bloch's favorite millenarian, Joachim of Fiore. Moltmann employs Joachim to advance a definition of the kingdom of God which begins with the kingdom of the Father. This kingdom, "consists of the creation of the world open to the future."[69] He sees the kingdom of the Father not as a "kingdom of power" but rather in terms of: "self-limitation," "self-emptying" and "the patience of love," all of which were manifest in the creation of the world.[70] In making this assertion, he continues the basic argument of his book, *The Crucified God,* and applies its main theme of the liberating work of the self-emptying and suffering crucified God to the entire Trinity. Logically, Moltmann sees the second Joachimite kingdom, the kingdom of the Son, in terms of "the liberating lordship of the crucified one."[71] Christ's liberation of mankind from sin consumates "the Fathers' patience." The third kingdom, that of the Spirit, is understood in the realization of "the Holy Spirit's energies;" in the Spirit "we" take part in the freedom granted to us by the Son and sense both "God in us and we in God."[72] Joachimite Trinitarian history illuminates Moltmann's basic argument—that the kingdom of God is, "the history of humanity's progressive and growing liberty," as it proceeds towards the kingdom of glory. For Moltmann this means the repudiation of "freedom as lordship" which "destroys community" and the final realization that, "the truth of human freedom lies in the love that breaks down barriers." Only this love can heal the wounds," which freedom as lordship has inflicted."[73] According to the Tübingen theologian, the second great flow of the traditional Western view of the Trinity is that it has led to, "the development of individualism, and especially possessive individualism" to the terrible detriment of social relations, society, and a proper sense of community. The person is granted preeminence over the community.[74] The social Trinity will end this imbalance and make possible what is for Moltmann a liberating and necessary social goal: "The abolition of property by means of a society that has become personal and authentically social" and which understands "the project of a common future," as a "common responsibility for all.[75] As was clear in *The Crucified God*, the new soteriology advanced by Moltmann has a direct social application. It serves to advance the progress of socialism. Social Trinitarianism is the prerequisite for the abolition of private property. The vehicle for this transformation is the "congregation," i.e. the dynamic basic element of the church.

It would have been impossible for Moltmann to develop his concept of the Trinity as a theological doctrine of freedom without first having evolved his idea of the crucified God. Historically, Moltmann is convinced that: "Jesus died, whether rightly or wrongly, a political death as a rebel on the cross."[76] The question which he raises in making this assertion is not merely a historical and a political one. It is a basic theological question which has both theological and social implications. The theological question which Moltmann raises finds its focus in Christ's cry of despair on the cross: "My God, why has thou forsaken me?"(Mark 15:34; Matthew 27:46; cf. Psalm 22:1-2). God abandoned Christ to die on the cross but at the same time his abandonment of Christ placed his own deity in question. It also raised a second issue. If Christ was in fact God's Son, did not his crucifixion mean that God suffered on the cross? If this is so, then we cannot claim that God is immutable and incapable of pathos, i.e. suffering.[77]

In posing both these questions Moltmann seeks to develop his idea of eschatological hope and to bring the development of his theology of liberation yet another step forward. The metaphysical underpinning which he employs to develop his argument is derived from Hegel and Fichte and involves the idea of the self-revelation of God which makes God a subject about which man thinks. If man thinks of God, then God is thinking of himself in man. If Christ knows himself as the Son of Man, God must know Himself in Christ. Such an approach is a deliberate departure from the traditional analogies of being which Moltmann wishes to reject, because they are based upon Aristotelian metaphysics and a conception of ethics which stresses the importance of achievement and works. This stress provides the foundation for the Protestant ethic of achievement and this is an ethic Moltmann cannot abide. The analogies of being which are derived from Aristotle's metaphysics also lead to a triumphalism in considering the risen Christ and makes the development of a theology of glory inevitable. Moltmann regrets that Luther's attempt to reject the theology of glory by asserting a theology of the cross was sabotaged by the humanists Erasmus and Melanchthon.[78]

Moltmann's use of Hegel and Fichte, as well as his rejection of the theology of glory, serve to provide him with the basis for his own interpretation of the crucifixion and the resurrection as a liberating event, the beginning of the eschaton, as the future of history; it is the final proof that the future had already begun.[79] In order to demonstrate that the drama of the crucifixion and resurrection were truly liberating events, Moltmann is at pains to demonstrate that Christ died because he was a political activist, "a rebel," and "of the poor." The consequences of this argument are that in Christ, God also suffered for his political and social commitment to the oppressed and poor who are his true followers.[80] The context for this argument is the state of the world then and now. Our modern technocratic society has reduced all human relationships to the level of things. The result is apathy on a massive scale.[81] The same problems were present in the social context of Jesus' own day and caused Jesus to rebel against the legalism of Pharisees and zealots, and to seek his friends among tax collectors and sinners as an act of love (agape) which in itself proclaims a new conception of God as a God of grace and love rather than as a sovereign ruler.[82] God's answer to the evil deed of the crucifixion was to raise Christ from the dead. The crucifixion was an anticipation (prolepsis) of liberating love in which the true God was not revealed through His power and glory but rather through His helplessness and death. The crucifixion presents God as a "human" God and not a God who resembles the rulers of this world and practices political repression.[83] This argument is of course the basis for Moltmann's rejection of the idea of a state church which seeks its base in "the political religion of a society."[84] It also serves his earnest wish to reject what he terms "theism" and by so doing to separate Christianity from the bourgeois religion of particular societies.[85] In sum Moltmann's understanding of the crucified God has ultimate significance: "For eschological faith, the Trinitarian God-event on the cross becomes the history of God which is open to the future and opens up the future."[86] The reader needs to remember that the liberation brought by love is for Moltmann necessarily also liberation in political life which is why he calls for the control of economic power by the producers.[87]

In the final chapter of *The Open Church* Moltmann defines the church as the "people of God" and complains that the hierarchy of both the Catholic and Protestant churches perpetuate "monarchism" which keeps the laity, "dependent," "helpless," and "in servitude." He wants the term *lay* to be employed in the original Greek sense of *laos*, which means a participant in, "the people of God."[88] The church dominated by the clergy is "the church for the people" but not "of the people," just as present day socialism is not for the people because both employ the language of rule (Herrschaft) and therefore offer no hope to the people in what Moltmann terms "their struggles."[89]

Moltmann identifies the theologian, the pastor, and the bishop with the scribes and Pharisees of the New Testament. It is clear to him that Jesus identified himself with the people in their conflict with the scribes and Pharisees. The people were obviously the "poor." He interprets Matthew 25:31-46 to mean that "the world judge" is already present in the world, hidden in the hungry, the thirsty, the alien, the naked, the sick, and the impoverished."[90] According to Moltmann, Christ identifies Himself not merely with the persecuted but with all "the people" and the Christ who is identified as the world judge is the Christ of the "passion . . . on the way of the hungry, thirsty, stripped, powerless Son of Man from Nazareth to Golgotha." Moltmann links both the "powerless Son of man" as world judge and the "exalted Christ" (after the resurrection) to Christ's presence through others both in the missionary activity of the believers, the apostolate, and in the suffering expectation of the least significant member of the community. These are Christ's brothers in the messianic kingdom. The missionaries explain "what the church is" and "the least of these say where the church belongs." This explanation prevents a one-sided emphasis upon the "Christ of the church," "the exalted, heavenly King," for "the Christ of the people was always the poor, homeless Son of man."[91]

Therefore, Moltmann argues that Jesus' function was to call the people, "from their position as objects of manipulation and rule by others to be subjects of the new history of God with the human race." The "folk movement . . . is the movement in which the people itself becomes the subject of its own new history in the liberation movement of God."[92] The people then become "the people of the coming kingdom and the coming kingdom becomes present through Jesus and his community." Through this process, "the people discover their own identity and worth" which cannot be taken away from them.[93]

On the basis of this definition, Moltmann questions the function and future of "large, established churches," because "the people" have difficulty identifying with them. To reach the people, a clear definition of the church has to be made.[94] Once the term church has been properly defined, then the church's mission can also be rightly understood: "The mission of the church is the mission of God, and the mission of God is aimed at the total liberation of the whole enslaved creation to the Kingdom of God and of freedom."[95] In the last analysis then, "Mission is taking part in the messianic sending of Jesus and as such taking part in the people, . . . to the extent that mission stands as a representative for him . . . Participation is an expression of solidarity."[96]

Moltmann looks for the realization of his concept of mission and participation with the people as a representative of Christ not in any hierarchical church which is concerned with religious power. The "universal priesthood of all believers" can only be realized in the tradition of the left wing of the Reformation. The "Protestant—bourgeois world" of the nineteenth century has been destroyed and no amount of grieving over it or over a failed divisive Reformation can bring it back.[97] For Moltmann the conventicles of the left wing of the Reformation beckon, because within their voluntary congregations, it will be possible to develop a "church for or by the people." The churches which care for the people, "from above" are becoming ineffective and must give way to the "congregation from below" in which hierarchy is absent and community dominates. In other words, the sect-type offers the only hope for Christendom as well as *the* escape from "the social isolation" of "mass society;" . . . in the last analysis, in times of contempt and persecution, the church stands or falls with the gathered congregation and with no one else."[98]

The assertion that the gathered church, i.e. the conventicle, is the only possible institution for today's church concludes the discussion begun almost twenty years before in *The Theology of Hope* and carried further in *The Church in the Power of the Spirit*. A few basic motifs in Moltmann's theology require notice before we conclude this essay. Moltmann began the *Theology of Hope* with the complaint that the reality of early Christian eschatology had been ignored and its impact deadened, because Christianity became the successor to the religion of the Roman state and quickly abandoned the revolutionary and critical elements which predominated in the eschatology of the primitive church. Despite the biblical witness to the messianic expectations. this element was neutralized in mainline Christian theology and relegated to a shadowy existence among the "enthusiastic sects" and "revolutionary groups" which flourished on the fringes of Christianity.[99] It was Moltmann's goal to restore eschatology to the central role it had occupied in the primitive church, in order to advance his own concept of what the modern church's theology and mission should be. His basic definition of eschatology was in fact traditional, but the use he sought to put the doctrine to was theologically and politically revolutionary. Eschatology was for Moltmann the return of Christ in glory which breaks into our time from the outside and puts an end to our time. This event means that the day of the "Last Judgment" is at hand, the dead do rise again, and all things experience a new creation which comes from beyond history into our experience.[100]

Drawing heavily on Ernest Bloch's conception of the hope and the future, Moltmann asserted that from the time of the crucified Christ's resurrection, the eschatological element in Christian thought became decisive because man had been given hope for the future by God. Thus the problem of the future had been made the central problem for Christian theology, because the church had a God-given promise and a goal for the future.[101] What was so remarkable about this fact was that the hope which was proclaimed by faith in Christ contradicted what should have been reality and thereby made truly new experiences possible, indeed made an exodus experience possible. In such a system, flight from the world to another world beyond and resignation were simply not possible; Christ's resurrection did not concern the next life but rather life in this world.[102] The peace with God which came with the hope granted through faith in Christ and his resurrection made the believer dissatisfied with the world.[103] This dissatisfaction with the world is the central element in Moltmann's idea of the role of the church congregation in the present; it is the focal point for the gathering of the dissidents of this world, so that they can express their dissatisfaction with the existing institutions of society, including the hierarchal church. This is the keystone for Moltmann's entire theology and his sect-type ecclesiology. Such a theology and ecclesiology had to become political, because the nature of Moltmann's definitional structures, especially that of his eschatology, make a forward-looking political theology inevitable; it had to be a theology which at least claimed to reject history and concentrated upon the injustices of today's world and its culture.[104] However, Moltmann's rejection of history could not be complete, because he was virtually compelled to employ the norm of the eschatological expectations of the primitive church to justify his revival of eschatology as the central theme of Christian hope. As soon as this happened, Moltmann joined the ranks of a very select few who employ a reductionism far more radical than that of the left wing of the Protestant Reformation to restore the church to the pristine purity which they believe she reflected in her golden age. Moltmann's historical norm was really the age of the primitive Jewish-Christian congregation at Jerusalem which awaited the speedy return of their Lord. But even this norm was partially obscured by Moltmann's vision of the modern church as a revived version of the exodus congregation which followed Moses out of Egypt to an unknown future in the wilderness of Sinai, because it trusted the promise of God.[105] The very fact that these norms oriented in the past creep into Moltmann's future-oriented theology inevitably weakens its eschatological thrust.[106] But it certainly did not prevent him from defining the rule of God, not in terms of a world-wide kingdom but rather in terms of God leading his people, namely the oppressed and cast out ones, into a landscape of promise, where new experiences were possible.[107] The context for the wandering people of God, the exodus congregation's journey, is a world which has constantly been in crisis since the French Revolution, and is therefore open to new experiences and free of the encumbrances of the past. The Industrial Revolution has, according to Moltmann, made the crisis in the world far more acute and the situation of God's people much more precarious. But this makes its future orientation all the more urgent if it is to change the world around it.[108]

To understand Moltmann's concept of the exodus congregation (*Die Exodus Gemeinde*), the question of who the members of the congregation should be has to be raised. In *Das Experiment Hoffnung* he says two very important things about the membership of the congregation. First, the author asserts that Christian theology must be done among and with the people. By the people Moltmann means "those without rights," "the poor," "the abandoned," and "the unrighteous," for these are the brothers of the crucified Christ.[109] To this description, he adds the assertion that the Bible is the book of the "poor" and the "hopeless" and not the book of priests and rulers. Only "the poor" and "the sinner" can really understand the Bible properly because they are able to recognize that it contains a history of freedom and liberation. Therefore, Moltmann concludes, the Bible is "a revolutionary and subversive book." Elsewhere he adds that the Bible tells the story of hope for the oppressed.[110] In making these statements, Moltmann has in fact defined the membership of the exodus congregation and evolved a new principle of election. The elect are the poor and oppressed, for only they can understand God's Word and enjoy true fellowship with the crucified Jesus.[111]

A further example of this economic conception of election is found in his open letter to José Miguez Bonino which is certainly sympathetic with but not uncritical of Latin American liberation theology. The letter closed with a bitter denunciation both of the Chilean military junta and a group of twenty-two Protestant churchmen who welcomed the junta's seizure of power.[112] He calls those who have praised the generals, adherents of a "murderous political religion." When they term Marxism "satanic," Moltmann answers them angrily that they make Christ "an anti-communist Satan." To Moltmann, the generals were worshippers of "Moloch," but the real cause of his anger is that they killed ten thousand "poor" people.[113] The killing seems to bother him far less than the fact that those who were killed were poor, or in other words belonged to the economic elect. In the seventeenth century, Puritans who wished to become full members of the Congregational Church in New England, which was the state church, had to prove that they possessed the marks of grace. In Moltmann's modern exodus congregation, poverty and marginality have become the marks of grace and the prerequisites for membership in the congregation. In developing the new doctrine of election, Moltmann has remained true to his own Reformed origins. He is clearly one with Theodore Beza and the Canons of Dordt in believing that Christ died for the elect. What is new in his doctrine both of election and of the church is that the nature of the elect has been redefined in terms of Marx, Marcuse, and Bloch, who are a remarkable modern trinity.

Only the elect can belong to the three dimensional church: the church before God, men, and the future. This church of the elect, Moltmann insists, is based upon a political and social concept of a church which combats injustice and inhuman social systems.[114] It fits perfectly the model of the sect-type organized from below, dominated by the laity, whose members are close to each other, are anti-hierarchical and sacramental,[115] and above all are eager to practice piety for their own benefit and that of the world, if the world either will listen or can be compelled to listen. Such an institution, which is really a microcosm of a "classless society," is also not far from the concept of the revolutionary elite which Lenin insisted was necessary to guide the revolution and to guard the revolution during the first stage of transition to the dictatorship of the proletariat. For Moltmann, the church's function is to free the congregation as the basic ecclesiastical unit from its sinister involvement with the middle class and the "political" religions of their societies.[116] This in turn will allow the exodus congregation, the conventicle of the truly chosen, to take part in the worldwide struggle to free the oppressed and exploited. This is the institution which lives in the Holy Spirit, "and thus is itself the beginning and earnest of the future on the new creation."[117] Perhaps, the greatest strength which this organization has is that it is led by a God whom Moltmann describes as nomadic.[118] Moltmann's sect will be guided by the nomadic God's spirit, i.e. the third person of the Trinity, the Holy Spirit, in its struggle for social justice in the world: "The history of the creative spirit . . . to be understood in dialectical-materialist terms as 'the movement,' 'the urge,' 'the spirit of life' . . . "[119] However, the Holy Spirit alone will not guide the exodus congregation in what Moltmann later calls the "messianic way of life;" it will also find its directives in the "apocalyptic interpretation of the signs of the times."[120] Moltmann believes that these signs point towards a revolutionary conflict against the rich men who oppose the poor which was given its "revolutionary keynote" by the French Revolution.[121] Christians have only one choice: to be either revolutionary progressives or anti-revolutionary conservatives—for Moltmann there is no middle ground and in fact to him Christians have no real choice. When they truly understand Jesus as the Son of God, they will work for the destruction of a stratified, caste-ridden society.[122] They will see to it that the exodus congregation will take its rightful place as a fighting unity in the framework of the "universal history of God's dealing with the world."[123] The congregation will glorify God in the suffering and struggle-filled liberation of creation, i.e. the "messianic liberation," for: "The true church is the church under the cross." Its gospel will be a partisan gospel which favors the oppressed as did the Messiah himself.[124]

Thus Moltmann explains further what he means by the exodus church—it is the people of the kingdom whose church has emigrated from society, i.e. bourgeois society, and its concern for a hierarchical state church, in order to join in the "universal movement" for the liberation of enslaved creation.[125] Seen historically, the exodus church under the guidance of the gospel of liberation is, "an eschatological movement away from the past and out of death, towards the future and into life.[126] The advance of the exodus church into the future naturally calls for the rejection of any idea of growth or progress, and an end to what Moltmann terms "imperialism" but never defines; by this he surely means the Hobson-Lenin interpretation of imperialism, though there are other definitions. The march of the exodus congregation in the desert also calls for the total repudiation of the capitalist ethos and a society which lives according to a market-oriented economy of supply and demand.[127] As the congregation battles for social justice, it will give up all idea of "private or group-oriented self-realization" and will follow "the line which Christianity in the world ought to follow . . . 'socialism' in the relationship of people with one another and 'socialism' in the relationship of humanity to nature."[128] The marks of "true church," as Moltmann understands them are: "Unity in freedom, holiness in poverty, catholicity in partisan support for the weak, and an apostolate in suffering are the marks by which it is known in the world."[129]

CONCLUSION:

Troeltsch would probably have been surprised not by the structure of the sect-type of ecclasiastical organization which Moltmann advocates but rather by the radically destructive mission which Moltmann assigns to the "saints in arms" who belong to his ideal exodus congregation. Sydney Mead's warning that every sect longs for social domination is more than justified by the worldwide aim of the struggle against oppression which Moltmann says the nomad God, the gospel of hope, the Holy Spirit, and the "signs of the times" assign to the exodus people, the elect congregation of the new Israel. However, Mead's assertion that in America the pluralistic nature of church life and the limiting effect of American civil religion prevent any one sect from dominating should reassure Troeltsch's wrath and the readers of this paper, as much as it will cast a shadow over Moltmann's pursuit of the "messianic life-style," the way of the future.

To anyone familiar with modern German political life, Moltmann's advocacy of the conventicle with a clear plan of political and social action aiming at the realization of worldwide socialism and socialist democracy which will set aside the remnants of bourgeois society for all time is very familiar. It is also very Prussian, aristocratic and Catonic. In today's context it is the extension of the German New Left's conception of participatory democracy, *Basisdemokratie*, into the realm of theology. Indeed, Moltmann's theological achievement is remarkable; he has presented us with a theology for the left which has transformed every major doctrine into a weapon in the struggle for world socialism. Few Americans would enjoy his form of participatory democracy at the congregational level. Even fewer would accept Moltmann's economic doctrine of election which would exclude over eighty percent of America's population from membership in the exodus congregation, because they persist in believing that they belong to the middle class. It is hard to accept the assertion that Christ died only for the welfare mother and shoeshine boy on the corner. When one contemplates the consequences of this doctrine, one is compelled to realize that most people never had the ghost of a chance of belonging to the Christian church and that they should give up the charade of attending church anyway. Moltmann believes that Augustine was wrong; the church in the earthly city is not a mixed body of the saved and the damned, it is a conventicle of visible saints, saints in arms. The "judgment of men" employed by Zwingli and the "judgment of charity" advocated by Calvin, so that all the members of the visible church could be called "elect," as long as they were on earth, is absent in Moltmann's theory of economic or sociological election. Indeed, there is little charity (love) in his theology. As one thinks about this, Thomas' assertion that Christ died for all men but that all men were not able to take advantage of the consequences of Christ's sacrifice appears an oasis of theological assurance in a desert of apocalyptic gloom.

There have always been Donatists. Why should one worry about Moltmann? The reason is that Moltmann has found many followers, especially in the theological seminaries and the administrative offices of the mainline denominations, who are eager to transform their churches into exodus congregations ready to wage war on bourgeois America, as long as the laity is foolish enough to pay for it. Their policies have caused the laity to leave the mainline churches in droves.

There is something very frightening about Moltmann's reductionist political theology and ecclesiology. Troeltsch has observed that the sects were able to smash the church-type at the end of the Middle Ages, but that the church-type resurfaced during the Reformation.

It is possible that Moltmann and his followers could play a very destructive role at this stage in western Christendom's development. They might well help to destroy the existing state churches in Protestant Europe; they certainly do aid guerilla movements in the third world and help to make propaganda for these movements which makes it hard to recognize the real goal of the guerillas, the creation of leftist totalitarian dictatorships, until it is too late. Elements of Moltmann's political theology have deeply influenced the 1967 Confession of Faith of the United Presbyterian Church in the United States, and the new German Reformed Confession of 1982 which numbers among the elect of God only those who oppose nuclear armaments. The Christian ethics of Paul Lehmann is indebted both to Moltmann and his Marxist sources. Lehmann agonizes over the need to use force to save "the revolution,' a term which he does not define, and concludes that killing for its sake is participation in Christ's transfiguration and therefore acceptable. He does not deal with killing on the part of the counterrevolutionaries but one is left with the impression that only the elect, i.e. the revolutionaries, please God when they kill.[130]

The twentieth century has been a killing time for Western European civilization. Moltmann himself experienced the killing associated with the "revolution of nihilism," i.e. the period of Nazi domination in Germany and Western Europe. At least in this writer's opinion, the question arises whether or not Moltmann's theology really continues the "revolution of nihilism" in another context. It remains to be seen in Germany whether *Basisdemokratie* is democratic or totalitarian; it appears to be a form of manipulative totalitarianism. Indeed, there is a good deal of authoritarian anti-authoritarianism in the idea of *Basisdemokratie*, as there also is in Moltmann's political theology. The model of the Trinity which Moltmann employs is derived from the social trinity of Eastern Orthodoxy. It is hard to believe that this form of the Trinity can serve anything but an authoritarian society; it has found its strongest supporters in traditionally authoritarian Eastern European, totalitarian society. Should Moltman's followers really achieve their political end, how would this churchly revolutionary elite treat the conquered bourgeois societies of the West? What kind of church-type would they found? They would certainly have to use force to coerce the majority to join their new Constantinian order. Is not Moltmann's exodus congregation essentially totalitarian and murderous? Is it not also another emergent church-type? Are the congregations not of necessity hunter-killer societies until they dominate Christianity? Observers as disparate as C. G. Jung and Edmund Burke have warned that the rejection of past traditions and history can cause collective psychic disturbances in whole nations. Does not Moltmann's rejection of the past and his one-sided futuristic gospel of hope, that is his reductionism, offer an ecclesiology and a theology which must inevitably end in violence and disruption, and only much later in institution building? Moltmann calls the generals of the Chilean junta worshippers of Moloch. Is he not in the Jungian sense obsessed by the archetype of Wotan? Can he and his followers avoid running amuck?

NOTES

1. Michael Novak, *The Spirit of Democratic Capitalism* (New York: American Enterprise Institute/Simon & Schuster, 1982), p. 255.

2. Sydney E. Mead, *The Nation with the Soul of a Church* (New York, Harper & Row, Publishers, 1975). With respect to this essay, Mead's warning that in every sect "absolutistic tendencies" are "inherent" is of particular importance. He sees neutral civil authority, based on the Enlightenment Religion of the Republic, as well as the very variety of the sects which flourish in America as the basic guarantees against such a development (Mead, pp. 58-60, 73-77). Chapter 4, entitled, "The Nation with the Soul of a Church," deals in detail with this question (Mead 48-77. cf., 118-123). Mead's criticism that for the last century, American biblical and theological scholarship has been so dominated by European scholarship that it is ignorant of the "American experience of Christianity" is also important for our consideration of Moltmann's theology (Mead, 65-66).

3. Kurt Dietrich Schmidt, *Grundriss der Kirchengeschichte* (Auflage, Gottingen: Vandenhoeck & Ruprecht, 1960), pp. 493, 502-503, 507.

4. Reinhold August Dorwart, *The Prussian Welfare State before 1740* (Cambridge: Harvard University Press, 1977), vii-viii, pp. 2-5, 12 ff, pp. 16-19, 20, 157-158, 204 ff, 211-213. *Polizeistaat* does not mean a modern police state. After 1500 the term *Polizeistaat* was used to refer to a state which sought to serve the "general welfare." According to Dorwart, "The only proper translation of *Polizeistaat* is "welfare state." (Dorwart, 3 ff). In asserting that the development of the *Polizeistaat* led to the

emergence of the power of the state at the expense of the individual, Dowart follows Fritz Hartuing's thesis (Dorwart, 5). The best discussion of the civil servant in a German context is Otto Hintze's "Der Beamtenstand" in: Otto Hintze, *Gesammelt Abhandlungen*, 3 Bde (Gottingen: Vandenhoeck & Ruprecht in Gottingen, 1964), II, pp. 66-125. (Hintze "Der Beamtenstand," pp. 71; 93, 95).

5. For Treitschke see G. P. Gooch, *History and Historians in the Nineteenth Century* (Boston, Beacon Press, 1959, pp. 139-141) (first published 1913). Treitschke's attacks on such thing as "socialism," "the Jews," and "Parliamentary Government" made an unforgettable impression upon his students (Gooch, p. 145). Above all, he believed in the necessity of a strong state, whose executive was free of party majorities. He also favored the education and training of "virile citizens." (Gooch, p. 145).

6. Leo Strauss and Joseph Cropsey offer a good short account of Hegel's conception of the state. Leo Strauss, and Joseph Cronsey, edd. *The History of Political Philosophy* (Chicago and London: The University of Chicago Press, 1981), pp. 686-687. Hegel spoke of the state as "divine" but according to Strauss and Cropsey did not deify it. (Strauss & Cropsey, p. 687).

7. Strauss and Cropsey, pp. 694-695.

8. Strauss and Cropsey, pp. 692-694, 696-697.

9. Strauss and Cropsey, pp. 692, 696-700, 701-704.

10. Strauss and Cropsey, pp. 706-708.

11. Strauss and Cropsey, pp. 704, 699-700. For a further discussion of Hegel's idea of "self consciousness" and of "objectivity" see W. T. Stace, *The Philosophy of Hegel* (New York: Dover, 1955) pp. 354 ff, 374-380.

12. Frank E. Manual, Fritzie P. Manual, *Utopian Thought in the Western World* (Cambridge, Mass.: The Belknap Press, 1979), p. 797. The quote is taken from the chapter entitled, "Freudo-Marxism, a Hybrid for the Times." The reader would profit from the Epilogue: "The Utopian Prospect," pp. 801-804.

13. Manual and Manual, pp. 798, 8, 792-796.

14. Moore sees the rise of Nazism as an example of "plebian anti-capitalism" which resulted from the intrusion of this system into neo-commercial agrarian life. He also cites Prussia as a model for a process which he terms "conservative modernization." Barrington Moore, Jr., *Social Origins of Dictatorship and Democracy Lord and Peasant in the Making of the Modern World* (Boston: Beacon Press, 1966), pp. 448, 441, 449-450. Moore derives the term Catonism from the example of Cato the Elder (234-149 B.C.). He defines Catonism as follows: "It justifies a repressive social order that buttresses the position of those in power. It denies the existence of actual changes that have hurt the peasants. It denies the need for further social changes, especially revolutionary ones. . . . Modern versions of Catonism arise out of the adoption by the landed upper classes of repressive and exploitative methods in response to the increasing intrusion of market relationships into an agrarian economy. . . . A key element . . . is the appearance of a great deal of talk about the need for a thoroughgoing moral regeneration, talk that covers the absence of a realistic analysis of prevailing social conditions which would threaten the vested interests behind Catonism . . . An aura of moral earnestness suffsses Catonist arguments. . . . policies are not advocated in order to make humanity happier (happiness and progress are contemptuously

dismissed as decadent bourgeois illusions) and certainly not to make people richer. . . . That Catonist views of the past are romantic distortions goes without saying." (Moore, pp. 491-492). The reader may feel that it is improper to apply this term to theology or the work of a theologian. The author feels that the term used more broadly than Moore chose to use it has a real application to theology, in particular to the theologies of Barth and Moltmann. Moltmann's theology avoids a realistic analysis of social conditions. It talks a good deal about "The need for a thoroughgoing moral regeneration;" his proposals would make few richer or happier. His view of society is a "romantic distortion" and the success of his ethics would strengthen his position in society. There is one other element in Moltmann's theology which needs mention. Inevitably his theology stresses violence which Moore sees as a very typical element in Fascism. The author feels that it has wider application: "Blood and death often acquire overtones of erotic attraction. . . ." There can be no doubt that Moltmann's theology does represent an attempt to re-establish the social position of a threatened segment of an establishment which has survived from an earlier age. Moore says that opposition to "plutocracy," "technology," and "technological expertise" are major themes in "the Catonist cacophony." Catonism is "anti-industrial" and "anti-modern." The privileged defend themselves and their position by means of an "anti-bourgeoise" view of the world which is "anti-materialist" and "anti-urban" and reflects a romantic nostalgia for the past (Moore, pp. 495-498). All these elements are clearly present in Moltmann's theology which is certainly anti-technology, the middle classes, and capitalism. The "Experiment Hope" is Moltmann's form of "moral regeneration." If his experiment were a success, the workers and the poor would certainly suffer most. From a German point of view, Moltmann's Catonism is as much that of the right as it is that of the left which in a German context is truly traditional.

15. The term "hunter-killer" is derived from information given in General Sir John Hackett's *The Third World War* about the *Jagdkommandos* (Hunter Groups) of the West Germany Army and their British equivalents. These special groups are conceived to serve the purposes of the new tactics being developed to combat massive Russian tank thrusts and to disrupt the forward areas of the Russian advance. The hunters are to move in small heavily armed groups through the area of the Russian advance. General Sir John Hackett *The Third World War* (New York: Macmillan, 1978) pp. 146, 156-157, 163, 241. There is also a "hunter-killer" submarine whose function is obvious. As yet NATO forces do not really possess such units but their creation is hotly debated. The author believes that the term is an accurate term to describe the type of ecclesiology which Moltmann advocates. This argument will be further developed in the course of the essay.

16. C. G. Jung, "Wotan," *The Collected Works of C. G. Jung*, edd., Sir Herbert Read, Michael Fordham, Gerhard Adler, William McGuire, 20 vols., Bollingon Series *XX* (Princeton: Princeton University Press, 1964, 1970, 1975), vol. X (*Civilization in Transition*), pp. 180, 184, 185, 187, 190-192. Jung sees the reemergence of "Wotan" as the result of the "weakness" of Christianity, i.e. its decline in the modern period. He also believes that National Socialism and Fascism in general are not, "the last word." Jung, "Wotan," *Collected Works, X*, pp. 180, 184, 189, 192. cf. also his

essay "After the Catastrophe" Ibid. X, in which Jung warns that excessive dependence on the state causes a whole nation to become a "herd of sheep" and the shepherds, "wolves." He feels that, the "Welfare State is a 'doubtful blessing' which robs people of their 'individuality' and 'turns them into infants and sheep.' " He also believes that the extension of welfare will make people more destructive. Moltmann's theology seems to prove Jung's point.

17. "Jürgen Moltmann," *Kurschners Deutscher Gelehrten Kalendar*, heraugegeban von W. Schuder, 14. Ausgabe, (Berlin, New York: Walter de Gruyter, 1983).

18. cf. footnote 16.

19. Kuhn defines scientific paradigms as " . . . universally recognized scientific achievements that for a time provide model problems and solutions to a community of practitioners." Thomas S. Kuhn, *The Structure of Scientific Revolutions*, Sec. Edition, *Foundations of the Unity of Science*, 2 vols. (Chicago: University of Chicago, 1962, 1970), vol. 2, no. 2, vii; cf. 176ff., 179ff., 182-183, 191ff., 195-196, 198ff., 202-204, 208-210.

20. Roland H. Bainton, *The Reformation of the Sixteenth Century* (Boston: Beacon Press, 1952 & 1953), pp. 17, 68-70, 80-81. See also P. O. Kristeller, "The Place of Classical Humanism in Renaissance Thought," *Journal of History of Ideas*, Vol. 4, January, 1943, pp. 59-63; P. O. Kristeller, *Renaissance Thought and Its Sources*, ed., Michael Mooney, (New York: Columbia University Press, 1979), pp. 33, 41-43, 46-49, 69-78, 85ff., 98-105.

21. Bainton, *The Reformation* . . . , p. 69.

22. Bainton, *The Reformation* . . . , p. 57-58.

23. Fritz Blanke, "Anabaptism and the Reformation; Franklin H. Littell, "The Anabaptist Conception of the Church," in *The Recovery of the Anabaptist Vision*, ed., G. F. Hershberger (Scottdale, Pa.: Herald Press, 1957 & 1962), p. 68, 127ff.; Franklin H. Littell, *The Anabaptist View of the Church* (Boston: Starr King Press, 1958), pp. 46, 48, 50ff., 55-62, 63-64, 65-72, 76-78; John M. Headley, *Luther's View of Church History* (New Haven and London: Yale Univesity Press, 1963), pp. 156-161, 167ff., 224ff., 270ff.

24. Manuel & Manuel, pp. 1-4, 5ff., 21-22.

25. Jürgen Moltmann, *Theologie der Hoffnung Untersuchungen zur Begruendung und zu den Konsequenzen einer christlichen Eschatalogie* (München: Chr. Kaiser Verlag, 1964), pp. 144-145, 280-281; Jürgen Moltmann, *The Church in the Power of the Holy Spirit* (London: SCM Press, 1977), pp. 83-84, 135, 305, 318-319, 325-326: Jürgen Moltmann, *Das Experiment Hoffnung Einfüehrung* (München: Chr. Kaiser Verlag, 1974), 15: Jürgen Moltmann, *The Crucified God* (London: SCM Press, 1974), pp. 194-195, 215, 320-322 (On Constantine and Christianity as the Roman State Religion), pp. 323-325, 326-328.

26. Moltmann, *Theologie der Hoffnung*, pp. 213-215, 275, 279, 284-285.

27. Lonnie D. Kliever, *The Shattered Spectrum A Survey of Contemporay Theology* (Atlanta: John Knox, 1981), p. 101. Kliever's general survey is probably the best one available and I have been glad to make use of it.

28. Kliever, p. 101.

29. Kliever, p. 121.

30. Manuel and Manuel, p. 806.
31. Manuel and Manuel, p. 806. I am following the Manuels' interpretation of Bloch and his disciples' goals in this section.
32. Manuel and Manuel, p. 810.
33. Christopher Morse, *The Logic of Promise in Moltmann's Theology* (Philadelphia: Fortress Press, 1979), p. 13.
34. As quoted by Morse, 13 from Ernst Bloch, *Atheism and Christianity*, p. 265.
35. Morse, p. 14.
36. Morse, p. 14.
37. Morse, pp. 14-15.
38. Morse, pp. 15-16.
39. Kliever, p. 99.
40. Moltmann, *Theologie der Hoffnung*, pp. 34-35 (Barth); pp. 37-41, 45-53, 57ff.
41. Moltmann, *Theologie der Huffnung*, pp. 39-43.
42. James Gustafson , *Protestant and Roman Catholic, Ethics Prospects for Rapproachment* (Chicago: The University of Chicago Press, 1978), pp. 60-61, 65.
43. Ernst Troeltsch, *The Social Teaching of the Christian Churches*, translated by Olive Wigen, 2 vols. (London: George Allen and Unwin, 1931 & 1949) I, pp. 331-332. Hereafter referred to as ET, ST, I or II.
44. ET, ST, I pp. 331-332.
45. ET, ST, I, pp. 341-42, 343-344.
46. ET, ST, I, p. 331.
47. The example of the origins of the Society of Friends refutes Troeltsch's assumption. In its first phase of development the Friends recruited from virtually all classes including the lesser gentry. Vann sees this as a demonstration of what Max Weber calls "vertical cleavage." Later the Friends ceased to recruit from the upper eschelons of English society and fulfilled Troeltsch's definition of a sect. Richard T. Vann, *The Social Development of English Quakerism 1655-1755* (Cambridge, Mass.: Harvard University Press, 1969), pp. 47ff., 59-60, 62-71, 73 (vertical cleavage), pp. 74-87, 197-208. cf. Max Weber, "Antikritisches zum Geist des Kapitalismus," *Archiv fuer Sozialwissenschaft and Sozialpolitik*, Bd., pp. 30, 1910, 188 n. 44.
48. ET, ST, I, pp. 331-334.
49. ET, ST, I, pp. 335.
50. ET, ST, I, pp. 336-337.
51. ET, ST, I, pp. 338-340.
52. ET, ST, I, p. 344.
53. ET, ST, I, p. 345.
54. ET, ST, I, p. 347.
55. ET, ST, I, pp. 381-382.
56. Jürgen Moltmann, "Political Theology," *Theology Today*, Vol. 28, No. 1, April, 1971, p. 6.
57. "Ihre Zukunft liegt in der Befreiung von dieser anchronistischen Symbiose von Kirche, Gessellschaft und Staat, die man heute euphemististisch 'Christentum' nennt." Jürgen Moltmann, "Das Volk des kommenden Christus," *Evangelische Kommentare*, No.4, 1979, p. 197. Hereafter Jürgen Moltmann abbrievated as JM.

58. JM, "Das Volk des kommenden Christus," pp. 197-198. Elsewhere Moltmann presents this development in another light. He argues that it sets off a continuous conflict between the Constantinian and the chiliastic wing of Christianity. He describes the chiliastic wing as, "united with the humiliated and oppressed in a revolutionary way." JM, "The Revolution of Freedom Christians and Marxists struggle for Freedom," *Religion, Revolution, and the Future*, translated by M. Douglas Meeks (N.Y.: Charles Schribners' Sons, 1969), p. 70. For Moltmann's loudest lament over the rise of the authoritarian monarchical episcopacy which really prepared the way for the creation of an hierarcy in the church see: JM *The Trinity and the Kingdom of God. The Doctrine of God* (London: SCM Press, 1981), pp. 200-203. Hereafter referred to as JM, TKG.

59. "Das Volk des kommenden Christus," p. 198. Moltmann gives another account in "The Revolution of Freedom. . . . ," where he asserts that the conflict between the Empire and the Papacy did free the Church from the Emperor's authority, but led to the clericalization of the church. JM, "The Revolution of Freedom. . . . ," p. 72.

60. Ibid, p. 198.

61. Ibid, p. 199.

62. To understand Moltmann's view of America, a very close look at his article: "De amerikanische Traum," which appeared in *Evangelische Theologie*, p. 37 (March-April) 1977, pp. 166-178 is necessary. In this article he is too quick first to identify the American dream with the aspirations of the "oppressed," "persecuted," "socially humiliated," and "racially defamed;" and then to see the birth of the Republic in terms of "political Messianism." The framers of the American Constitution were after all followers of the moderate English Enlightenment. "Der amerikanische Traum," pp. 167, 166-170. Political Messianism is also not the only theme in American history. In the course of his article, Moltmann makes it clear that he believes Carter's "moral conscience" cannot prevail over the influence of "big business" as the champion of American security. This view only reflects Moltmann's paranoid view of capitalism. A close look at Michael Novak's, *The Spirit of Democratic Capitalism*, especially the second part of Chapter I which is entitled "Pluralism" (pp. 49-80), would greatly enlighten Moltmann. (Cf. especially page 56 and 57) Novak remarks: "The fact that humanists and political scientists have scarcely studied the history and workings of the economic system . . . has probably created a larger gap in our culture than the celebrated gap between the two cultures of literature and science . . . " (Novak, 57); See also Ronald Nash, *Social Justice and the Christian Church* (Milford, Michigan: Mott Media, 1983) pp. 6-7, 9-15, 24-25, 27ff., 74ff. Moltmann's description of the two faces of eschatology in American thought is not wrong but only exaggerated to fit his cultural pessimism and possibly a latent anti-Americanism. Of course, the messianic and apocalyptic eschatology which he discovers in the American experience are yoked to his conception of "Exodus history." He carries this motif further to explain not merely American developments but also the origins of Latin American "liberation theology," as well as the nature of American anti-communism. JM, "Der amerikanische Traum," pp. 171-173. Of course, Moltmann notes the failure of the founding fathers to realize how numerous the oppressed were and he is glad to assert that only the few who belonged to the upper class could really take part in the "abstract

Jürgen Moltmann's Theology of Hope

concept of freedom" propounded by the founding fathers. Bellah's assertion that the "covenant" is broken delights Moltmann. JM, "Der amerikanische Traum," p. 175. He concludes that the American covenant has to be renewed and to him this can take place only if America embraces the "Religion of freedom" which he preaches. Naturally, this means economic and social liberation. Moltmann draws on such writers as Daniel Boorstin to envisage the realization of "life as an experiment in America." JM, "Der americanische Traum," pp. 175-177. He does rightly see that there is a "messianic dynamic of the present" in America which is weakened by the provisional life" found among Americans. What he wants is for Americans to correct the "provisional" in their lifestyle with the "Experiment of Hope." JM, "Der amerikanische Traum," pp. 177-178. My question is, does any American need Moltmann's Hegelian "Experiment Hope?"

63. Jürgen Moltmann, *The Open Church Invitation to a Messianic Life Style* (London: SCM Press, 1978); hereafter referred to as JM, OC; JM, TKG.

64. JM, TKG, p. 192.

65. JM, Ibid., p. 198.

66. JM, Ibid., p. 202.

67. JM, Ibid., p. 202.

68. JM, Ibid., p. 202.

69. JM, Ibid., pp. 203-208, 209.

70. JM, Ibid., p. 210.

71. JM, Ibid., p. 210.

72. JM, Ibid., p. 211.

73. JM, Ibid., pp. 214, 216-217.

74. JM, Ibid., p. 199.

75. JM, Ibid., pp. 217-218.

76. JM, *The Crucified God*, p. 69; hereafter abbreviated at CG.

77. JM. CG, pp. 146-150; D. G. Attfield, "Can God be Crucified? A Discussion of J. Moltmann," *Scottish Journal of Theology*, Vol. 90, No. 1, Feb. 1977, pp. 47-48. Attfield attempts to classify Moltmann's concept of the crucified God in terms of a distinction between the incarnate and discarnate Christ. Attfield, "Can God . . . ?", pp. 55-57. Attfield's argument is that at least the terminology of the theology of glory cannot be avoided when one speaks of the risen Christ. Attfield, "Can God . . . ?", p. 50. The term "The crucified God" is taken from Luther.

78. JM, Ibid., pp. 71-72, 90, 205-207, 208-210. In his remarks about Erasmus, Moltmann reveals that strange prejudice common to many modern German theologians against humanism. Melanchthon, though a loyal and creative follower of Luther, is criticized, because he was so friendly to humanists, like Erasmus. Perhaps, at least in Moltmann's case, the antipathy represents an instinctive dislike of the program of "good style and clarity" championed by Renaissance humanism which was after all a literary and not a philosophical movement.

79. JM, CG, pp. 162-163, 170-173.

80. JM, Ibid., pp. 122-136.

81. JM, Ibid., p. 68. Here Moltmann follows Marcuse among others. The best refutation of this kind of argument which assumes that all the workers are exploited,

because they have been corrupted and coopted by the establishment is found in the section entitled, "Socialism and Human Freedom" in Ronald H. Nash's *Freedom Justice and The State* (Washington, D.C.: University Press of America, 1980), pp. 140-145. According to Marcuse, everyone is enslaved, because they have been manipulated into "false needs" and the pursuit of "false satisfactions." Nash's answer is that Marcuse is unable to show how liberation is possible; all he can complain about is "Repressive Tolerance." Marcuse assumes that small groups of his own followers, i.e. "revolutionary minorities," question this tolerance. But Nash observes that even if the revolutionary elite were to be successful, how can it free itself from "a conditioning which blinds everyone else?" He also asks who can protect society against the revolutionary elite's "repressiveness?" Nash says that the dilemma which Marcuse has created had led some to call him a neo-Nazi. (Nash, pp. 143-144. It would be better to say that philosophically Marcuse and theologically Moltmann have continued the "revolution of nihilism" of which Nazism was a part. According to Nash, Marcuse's arguments, especially those concerning the inability of anyone to evolve a critical theory, are self defeating and in fact irrational (Nash, p. 145). Moltmann seeks to escape this dead end with his interpretation of the meaning of the crucified God.

82. JM, CG, pp. 65, 68, 227-228, 245.

83. JM, Ibid., pp. 178-179, 185-186, 192, 194-195.

84. JM, Ibid., p. 195.

85. JM, Ibid., pp. 215-216.

86. JM, Ibid., p. 255. There is no space here to deal with Moltmann's discussion of Freud and liberation from neurosis. It is interesting to note that Moltmann believes Christianity can adopt Marxism and its criticism of religion to free "the fellowship of Christ" from bourgeois capitalist fetishes of gold and consumer goods. He also believes that Christians can use Freud to detach "liberating faith" from "the religious superstition of the heart." Moltmann is sure that his conception of the "crucified God" will liberate Christians from the obsessive performance of religious ritual and permit the Christian Church to cleanse itself from its taboos. JM, CG, pp. 294-296, 298-302, 304-306, 312-314.

87. JM, CG, pp. 319-320, 332-335. In Moltmann's discussion of the "Political Theology of the Cross" he asserts that Puritanism abolished the feudal system which it replaced with the idea of a covenant or constitution. JM, CG, p. 328. This is quite inaccurate and it is truly unfortunate that Moltmann knows so little of Puritanism. He remains in his thinking a nineteenth century "Whig." It would help him greatly to read (Sir) Herbert Butterfield's, *The Whig Interpretation of History*, 6th edition (N.Y.: W. W. Norton & Co., 1965). Butterfield defines a whig historian very aptly as one who believes in Protestantism and progress and he explains exactly what he means on pages 3-33. Butterfield states: "There is a common error into which the Whig historian is bound to fall. . . . He is apt to imagine the British constitution as coming down to us by virtue of the work of long generations of Whigs and in spite of the obstructions of a long line of tyrants and Tories." (Butterfield, p. 41). The example which Butterfield uses here to prove his point is the Whig view that Luther was a champion of religious liberty. (Butterfield, pp. 41-63). Like Marx before

Jürgen Moltmann's Theology of Hope

him, Moltmann's approach to history is hopelessly Whig. Cf. Moltmann's inaccurate remarks on Calvinism as the "motive power for the democratic development of the political polity." JM, *The Church in the Power of the Spirit*, pp. 178, 330-331. Hereafter referred to as JM, CPS.

88. JM. The Open Church, pp. 98-99; hereafter referred to as OC.

89. JM, OC, pp. 98-99, 102-103.

90. JM, Ibid., p. 104.

91. JM, Ibid., p. 104-107.

92. JM, Ibid., p. 107.

93. JM, Ibid., pp. 107, 108-109.

94. JM, Ibid., p. 109.

95. JM, Ibid., p. 109.

96. JM, Ibid., pp. 110-111.

97. JM, Ibid., pp. 114-115, 116-118.

98. JM, Ibid., pp. 118, 120-126. The corollary to Moltmann's concept of the ultimate value of the sect-type is his identification of its goals with those of Marxism and his desire to encourage cooperation between the two groups. JM, *Religion Revolution and the Future*, (N.Y.: Charles Schribners' Sons, 1969), Chapter IV, "The Revolution of Freedom: Christians and Marxists Struggle for Freedom." pp. 74, 76, 81.

99. JM, TH, pp. 10-12.

100. JM, TH, pp. 10-11. When he emphasized this development, Moltmann followed closely the latest development in New Testament research. Cf. Ernst Kåsemann, "An Apologia for Primitive Christian Eschatology," *Essays on New Testament Themes* (London: SCM Press, 1981), pp. 169ff., 178, 188ff., 192ff.

101. JM, TH, pp. 12-13; cf. *Diskussion uber die "Theologie der Hoffnung"* herausgeben von Wolf Dieter Marsh (Muenchen: Chr. Kaiser Verlag, 1967).

102. JM, TH, pp. 13-16.

103. JM, TH, p. 103.

104. See his discussion of the rejection of history. JM, TH, p. 25ff.; as well as his criticism of Kant, Barth, and Bultmann, JM, TH, pp. 40-57, 60ff.; indeed Moltmann was even less kind to Greek influences. JM, TH, pp. 74-75, 82ff., 127 (The rejection of the identification of God with Plato), pp. 187ff., 288ff.

105. JM, TH, pp. 86-98; cf. 114ff., 127ff., 280 ff., (the wandering people of God); cf. Moltmann's appeal to return to the Israelite origins of Christianity in JM, CPS, pp. 135-137, 349-350.

106. The author of this essay employs the same logic here which Moltmann employs to reject a view of the incarnation which enthrones the risen Lord, i.e. the theology of glory. This theology was in part the result of the Hellenization of Christian thought. JM, TH , p. 143 ff.

107. JM, TH, p. 197.

108. JM, TH, pp. 212-214; cf. the wandering people of God motif in the Exodus congregation JM, TH, p. 280; cf. also Moltmann's discussion of the deepening crisis in today's world in: JM, *Das Experiement Hoffnung Einfüerhrung* (München: Chr. Kasier, 1974), pp. 12-14, 16ff., hereafter referred to as EH. p. 109. JM, EH, pp. 16-17.

110. JM, EH, pp. 20-21, 65-66.

111. JM, CPS, pp. 97-98.

112. However, the letter does make it clear that Moltmann is willing to accept a temporary dictatorship of the left to achieve socialism and democracy.

113. JM, "On Latin American Liberation Theology: An Open Letter to José Miguez Bonino," *Christianity and Crisis*, Vol. 36, No. 1, Feb. 1976. pp. 62-63.

114. JM, CPS, pp. 2, 5-6.

115. Cf. Moltmann's discussion of baptism and the Lord's Supper, JM, CPS, pp. 235-236.

116. JM, CPS, pp. 11-12, 21-22, 25-26, 27-29.

117. Here Moltmann merely paraphases the goals of the theology of Revolution with approval and he repeats his view that only the poor can really understand the Bible. JM, CPS, pp. 16-19; cf. Moltmann's discussion of a classless society and friendship a la Bloch. JM, CPS, pp. 115-117, 316, 318-320.

118. JM, CPS, pp. 33, 268.

119. JM, CPS, pp. 34, 197-198.

120. JM, CPS, pp. 41, 275.

121. "Today it is the protest against the North Atlantic centers of power, the anticolonist and anti-imperalist struggles for freedom carried on by the oppressed nations, and the ever wider class conflicts which give those revolutionary keynotes a worldwide connotation." JM, CPS, pp. 47, 79.

122. JM, CPS, pp. 47, 48-49, 51.

123. JM, CPS, p. 51; later Moltmann calls these "independent communities of action." JM, CPS, pp. 226, 124. JM, CPS, pp. 65, 68.

124. JM, CPS, pp. 79-80, 82.

125. JM, CPS, pp. 83, 152-153, 166-167, 190, 304-305, 324-325.

126. JM, CPS, pp. 84-86.

127. JM, CPS, pp. 84-86.

128. JM, CPS, pp. 175, cf. also 179, "Christianity must stay on this path of secularization, desacralization and democratization of political rule. . . . " JM, CPS, pp. 179; cf. also 225, 280-282 (Moltmann praises the Social Democrats for looking ahead), p. 331.

129. JM, CPS, p. 360.

130. Paul Lehmann, *The Politics of Transfiguration* (N.Y.: Harper & Row, 1975) pp. 261-265.

LIBERATION THEOLOGY AND THE SCRIPTURES

Carl F. H. Henry

Carl F. H. Henry

Carl F. H. Henry is a noted evangelical theologian, educator, lecturer, and author of more than twenty-five books. His major six-volume work on *God, Revelation and Authority* is available in Mandarin and Korean as well as in English. Dr. Henry was founding editor of *Christianity Today* from 1956-1968. Currently lecturer-at-large for World Vision International, he is also serving as distinguished visiting professor of religion at Hillsdale College during the 1983-84 academic year.

LIBERATION THEOLOGY AND THE SCRIPTURES* — Five Objections to Liberation Theology

With regard to liberation theology, two major points need to be made. First, liberation theologians are correct that the Christian church should express concern and support for the poor in word and deed. But liberation theology falls far short of what the church has a right to expect from theologians who purport to represent the biblical Christ and to theologize on the authority of God's revealed Word.

THE PROPER CALLING OF THE CHRISTIAN CHURCH

The Christian church must reject attempts to politicize an unregenerate world into the kingdom of God. It must also reject interpretations of evangelical conversion devoid of active social concern as fulfillments of Christian responsibility. God works through the Christian community to change the world. Its task is not to force new structures upon society at large, but to be the new society, to exemplify in its own ranks the way and will of God.

Karl Barth rightly warned against confusing the changing politico-economic ideals of our time with the content of God's new covenant, lest nationalism be confounded with the political objectives of the kingdom. The church has far more to offer than mere negations, however; its theological existence involves an inescapable political dimension and political action of a particular sort. It has a joyful good word to speak in the sphere of politics: that God is the true King; that God's faithful and gracious action toward man puts his seal on the dignity of the individual; that the coming kingdom is not merely a future possibility but is already in some sense actual; that even in the political arena God's main concern is not ideology, isms or ideals, but rather persons and their relationships to God and one another. While the orders of creation and preservation are permanent, the present structures are not necessarily so. The latter must

*Abridged from Carl F. H. Henry, *God, Revelation and Authority, Volume IV: God Who Speaks and Shows* (Waco: Word Books, 1979). Used by Permission.

be challenged, can and ought to be changed to remedy the afflictions of the oppressed. But like Barth, we must always ask what any proposed revolution has to do with the resurrection of Jesus Christ and with God's liberation.

THE DILEMMA OF LATIN AMERICAN CHRISTIANS

In Latin America, many young evangelicals are now torn between extremes because recent evangelical Christianity has failed to expound a viable alternative to either reactionary social withdrawal or socialist commitment as the framework of hope for the poor and downtrodden masses. The issue is especially urgent in those Latin American nations tottering on the brink of social revolution. In many countries of that vast continent, four hundred years of Roman Catholicism and a century of Protestant missions have done little to change the plight of the multitudinous poor. Since Marx once scorned the Russian Orthodox Church as historically identified with the oppressors, Roman Catholic leaders are today promoting social change in order to rescue the ecclesiastical image from being similarly deployed by present-day social revolutionaries. Many younger evangelicals consider traditional evangelical churches as too lacking in moral earnestness and spiritual resources to cope with the deepening predicament of the alienated masses. Something more dynamic and radical seems imperative for confronting the staggering social crisis.

These dispirited evangelicals increasingly opt for one of two alternatives. Either they are attracted by the Pentecostal offer of a spiritual environment whose charismatic dynamisms compensate internally for the material deprivation of an underprivileged humanity, or they are tempted to join social revolutionaries who stress dramatic material and physical improvements as an indispensable moral commitment. Both groups call for change and commitment more radical than the usual evangelical conversion. They insist on grasping a new world of human experience where the old life and circumstances are not only astonishingly inverted, but where hope also has already become a spectacular present reality. Charismatics and revolutionaries both reject status quo Christianity of the "evangelical establishment" type, not unlike the American counter-cultural Jesus movement or the so-called coalition of "young evangelicals" burdened by social concern who consider it either too spiritually bland or too socially unconcerned to serve as an adequate carrier of human hope. Traditional evangelical churches are thus judged as being either spiritually compromised or socially indulgent.

THE LIBERATING MESSAGE OF THE GOSPEL

The gospel resounds with good news for the needy and oppressed. It conveys assurance that injustice, repression, exploitation, discrimination and poverty are dated and doomed, that no one is forced to accept the crush of evil powers as finally determinative for his or her existence. Into the morass of sinful human history and experience the gospel heralds a new order of life shaped by God's redemptive intervention.

Christ's gospel is comprehensively liberating. While Liberator is less than a fully adequate title for Jesus Christ, it nonetheless declares that whatever else Jesus is and does, he also singularly unshackles the chains that enslave the human race. Not only will Jesus Christ the coming King some day topple every oppressive power, but he has also served notice that the battle is already underway to the very death. In his own person Jesus has already struck the forces of iniquity a mortal blow; their very days are numbered and the ways of wickedness are surely doomed. Moreover the emancipating Redeemer grants new life to the penitent and enlists them as a committed community, as the new society, to his ongoing victorious combat over the forces of evil. Even now the risen Christ is active in history, leading his followers in resistance against sin and Satan whom the wicked serve.

THE SOCIAL RESPONSIBILITY
OF THE CHRISTIAN CHURCH

The groan for liberation from hostile powers echoes creationwide. Everywhere evident is the demonic perversion of human relationships and the accommodation of human institutions to social injustice, be they cultural, political, racial, technological or economic. In our era prevalent conditions in many nations not only deny survival needs to the destitute, but also proffer no human hope whatever of reversing these sorry circumstances. Even if Christians should and must deplore pseudotheologies that deal inadequately and objectionably with human oppression, they nonetheless must recognize the positive concerns of theologies of liberation and of revolution with their indictment of political, economic, and other injustice against the human spirit. The critically desperate condition of vast masses of people strangled by oppression pleads for evangelism and social engagement. Concern for a theological orthodoxy devoid of justice and compassion is not orthodoxy but heterodoxy.

If in its own ranks the church even now unduly esteems the mighty and the affluent at the expense of the weak and the poor, and bows to the preferences, prerogatives and programs of the specially privileged, it can hardly hope to signal good news in countries where those rich in power and property exploit the underprivileged masses. Christ's church is not a church for the middle class or even of the lower middle class only, any more than it is limited to the rich over against the poor. Whenever the church becomes a society whose lifestyle and interests center mainly in the "haves" over against the "have nots," it threatens and obscures its identification with the needy and oppressed.

Christ's church cannot signal hope to those whose destitution and deprivation annul the dignity and the meaningfulness of human survival if it uncritically condones as members those who profess devotion to Christ while they consciously support socially and politically oppressive powers, policies and programs; or if it communicates the notion that a believer's only response to political or economic injustice is passivity and acquiescence; or if it closes its eyes to the public or private abuse of the poor by those who augment its coffers; or if it proclaims evangelism as its only interest in the needs of mankind so that other agencies must implement the concern for social justice. If wicked political regimes require what God forbids or disown what God commands, then the Christian community may not espouse an ethic of political neutrality and social noninvolvement; rather it must be clearly and openly devoted to the Lord of all principalities and powers and stand unequivocally only for those purposes for which civil government was divinely intended in a fallen society.

OBJECTIONS TO LIBERATION THEOLOGY

Having stated our conviction that Christianity must take an activist role toward an abuse of the poor, what is our evaluation of the particular form of social activism that goes by the name of liberation theology? While liberation theologians are not a monolithic class, they do share agreement on enough basic issues (discussed elsewhere in this volume) to allow some general criticisms.

1. *The Marxist ideals of the New Man and the New Society are a poor substitute for the analogous Christian ideals.* When Christianity speaks of *the new man*, it points first and foremost to Jesus of Nazareth. In His sinless earthly life Jesus manifested the kingdom of God and in His resurrection He mirrored the ideal humanity that God approves for eternity.

When Christianity discusses *the new society*, it speaks not of some intangible future reality whose specific features it cannot as yet identify, but of the regenerate church called to live by the standards of the coming King and which in some respects already approximates the kingdom of God in present history.

Marxist exegesis is notably vague in stating what precise form the socialist utopia is to take, and where in history it has been concretely realized. Radical neo-Protestant theologians needlessly accommodate much of this Marxist obscurity over the new man and the new society. For they fail to identify Jesus Christ as the ideal man, fail to emphasize the new covenant that Scripture associates with messianic fulfillment, and fail to center the content of the new society in the regenerate church's reflection of the kingdom of God.

The Marxist movement has been unable to make up its mind conclusively concerning the new man; it envisions him, assuredly, as intolerant of the status quo, hateful of the capitalist system, devoted whole-soul to politico-economic revolution, disdainful of belief in the supernatural as a hurtful myth, and committed to dialectical materialism and state absolutism as the keys to future utopia. But for Marx, the new man meant the proletariat; for Lenin, members of the Communist Party (although he, too, looked for the coming proletarian kingdom); for Mao in the earlier period, the destructive Chinese Red Guards epitomized the ideal; for Castro the ideal was the Cuban guerrilla devoted more to demoralizing the uncommitted than to violence and murder. In Latin America some followed Trotsky for whom the ideal man anarchically rejects any given structures; others naively idealized the Bolivian peasant Ché Guevara as the model for the coming Latin American revolution.

Marxist claims for the new society are weakened by the bewildering varieties of socialism in existence today. None whatever has fulfilled utopian expectations, some have in fact been conspicuous failures, while many others of the present experiments are in deep trouble. When pressed to stipulate the precise form their postulated utopia will ultimately take, Marxists now tend to beg the question. The definitive form, we are told, will emerge only through the ongoing process of history, and will be expedited by revolutionary rejection of the status quo. The world still awaits any formulation of an identifiable coming socialist utopia. The same criticism may be leveled at many young evangelicals in America, whose burning discontent with the status quo issues largely in a series of isolated and disorganized proposals rather than in a comprehensive social vision. Boldly proclaiming their imperatives, many contemporary social activists have little awareness of how powerless their isolated proposals for concrete action are when considered alongside the content of God's covenant.

2. *The Marxist hermeneutic subverts the biblical revelation.* Instead of first focusing on Christ and the Bible as the revelational center of human history and destiny, and by that light illuminating the cultural context, liberation theologians like Gustavo Gutiérrez make existing social and political conditions the necessary lens for viewing and interpreting scriptural data. Man's factual historical condition is considered the necessary starting point; from the outset faith gains a political dimension and reference. What specially characterizes liberation theologians is their insistence that theological reflection must begin with the historical situation rather than with the biblical revelation, and thus becomes directed toward a prestipulated social reconstruction.

When Marxist interpretation confers this decisive role in hermeneutics upon the sociopolitical situation, it proposes to judge the cultural status quo by the socialist vision of utopia. Liberation theology demeans all theologizing outside such commitment to a socialist society as inexcusably subservient to an ahistorical world view; it deplores nonliberation theology as resigned to the "ideology" of the status quo, and hence as aligned in spirit and fact with oppressive secular forces identified as imperialism, capitalism, communism, and big business linked expressly to technology or covertly associated with the missionary enterprise. It welcomes Marxism for supplying the scientific content of Christian social ethics, and considers Christian theology authentic only when and as it applies the demand for socialist reconstruction to the concrete historical situation. By appealing to the present historical milieu as the only legitimate context for theological reflection, liberation theology thus readily colors, limits and even subverts the scripturally given revelation even while it does not necessarily displace it. The biblical heritage is glossed over to advance the modern ideology of socialism.

3. *Liberation theologians accept a Marxian analysis of class struggle and proposed Marxian solutions as gospel.* Like Marx, liberation theology presupposes that social classes are byproducts of a capitalistic society, and that all ethical ecclesiastical thought and effort must promote the overthrow of that society and replace it with a socialist alternative. Hence liberation theology opposes reformist effort—economic assistance to churches in poorer lands by churches in wealthier lands, for example—on the ground that such "superficial changes" would only postpone radical alteration of basic economic structures.

The call for an authentic Latin American theology gains ironic overtones when the theology of liberation is identified precisely and superlatively as just such an authentic theology. On the one hand, it exalts Latin American heritage, music and literature, but at the same time it welcomes Marxian ideas as if they were native to the Latin American continent. North American and European theological systems are derided by liberation theologians as abstract and irrelevant, because they were formulated not in the context of the Third World but in the context of the technologically oriented First World, which the Latins repudiate as exploitive and oppressive.

Liberation theologians romanticize the Latin American temperament and demean Western logical constructs and thought categories, although they must of necessity employ these very categories in order to present their own alternatives intelligibly. Any abandonment of universally valid logical rules would only reduce liberation theology to sheer nonsense. Sometimes it even seems to be forgotten that Latin Americans and non-Latins share an essential common humanity; the Christian message itself is sometimes treated as if it implies a contrary if not contradictory content inside and outside Latin America.

Liberation theology cannot see and will not accept more than two possible alternatives: either the status quo or a social revolution predicated on a Marxist critique. Indeed they rarely suspect how easily socialism itself reduces to an oppressive alternative that in its own way becomes the inflexible status quo.

4. *Liberation theology proceeds on the basis of a distorted Christian gospel.* Gustavo Gutiérrez is so one-sidedly concerned with political implications of the gospel—which he then expounds in an additionally one-sided way—that one wonders what his gospel truly is. The authentic faith that he liberates from so-called religious baggage seems—contrary to the Apostle Paul's statement in I Cor. 15:1-4—to retain no decisive centrality for the atoning death and bodily resurrection of Jesus Christ. The saviorhood and lordship of Christ is interpreted instead as the universal prospect of equality and justice assured by a particular social ideology.[1]

Liberation theology subserves a special interest not found in the biblical witness: socialism (rather than God) is presented as the liberator. God's people, says Gutiérrez, are becoming increasingly aware that the process of liberation "implies a break with the *status quo*, that it calls for a social revolution."[2] The goal of theology and evangelism is "a socialist society, more just, free and human."[3]

Instead of presenting a scripturally oriented doctrine of salvation, the secularized theology of liberation thinkers blurs the biblical representation of sin and death and of the alternatives of heaven or hell. Universal salvation, Gutiérrez tells us, is no longer a matter of theological debate.[4] Man everywhere, Christian or not, "is saved if he opens himself to God and to others, even if he is not clearly aware that he is doing so."[5] The notion of salvation here is unbiblically universalistic; all men are potentially saved, and actually so if they share in political liberation. The whole scheme of liberation therefore dispenses with the act of saving faith, and with the condemnation of those who do not have this faith (John 3:18, 36).

The radical orientation of Christianity espoused by liberation theologians results in a redefinition of salvation, christology, eschatology and the church. Under the imperative of human liberation, Christian commitment is restated in terms of conversion to man and his history; the incarnational character of the gospel requires faith that acts in the service of others through participation, identification and solidarity, rather than sporadic efforts to salvage individuals and momentary social relief. When considered abstractly, the plea for human solidarity has much to commend it; when formulated specifically by liberation theologians, however, it means an unwavering devotion to socialist structures.

The use of scripture by liberation theologians is notably tendential. To restrict theology to the historical sociopolitical context sidelines all elements of the biblical revelation that pertain to transcendent reality—the nature of God as He objectively is, the divine nature and work of Christ, the transcendent aspects of the kingdom, and so on.

The Marxist repudiation of transcendently disclosed absolutes prepares the way for relativizing revealed theology and for substituting a conjectural absolute, namely, the Marxist ideology itself. The Marxist welding of theory and praxis requires rejecting the permanent self-identity of the Christian faith, and losing Christianity's ongoing self-identity in the process of history. If consistently applied, of course, this view would also cancel whatever absolutist claims are made for the Marxist alternatives, yet social critics seem to absolutize Marxism while they relativize Christianity.

5. *Liberation theology almost everywhere reflects the perils of a situationally controlled hermeneutic.* Biblical teaching has merely an illustrative and supportive role; only political reflection is considered "scientific" or authentic theological engagement. The consequence is that scriptural teaching is relativized, while contemporary sociological concerns are absolutized. It is clear that whatever profession of biblical fidelity such theology of liberation may make, in practice it disavows Scripture as the normative authority.

Liberation theology views man as divinely endowed with a creative nature that enables him to shape his own history. Although Christ is said to supply fulfillment in the emergence of a new people, Christ and the church are redefined in terms of man, salvation is restated in terms of man's political liberation, and the concept of grace is subordinated to human ingenuity. God becomes merely a co-worker in an essentially man-centered program. The disposition to make sociopolitical factors primary dissolves the biblically controlled message and substitutes an anthropocentric theology for the theology of revelation, and does so in the guise of preserving and guaranteeing the relevance of biblical theology to the human predicament.

In short, the whole concept of salvation is given a speculative character, in terms especially of contemporary liberation from all sociopolitical oppression; the value of human existence in history is maintained without an other-wordly reference and without a struggle against sin and death in its full dimensions. The exodus becomes a paradigm for the political history of mankind.

6. *Marxist exegesis of the Bible is selective and one-sided.* Marxist exegesis of the Bible in no way deals with man's whole existence either in theory or practice; its hermeneutic is reductionistic and misleading. On the theoretical side, Marxism involves an uncritical denial of God, and thereby extends the alienation of man to the fundamental relationships of human existence by trying to suppress God-man relationships. On the practical level, Marxism ignores the fact that wherever its socialist program has triumphed, as in Eastern Europe, alienation does not in fact disappear. The highly prejudiced nature of the Liberationist appeal for the socialist alternative is evident from its silence over Marxism's failure to achieve its promised liberation. In Marxist lands the ruling clique becomes the new privileged class in a supposedly egalitarian society. What present-day socialist country, economic hardships apart, has not surrendered some of the dignity of human life through a loss of freedoms? Which has actually liberated human beings from fear?

CONCLUSION

So-called Marxist exegesis of the Bible perpetuates a materialistic understanding of reality and life. It transmutes the Savior and Lord of scriptural revelation into a sociopolitical liberator who promotes a modern socioeconomic idealogy. For the redemptive conflict with Satan and sin and death at the heart of the gospel, it substitutes the class struggle; it ignores supernatural aspects of the kingdom of God and substitutes a temporal sociopolitical utopia; it miscasts the promised Messiah as a political-economic liberator and dilutes the content of the new covenant which seeks inscription of God's moral law on man's inner nature, and it does all this in accord with a partisan modern social ideology.

Much like the theology of revolutionary violence, the theology of liberation encourages excessive materialistic expectations among the masses because it takes the plight of the poor and oppressed as its definitive starting point rather than the comprehensive principles of Scripture. Since the demand for restructuring the status quo permeates all theological proclamation, liberation theology proclaims itself an "ethic of change" in contrast with the traditional evangelical "ethic of order." Consequently the divine orders of creation and preservation on which evangelical theology insists, already obscured in the forepart of the twentieth century by evolutionary social ethics, are eclipsed even further by a radical or revolutionary view of social change. Dialectical materialism tends to crowd out any governing divine creation and preservation as a controlling perspective, and relates history to the special goal of Marxist transformation.

Moreover, liberation theology is inadequately aware of the imperfection of all human efforts to achieve justice in a fallen world history. To restate the fall of man in terms of private property and economic disparity caricatures the depth of human sin. The Old Testament prophets not only demanded justice—always in the name of Yahweh—but they called also for the personal appropriation and internalization of God's law as an irreducible spiritual goal and moral requirement. And they pointed to the coming messianic kingdom as the reality in which violence is done away and universal justice and peace prevail. These biblical emphases contributed to a sobering of human pride, quite in contrast to the almost exuberantly millennial prospect imported by the theology of liberation into the present. Liberation theology therefore offers no adequate guidance for those whose sincere and justifiable social and political grievances are unappeased by the existing mechanisms. Sociopolitical emphases are given priority over the theological-revelational; the social sciences are considered the contextual starting point for theological and moral reflection.

We must stand firmly for a championing of the gospel's irreducible relevance for oppressed multitudes, and in places of human exploitation and oppression we must actively identify evangelical Christianity with the justice that God demands. Many evangelicals polarize the individual and social aspects of salvation, and overlook the fact that structural interrelationships are critically important for meeting the problem of social justice. If evangelical Christianity is to rescue the perception of the dire needs that plague masses of men on every continent from secular ideologies or radical theologies, then we must aggressively cope with injustice and immorality, sin and starvation, pride and prejudice in a principled and practical way.

While the church of Christ may well be disconcerted that it took Christianity almost nineteen centuries to eradicate slavery, the whole world should be terrified, as missionary church historian Samuel H. Moffett notes, that it took communism only a single generation to bring it back.

NOTES

1. See Gutiérrez's *A Theology of Liberation*, pp. 231-232.
2. Ibid., p. 102.
3. Ibid., p. 274.
4. Ibid., p. 150.
5. Ibid., p. 151.

A CRITIQUE
OF CHRISTIAN MARXISM

Dale Vree

Dale Vree

Dale Vree is the Executive Editor of the *New Oxford Review*. He received his B.A., M.A. and Ph.D. degrees in political science from the University of California at Berkeley. He is the author of the book *On Synthesizing Marxism and Christianity*. His articles have appeared in many journals including *The New Leader*, *American Political Science Review*, *National Review*, and *The Reformed Journal*. In addition to teaching political science at Earlham College and Christian social ethics at the Anglican Theological College in Berkeley, he has been a Rockefeller Fellow at the University of California at Berkeley and an NEH Fellow at the Hoover Institution at Stanford University.

A CRITIQUE OF CHRISTIAN MARXISM* — *A Centuries Old Heresy in Disguise*

A serious dialogue between Marxists and Christians has been going on in Europe for almost twenty years. This dialogue, which has frequently led to theoretical attempts to synthesize Marxism and Christianity, has certainly been intellectually innovative and stimulating. Collaborative political action between Marxists and Christians has been an important factor in the politics of Italy, France, Spain, Czechoslovakia, and Yugoslavia, but in terms of depth of commitment and readiness to resort to violence, such action has not yet been matched by what can be found in Latin America. There, important segments of the Catholic priesthood and hierarchy have been dramatically radicalized. It is not unusual to see bishops issue statements generally critical of the domestic and inter-American status quo and supportive of socialist and nationalist alternatives. Nor is it unusual to see priests—such as the late, "martyred" Camilo Torres—throw off their cassocks, pick up rifles, and run off with a band of guerrilla warriors. But in terms of political theory, the Latin Americans have been well behind the Europeans and North Americans who, having felt less urgency to act, have enjoyed more time for scholarship and reflection.

A Theology of Liberation[1], by the Peruvian theologian and activist, Gustavo Gutiérrez, is an important attempt to begin to redress the imbalance in theoretical output. Although the thought of Gutiérrez is not as original or complex as that of European dialogue-makers such as Jürgen Moltmann, Ernst Bloch, Johannes Metz, Roger Garaudy, and others, his book is generally recognized as a unique intellectual breakthrough; indeed, as perhaps the most sophisticated voice of Marxist-Christian dialogue in Latin America to date. Contrary to most books of this genre, its significance seems to grow with each passing year. Gutiérrez has emerged as the intellectual spokesman for a new worldwide current in Christian social ethics known as "liberation theology." In the United States,

* Originally published as "Political Transubstantiation" in *Freedom at Issue*, May-June, 1976. Reprinted by permission.

liberation theology has served as the idiom for Christians anxious to promote their favorite liberation movements—particularly black and women's liberation.

More recently, liberation consciousness has been expanding to encompass the entire third world. In 1975, the Latin American Secretariat of the U.S. Catholic Conference and the Latin American Working Group of the National Council of Churches sponsored a week long conference on liberation theology in Detroit—the significance of which was noted in *Time* magazine[2] with a full-page story. An appearance by Gustavo Gutiérrez was the main attraction of the conference. Beyond the United States, the World Council of Churches—much like the United Nations—effectively functions as a forum for third world causes and interests. The World Council has already committed its prestige and its money to the liberation movements directed against the white governments of southern Africa. Indeed, the "pervasive philosophy" of the World Council has become a " 'solidarity with the oppressed' liberation theology which recognizes no challengers."[3] Israel is not much more popular with the Council than South Africa, and one wonders when Israel too will feel the lash of the Council. Because of the popularity of liberation theology in World Council circles, it would be well to have a closer look at Gutiérrez's *A Theology of Liberation*, the basic guidebook of liberation theology.

Although Gutiérrez borrows frequently from European thinkers, his politico-theological thought is unparalleled by Europeans because he is responding to the Latin American experience. Gutiérrez is not primarily reacting to other people's ideas, but rather to his own existential condition as an inhabitant of the third world. The difference between the third world and the developed world is not only geographical: it is also psychological. For the theologian, the situation of the developed world is as Dietrich Bonhoeffer described it: the *mündige Welt* (the world come of age) where technologically competent people no longer feel a need for God. In Latin America, on the other hand, the theologian must respond to quite another situation, a situation where people feel incompetent and helpless, and where suffering is a way of life with no end in sight. Here people *do* feel a need for God, but are at pains to understand how a loving God could have created such an unlovely world.

A Critique of Christian Marxism

Inasmuch as the church is now widely regarded as the most "progressive" institution in Latin America, and insofar as much of Latin America is in a potentially revolutionary situation, we must have further reason to examine Gutiérrez's *magnum opus* with some care. It is easy enough to applaud Gutiérrez's book as a reflection of the Latin Catholic Church's turning from corruption and concubinage, and toward commitment and change. Be that as it may, "progressive" Latin American Catholic thought (or liberation theology, as it is now called) need no longer be patronized in that way. Liberation theology is ready to stand on its own feet, to stand up to normal intellectual scrutiny.

ESCHATOLOGY AND MARXISM

A central motif in the international Marxist-Christian dialogue is eschatology, or the doctrine of last things. The theological locution most often associated with eschatology is the "Kingdom of God." Christians have traditionally equated the fullness of the kingdom of God with the experience of heaven after death. The kingdom has also been thought to be embryonically present in the heart of the believer as a kind of foretaste of heaven. But rarely has the kingdom been thought to have any bearing on political matters. However, those Christians who have engaged in dialogue with Marxists have tried to expand the notion of the kingdom into the hope for an earthly millennial society built—in part at least—by human political action. If this notion of the kingdom is accepted, and if the full-blown communism of which Marxists-Leninists speak can be understood as a secular version of millenialism, then it is obvious that Christians and Marxists have much in common and every reason to engage in dialogue.

Making eschatology a central motif allows for a much more interesting dialogue than if, say, ethics is made a central motif. A generation ago, such "First World" Christians as Hewlett Johnson (the "Red" Dean of Canterbury) and Harry F. Ward of Union Theological Seminary, tended to focus on the ethics of Jesus as the basis for cooperation with Marxists (in particular, with Stalinists). The problem with that approach is twofold: First, Christianity has clearly been more than an ethical system; it has been a *theological* system which presumes to talk of God, the mystery of the kingdom, the meaning of history, and the life of the world to come. To stress ethics is to seem to be too rationalistic and too neglectful of the mystical dimensions of the faith. It is to reduce the kingdom to an ethical metaphor. Those Christians who get themselves fixated on ethics are too easily suspected of being nothing but ethical humanists—eccentric ones, to be sure. Second, Marxist-Leninists are not really interested in ethics. They are interested in the laws of history and the economy, of which ethics is only an epiphenomenon. A concern with ethics is the hallmark of utopian, not scientific, socialism. Hence, it is very difficult to achieve a sustained intellectual interchange between Christians and Marxists when attention is limited to ethics.

Because of their eschatological focus, present-day Christian dialogue-makers are in a better situation. Yes, they do talk about ethics. But they are really interested in the *dynamics* of historical, economic, and political change—just as the Marxists are. Furthermore, they do not *seem* to be ethical humanists because they are very anxious to talk about God, salvation, providence, prophecy, the Kingdom, etc.—almost all of the paraphernalia of traditional Christianity—in the same breath with which they talk of the dynamics of change. Finally, by going beyond ethics they are better able to sidestep embarrassing questions about the alleged pacifism of Jesus.

This brings us directly to Gustavo Gutiérrez and his *Theology of Liberation*. Without doubt, Gutiérrez is interested in salvation, and his interest in political liberation for Latin America (namely, "liberation" from American hegemony and domestic capitalism) is an integral part of his interest in salvation; indeed, liberation is part of a single salvational process. This is where matters get intriguing— and sticky. Since the Second Vatican Council, the Catholic Church has been willing to say that political action (or "liberation") has something to do with the kingdom of God, although it has refused to specify exactly what the relationship is, and has insisted that political goals cannot be identified or equated with the kingdom.

Were one to say that the kingdom is political liberation and that liberation is the product of human action, one would all too easily fall into the classical *Pelagian* heresy—that is, one would be saying that man is saved by good works, not grace. To say that is to deny the salvational significance of Christ's atoning sacrifice on the cross and his second coming. It is to deny that God in Christ is the source of salvation. Without Christ, there is no authentic Christianity. Hence, it is impossible for a *Christian* to equate liberation with salvation.

But Gutiérrez is unhappy with the recent Catholic position that political action has some (unspecified) relation to the kingdom. Says he: "It is not enough to say that Christians should not 'shirk' their earthly responsibilities or that these have a 'certain relationship' to salvation."[4]

Although Gutiérrez wants to relate eschatology to politics by uniting liberation and salvation into a single process, he also wants to keep liberation and salvation separate—for fear of sliding into Pelagianism. Traditionally, both Catholics and Protestants have said that salvation—or the kingdom—is an act, a gift, of God. After all, God saves man, man does not save himself: "For by grace are ye saved through faith, and that not of yourselves, it is the gift of God" not of works, lest any man should boast" (Ephesians 2:8-9). According to official Catholic theology, the kingdom "will be the effect solely of divine intervention."[5] The problem for any *theology* of liberation is to talk of salvation as a gift without inducing passivity and indifference to politics—which is frequently what happens. So Gutiérrez's problem is twofold: How can man's political liberation be seen to be a part of a salvational process which finds fulfillment in God's kingdom—without opening the door to Pelagianism? And how can one talk like a Christian out of one side of one's mouth, and like a Pelagian out of the other, without choking on the law of noncontradiction?

Let us hear what Gutiérrez has to say: He sees man "assuming *conscious responsibility* for his own destiny." The result will be "the creation of a new man and a qualitatively different society."[6] And yet Gutiérrez also says that, "The Bible presents liberation—salvation—in Christ as a *total gift* . . . "[7]

But how can the integral salvational process be a product of both men's "conscious responsibility" as well as a "total gift" from Christ? Is liberation-*cum*-salvation something humans must go out and earn for themselves or not? If so, then it cannot be a "total gift." If not, then it is something humans are not fully responsible for. Gutiérrez does not seem to know whether he wants to be a Christian, a Pelagian, or both. If it is possible to grant that Gutiérrez avoids complete capitulation to Pelagianism, it is not possible to grant that he escapes logical contradiction.

But perhaps what Gutiérrez wants to say is that man must initiate his liberation while God will have to finish it by turning liberation into salvation. This is the most generous interpretation I can come up with. Says Gutiérrez: "*Without liberating historical events, there would be no growth of the kingdom.* But the process of liberation will not have conquered the very roots of oppression and the exploitation of man by man without the coming kingdom, which is above all a gift.''[8] Gutiérrez is trying to protect man's autonomy and free creativity as well as God's sovereignty. But Gutiérrez actually succeeds both in truncating man's autonomy (because man cannot finish what man has started) and compromising God's omnipotence (because God cannot start what God alone can finish). For Gutiérrez, salvation is obviously *contingent* on man's *prior* action. Gutiérrez *wants* to affirm that the coming kingdom is above all a gift, but one must conclude from what he has said that the coming kingdom (which he described as the "complete encounter with the Lord" which will "mark an end to history")[9] is first and foremost a product of human action. Enter Pelagius! Enter Thomas Müntzer and a whole host of heretical chiliasts whom Friedrich Engels correctly identified as forerunners of Marxism.

MARXISTS DOING GOD'S WORK?

At the root of Gutiérrez's tortuous theologizing is his attempt to blend Marxism with Christianity. By making political liberation a necessary part of the salvational process, Gutiérrez is able to bring Marxism into the drama of Christian salvation. As a result, it is obvious that Marxists are *really* doing God's work. Furthermore, by liberating man, Marxists are *quite literally* freeing God's hands so he can usher in the kingdom. Hence, Marxists are really Christians incognito.

Gutiérrez says he believes in salvation for everyone—believers and non-believers alike. There is no doubt in Gutiérrez's mind that God will grant salvation to Marxists, but curiously, there seems to be some doubt that all Christians will be saved. Lest one think Gutiérrez to be a modern ethical humanist, he reminds us that he *does* believe in divine judgment: "we will be definitively judged by our love for men, by our capacity to create brotherly conditions of life."[10] And there is no doubt in Gutiérrez's mind that many, perhaps most, Christians are not measuring up to that standard. So his best pastoral advice to Christians would be to join with Marxists, who are presumed to be actively creating brotherly conditions of life. This is the safest bet—Gutiérrez's version of Pascal's wager! Such counsel sounds bizarre coming from a Catholic priest, but Gutiérrez does not seem to be kidding. Liberation is a precondition for salvation, and, as Gutiérrez repeatedly makes clear, liberation is another term for revolutionary (not social democratic) socialism. And for revolutionary socialism to be efficacious it must be a "scientific" socialism, Gutiérrez tells us. Finally, he leaves no doubt in the reader's mind that he considers Marxian socialism to be scientific (although not necessarily atheistic).

Not only do the Marxists—unknowingly—hold the keys to the kingdom of God, but they are undoubtedly spiritually gifted. Since Marxists are very adept at loving mankind, and since loving mankind is the "only way" to have a "true encounter with God,"[11] and since a "knowledge of God" is actually a "necessary consequence" of loving mankind,[12] one is forced to conclude that Marxists are remarkably religious people. Never mind the fact that Marxists do not seem to be aware of their spiritual gifts; Father Gutiérrez is aware of them and that seems to be what counts. The good father is empowered to turn bread and wine into Christ's body and blood. Now he presumes to turn Marxists into Christians.

But sometimes I wonder what all this has to do with helping the poor and the powerless. Priests have been notorious for sprinkling holy water on whatever political organization seemed to be the going concern at the time—or the coming concern (in the case of far-sighted priests). Perhaps Marxists should allow themselves to be amused—and tickled—by this sacerdotal sprinkle. Perhaps the water is a good omen for them, signifying that Marxism holds the winning ticket in the race for power in Latin America. (Indeed, Gutiérrez says again and again that he bases his thought on a reading of the "signs of the times" in Latin America.)

But Marxists would do well to bear in mind that the good *padre*, despite his frequent genuflections at the altar of scientific socialism, is no scientific socialist himself. He has *his own—utopian—*reasons for blessing Marxism. For him, "utopian thought" is the basis of scientific knowledge; indeed, it is the source of political action and a "driving force of history."[13] Marxists will perhaps not be surprised that behind this socialist priest there lurks a visionary dreamer. Neither perhaps will more orthodox Catholics (not to mention Protestants and Jews) be surprised that one who places Marxists at the head of God's elect is nothing but a fanciful utopian.

But let us not forget the prerogatives of priestcraft. In the old pre-Vatican Council days, priests used to stand at the altar with their backs to the people mumbling Latin words through a cloud of incense faster than the speed of sound. "Mumbo-jumbo," the irreverent were wont to call it. Now the priests stand in back of the altar, face the people, and—with the help of microphones—clearly enunciate the words of the Mass in the vernacular of the people. No more mumbo-jumbo. That they save for their books on politics—where Marxists are transformed into Christians by transforming Christians into Marxists.

NOTES

1. Maryknoll, New York: Orbis Books, 1973.
2. Sept. 1, 1975.
3. Elliot Wright, "The Good Ship *Oikoumene*," *Worldview*, November, 1975, p. 18.
4. Gutiérrez, op, cit., p. 46.
5. M. J. Cantley, "Kingdom of God," *New Catholic Encyclopedia* (New York: McGraw-Hill, 1967) Vol. 8, p. 191.
6. Gutiérrez, op. cit., pp. 36-37; italics added.
7. Ibid., p. x; italics added.
8. Ibid., p. 177; italics added.
9. Ibid., p. 168.
10. Ibid., pp. 198-199.
11. Ibid., p. 202.
12. Ibid., p. 206.
13. Ibid., pp. 232-234.

LIBERATION THEOLOGY AND THE CULTURAL CAPTIVITY OF THE GOSPEL

Richard John Neuhaus

Richard John Neuhaus

Richard John Neuhaus is prominent as a Lutheran pastor who for many years has been active in inner city ministries, civil rights, and Christian ecumenism. In 1970, he was a Democratic candidate for Congress. He is editor of *Lutheran Forum* and the author of nine books including *In Defense of People*, *Theology and the Kingdom of God*, *Christian Faith and Public Policy* and the forthcoming *The Naked Public Square: Religion and Democracy in America.*

LIBERATION THEOLOGY AND THE CULTURAL
CAPTIVITY OF THE GOSPEL* — Political Kingdoms

Gustavo Gutiérrez is widely credited with having coined the term "liberation theology." With the publication of his book, *A Theology of Liberation*, North American readers were challenged by a major systematic effort to articulate the meaning of the Christian gospel in terms attuned to the revolutionary ferment in South America. The importance one attributes to Gutiérrez's effort is hinged in large part upon where one thinks we (the world generally and Christians particularly) are in this latter part of the twentieth century. If one agrees that relations between poor and rich countries are a, if not the, major challenge of the second half of this century, and if one agrees that what happens in Latin America is central to the hope of rectifying current injustices, and if one agrees that institutional Christianity is critical to social change in Latin America, and if one agrees that theology is the intellectual side of the church's life and work, both reflecting and shaping the Christian mission, then one must take Gustavo Gutiérrez very seriously indeed. The above proposition admittedly involves many ifs, but I think it fair to say that these are assumptions that inform mainstream theological exchange across denominational lines today. Even if, however, one doubts one or more of these assumptions, Gustavo Gutiérrez must be reckoned with as a theologian of stature, whose stated determination is to address himself to the theological consciousness of the universal church, even as he wants the peculiar form of that address to be determined by the particularities of the church's struggle in Latin America.

Talk about "liberation theology" is haunted by understandable suspicions. The term liberation, with its socialist and frequently revolutionary content, invites the suspicion that theology is somehow being enlisted to legitimate a specific political option. Certainly recent years have witnessed the enlistment of sociology, political

*Originally published as "Liberation Theology and the Captivities of Jesus" in *Worldview*, June, 1973. Reprinted by permission.

science, history and economics, as well as of theology, in various directions of social change. While we may have no illusions about the absolute "objectivity" that can be sustained in any discipline, we might still want to insist that the integrity of a discipline depends in part upon a serious effort to maintain some critical distance from any form of advocacy.

Before examing Gutiérrez's work in greater detail, we should be more specific about the peculiar difficulties that plague theology's effort to maintain critical distance. Anyone who today might write a "theology of imperialism" or a "theology of capitalism" would be considered very marginal indeed; it would be alleged, probably with some justice, that he is impossibly rightist. Yet in other times, and in less intellectually respectable circles today, religious legitimations of the status quo are no occasion for scandal.

Successive cultural waves have each offered us their new version of Jesus and his gospel: the gospel of wealth, of peace of mind, of therapeutic triumph, of Consciousness III. From Orison Swett Marden (1850-1924) and Andrew Carnegie through Norman Vincent Peale and Charles Reich, Americans have been adept at tailoring the message to fit the mood. Among thoughtful Christians such efforts to take Jesus culturally captive have been generally deplored. They are put off by the prayer-breakfast athlete's description of Jesus as Life's Great Quarterback or the businessman's assurance that He is the Chairman of the Biggest Board of All. Such images appear as outrageous, perhaps blasphemous, cultural constrictions of the Christ figure.

Our protest should, however, be tempered by several considerations. First, many sides can play the game of taking Jesus culturally captive. Second, there is an element of inevitability about playing the game, whereby one distortion can only be countered by another distortion. Finally, running the risk of cultural captivity is inherent in the church's mission.

On the first score, Peter Berger has noted that were he to rewrite his *The Noise of Solemn Assemblies* (1961), his critique of American religion would be much the same. The difference is that at the end of the 1950s he saw religion captive to the regnant Protestant culture, while at the end of the 1960s it was captive to the minority counter-culture. The essential similarity, he contends, is that both situations represent cultural religion in bondage to something less than the transcendent dimensions to which Christianity ought to witness. Whether or not one finds Berger's analysis entirely satisfactory, the thrust of his argument can be verified by visiting any moderately radical bookstore selling "Wanted" posters portraying Jesus as a societal dropout and political subversive or, less moderately, as a guerilla fighter complete with submachine gun. The extent to which the image of Jesus is locked into a particular cluster of political and cultural perceptions may not be qualitatively different from the contraction represented by Bruce Barton's Jesus.[1]

It might be argued—and Gustavo Gutiérrez is among those who make this argument—that the qualitative difference lies not in the formal but in the material aspect of the question. That is, while the image of Jesus might in both cases be formally tied to a particular worldview, the dramatic differences between worldviews makes one image more legitimate than the other. It makes all the difference in the world, for example, whether an image places Jesus with the poor or with the rich, with the oppressed or with the oppressor. The problem, of course, is that terms such as oppressed and oppressor and notions about what might be done to change their relationships are uninteresting abstractions until related to concrete and usually conflicting movements, struggles and political parties. Jesus, knowing the temptations we would face, cautioned his disciples against saying "Lo here!" or "Lo there!" as though we could with absolute certainty identify the presence of the kingdom in history. Since almost every movement claims to be on behalf of the oppressed, and since even those movements which seem to us to represent the interests of the poor have within them dynamics directed against the rule of God ("sin" is the conventional and still distressingly accurate term for such dynamics), it is not enough to enlist the gospel "on the right side." Serious Christians have been forced again and again, often reluctantly, to respect the gospel's stubborn resistance to being used; it remains unenlistable and unrecruitable.

Yet there is a degree of inevitability in our tendency to take the gospel culturally captive. As Sartre observed that there are no privileged observers, so it might be said that there are no privileged believers. Critics of liberation theology should be pressed as to which adjectives—equally conditioned by culture and political perspective—are appropriate to their own theologies. It is more a boast than a description to say that one is doing simply "theology" or "Christian theology." Such a boast reflects a certain superficiality, a lack of modesty about one's placement within history. To be sure, we aspire toward the universal and catholic, but our grasp falls far short of our reach. Nor is this entirely lamentable, for (and this is the third consideration) running the risk of limitation, of the narrowing represented by cultural captivity, is inherent in the church's mission.

Running the risk is not the same thing as making a virtue of necessity. Whether the limitations be national, denominational, sexual, racial or ethnic, we ought not to glory in our parochialisms. That way lies the cacophony of competing chauvinisms and the impoverishment of us all. Nonetheless, a religion that affirms the Incarnation and the proposition that the finite can contain the infinite can afford to run some risks. In fact, it has little choice in the matter.

In one of the great prayers in the eucharistic liturgy Jesus is spoken of as "the new man for all men." Over the centuries Jesus has been pictured with the clothing, mannerisms and physical characteristics of Africans, Orientals, Mexicans and others who have appropriated His image. Today in Africa hundreds of burgeoning "independent churches" are bringing together traditional Christian and tribal imagery into something genuinely new under the sun. Historically the church has had an extraordinarily difficult time drawing the line between creative appropriation and distortive syncretism, but in its healthier moments it has sinned on the side of sympathy with the restatements generated by its missionary impulse. In any case, every cultural appropriation involves some limitation; there is a choice, conscious or not, of accents, a muting or even exclusion of discordant themes. Indeed it is precisely the multiplicity of culturally biased imaginations that has made it possible for countless culturally captive Christians to identify with Jesus as "one of us," and for the more catholic-minded to be gripped by the exploration of the inexhaustible diversity of the Christ figure.

The alternative to running the risk of cultural captivity is to surrender to the theologian's propensity to present the Christ as a cluster of theological propositions. José Comblin describes this failure to culturally enflesh the central figure of Christianity as the "iconization" of Jesus. Gutiérrez's protest against the iconization of Jesus and the resulting version of the gospel as a revolutionary manifesto will inevitably be compared with efforts to construct a theology of black liberation in this country, efforts associated notably with James Cone of Union Theological Seminary. Cone's main themes are reflected in the statement of the National Committee of Black Churchmen, issued during the height of the debate about the "Black Manifesto," which demanded reparations from white churches:

> Black Theology is a theology of black liberation. It seeks to plumb the black condition in the light of God's revelation in Jesus Christ, so that the black community can see that the gospel is commensurate with the achievement of black humanity. . . . The message of liberation is the revelation of God as revealed in the incarnation of Jesus Christ. Freedom *is* the gospel. Jesus *is* the Liberator!

Like Gutiérrez, Cone has taken care to relate his theology to the larger, more universal, Christian tradition. Again like Gutiérrez he has been most commonly criticized for reducing the gospel, for repackaging it, so to speak, in order to serve partisan purposes of social change. He has also been criticized from the other side. For example, Gayraud Wilmore (*Black Religion and Black Radicalism*) has suggested that it is not necessary to "validate" black theology in the terms of "white Christianity." Indeed the black religious experience, he writes, has its own integrity, which need not be in any exclusive sense related to Christianity at all.

The parallels between Cone and Gutiérrez deserve more careful examination than is possible here. The point is that both are wrestling with the tension between what is indigenous and what is catholic. Both acknowledge the danger of liberation theology becoming captive to a political ideology that is foreign to the believing community within which any significant theological statement must be appropriated and sustained. In Cone one detects a growing respect for the black church as it actually is, and not as the revolutionary vanguard we may want it to be. Similarly, Gutiérrez strives to relate his work not only to world theological discourse but also to papal and episcopal statements in which he seeks warrants for his own arguments, which he clearly views in terms of development rather than repudiation. Although both Cone and Gutiérrez frequently, and carelessly, represent their views as something "entirely new" and as a "complete break with the past," such rhetoric must be discounted in view of their evident consciousness of themselves as members of a continuing community of theological reflection. Gutiérrez is determined to relate not only to what is contemporarily catholic but also to what is chronologically catholic. That is, the referents from the past are permitted to impinge in an authoritative way upon present reflection. Writing in *Worldview* (September, 1972), Gutiérrez contends, for example, against the view of Jesus as an "apolitical" figure. "A serious reconsideration of this presupposition is necessary." But then he quickly adds, "But it has to be undertaken with a respect for the historical Jesus, not forcing the facts in terms of our current concerns. If we wished to discover in Jesus the least characteristic of a contemporary political militant, we would not only misrepresent his life and witness and demonstrate a lack of understanding of politics in the present world; we would also deprive ourselves of what his life and witness have that is deep and universal and, therefore, valid and concrete for today's man."

The "therefore" in the last sentence is crucial. It contains a host of assumptions about the theological enterprise and about rational discourse in general. The sentence is representative of Gutiérrez's acceptance of the tension between particularity and universality, between an indigenous church and a catholic church. It is therefore both fair and necessary to hold Gutiérrez to his "therefore" in reading his *A Theology of Liberation*.

Gustavo Gutiérrez clearly belongs to that company commonly described as the theologians of the future. The phrase does not refer to the expectation that they will dominate the theological enterprise in the years ahead, although that may well be the case, but to the key role that the future, under the metaphor of the kingdom of God, plays in their thinking. The approach is also described as the "theology of hope" or "theology of promise." Its chief luminaries are Wolfhart Pannenberg and Jürgen Moltmann and, on a somewhat lower elevation, Johannes Metz and another Latin American, Ruben Alves. All draw heavily on the German Marxist philosopher, Ernst Bloch. The extraordinarily rich notes that accompany *A Theology of Liberation* reveal the earnestness with which Gutiérrez has tried to combine these various contributions with his consciousness of contemporary Latin America.

Liberation Theology and the Cultural Captivity of the Gospel

Contrary to Pannenberg and much more relentlessly than Moltmann, Gutiérrez "politicizes" the idea of the kingdom. He suggests that the significance of any theological statement is in direct proportion to its applicability to the process of liberation. Indeed, theology, we are told at several points, is reflection on the *praxis* of liberation. In this respect he goes beyond Johannes Metz, to whose "new political theology" he is admittedly indebted. Of course, the "process of liberation" in its most expansive sense comprehends the totality of God's purpose in history. More immediately, it might mean the student confrontation with the regime's police in the *plaza de armas* last Thursday afternoon. Unfortunately, Gutiérrez's appeals to the process of liberation are often spectaculary indifferent to the time factor, which leads to no small confusion.

While Gutiérrez does not cite Arend van Leeuwen, the latter's appreciation of Marx as a theologian is consonant with the ways in which Gutiérrez employs Marxist categories in the definition of "the world" that is the object of theological reflection. "Alienation" is perhaps Gutiérrez's dominant metaphor for sin. For example, Ruben Alves has cautioned[2] against the use of Marxism as a "guarantee of faith." That is, he detects a tendency in liberation theology to replace the risk of Christian hope with the certitude of a Marxian "scientific" projection of the future. The tendency could no doubt find support in selected passages from *A Theology of Liberation*, but in general Gutiérrez steers away from the more dogmatic uses of Marxian scenarios and leaves, at least theoretically, wide range for the contingencies of the genuinely new, for divine initiative. This openness to the unexpected is, one must admit, obscured by his frequently uncritical legitimation, in theological terms, of the act of liberation at hand.

Gutiérrez's theologizing about liberation is complementary to the well-known secular use of liberation language. Along with most Latin Americans of the Left, Gutiérrez rejects the notion of development. Developmentalism is implicitly imitative of the oppressor and hopelessly wed to the indefinite projection of capitalist scenarios that can only mean tightening the circle of dependence which enslaves the poor. "In this light, to speak about the process of *liberation* begins to appear more appropriate and richer in human content. Liberation in fact expresses the inescapable moment of radical change which is foreign to the ordinary use of the term development." The terminological ambiguity in this sentence is increased as Gutiérrez continues: "Only in the context of such a process can a policy of development be effectively implemented, have any real meaning, and avoid misleading formulations."

While the particular forms of the future's arrival may be unclear at points, there can be no doubt that theology's business is with history and its future. Drawing directly from Pannenberg's insistence upon "universal history," Gutiérrez's hoped-for liberation assumes that "history is one." There is not a spiritual history that is the proper concern of theology and a temporal history that is left to the world, the devil and the flesh. Repudiated with equal vigor are the dichotomies between "salvation history" and "secular history," or between the realm of redemption and the realm of creation. All history is ultimately, and now in process of becoming, salvation history, and "all of the creation must be included in the order of redemption." There is but one promised kingdom which is the fulfillment of history in its totality.

Gutiérrez departs from Pannenberg in his greater certainty about what the kingdom looks like "in process of becoming." The dimension of mystery, which is closely tied to a sense of historical modesty, is frequently absent. Gutiérrez does not exclude as carefully as he might, and apparently intends, a simplistic progressivism of the onward and upward variety. This is the tone that marked much of the American social gospel movement and that provoked Reinhold Niebuhr to his polemic against the belief that "history is the Christ." The liberation struggle is the unfolding of history's script, and "the people" are the motor force of the unfolding and are, therefore, the Christ. Frantz Fanon is quoted favorably: "Everything depends upon the masses . . . there is no such thing as a demiurge. . . . the demiurge is the people themselves and the magic hands are finally only the hands of the people."

History, writes Gutiérrez, is a "Christo-finalized" history. The mission of the church, it is suggested, is not to juxtapose Christ and history, nor merely to help the world perceive the presence of Christ in history, but to see history as the Christ. Among the more attractive features of Gutiérrez's work is the seriousness with which he applies himself to the question of the church. He shuns both the fashionable mood of anti-institutionalism and the facile Marxist indictment of religion as false consciousness. He wants to affirm and seize upon the religious impulse, turning it toward the task of history and away from the suprahistorical preoccupations that characterize most religious life at present.

The task of history is thus the task of the church. There can be, then, no question of "mixing" religion and politics; the business of religion is history, including politics. Gutiérrez therefore assaults the notion of the "distinction of planes" whereby it is said that the church ought to work on the "spiritual plane" and leave the "temporal plane" to others. He notes the irony that in most Latin American countries it used to be assumed that the church would legitimate the political, economic and social status quo. At that time it was the people who wanted change who promoted the idea of the "distinction of planes." Because the church's influence tended to place a halo around repressive systems, the progressives demanded that the church stop mixing in politics. Now that the church has been stirred, and in part enlisted, by revolutionary forces, "the distinction-of-planes banner has changed hands," and it is the conservatives who are insisting that the church stay out of politics. In fact, writes Gutiérrez, in our one history "the political options have become radicalized," and for the church to stand aside from the struggle is to choose against the struggle.

The last proposition has been a perennial problem for the Christian community. At one point Jesus said, "He that is not with me is against me" (Matt. 12:30). Then again he said, "For he that is not against us is for us" (Mark 9:40). Gutiérrez's Jesus is clearly the former and, for those who want to be with Jesus, Gutiérrez seems to have a pretty clear idea of where Jesus is doing business in our generation. While Gutiérrez appears to have an unseemly confidence in his locating of Jesus' present-day activity and while Gutiérrez tends to propose the church as a recruitment office for the revolution, one should also keep in mind that not everywhere have "the political options become radicalized" as they have in many Latin American countries. Fastidiousness about maintaining the church's critical distance from the parties that would capture it is perhaps a luxury that can be afforded only in societies where the options are not so restricted as to force to the forefront the revolutionary alternative.

Nonetheless, there is, one hopes, an approach between fastidiousness and recklessness.

Gutiérrez's approach, it is important to note, seems aimed more at gaining the attention of the revolutionary than at converting the enemies of the liberation struggle. He recognizes that many Latin Americans have chosen the revolution despite Christianity—or at least despite the Christianity they were taught in years past. "If they are not always able to express in appropriate terms the profound reasons for their commitment, it is because the theology in which they were formed . . . has not produced the categories necessary to express this option, which seeks to respond creatively to the new demands of the gospel and of the oppressed and exploited peoples of this continent." Certainly they were not taught the Christian rationale for the revolutionary alternative by a church that "is so static and devitalized that it is not even strong enough to abandon the gospel. It is the gospel which is disowning it." Although Gutiérrez intends to do more than this, *A Theology of Liberation* is in part an effort to provide for radicals the "appropriate terms" in which to express "the profound reasons for their commitment." It is one version of what it means to obey the biblical injunction to "be always ready to give a reason of the hope that is in you" (I Peter 3:15).

In offering a politicized theology, Gutiérrez recognizes that religion encompasses much more than what is included in the conventional definition of politics. He realizes that, if it is to be relevant to the life of the faithful who actually make up the church, theology must deal with prayer, the Eucharist, ecclesiastical structures and so forth. Each of these subjects receives careful and even loving attention. His systematic effort is to recast each of these topics and to place it within a greatly expanded idea of politics, in which politics becomes almost synonymous with history. One chapter is devoted, for example, to traditional piety regarding poverty and seeks to demonstrate that the beatitude "Blessed are the poor" is not a statement of resignation or passivity but an assurance that the poor are blessed because they are the revolutionary vanguard. Neither does Gutiérrez neglect the pronouncements of the church's magisterium. He seeks rather to demonstrate natural developments toward a theology of liberation, arguing, for example, for the continuity between Pope Paul VI's *Populorum Progressio* (which he interprets as "a transitional document") and a commitment to revolutionary change.

Although Gutiérrez does not, then, disdain even the most traditional concerns of religion, it is nonetheless accurate to say that he finally equates the church's mission with the revolutionary struggle. "The scope and gravity of the process of liberation is such that to ponder its significance is really to examine the meaning of Christianity itself and the mission of the church in the world."

As we have seen, the phrase "process of liberation" is used in varying ways, with dramatically different degrees of inclusiveness. The goal of liberation's process remains elusive, although one or two summary statements are offered:

> The historical plan, the utopia of liberation as the creation of a new social consciousness and as a social appropriation not only of the means of production, but also of the political process, and, definitively, of freedom, is the proper arena for the cultural revolution. That is to say, it is the arena of the permanent creation of a new man in a different society characterized by solidarity. Therefore, that creation is the place of encounter between political liberation and the communion of all men with God.

The specifically socialist character of the process and its goal is explicit:

> The underdevelopment of the poor countries, as an overall social fact, appears in its true light: as the historical by-product of the development of other countries. The dynamics of the capitalist economy lead to the establishment of a center and a periphery, simultaneously generating progress and growing wealth for the few and social imbalances, political tensions and poverty for the many.

The conclusion is clear: "autonomous Latin American development is not viable within the framework of the international capitalist system." The socialism he envisions is not, Gutiérrez writes, monolithic nor slavishly imitative of the socialist constructions of others. It will be a distinctively Latin American construction.

"Socialism" is presented more as a conceptual model than as a political or economic blueprint. There seems to be greater clarity regarding the role of nationalism in the liberation process, although nationalism is in this context really Latin American continentalism. "It is becoming more obvious that the revolutionary process ought to embrace the whole continent. There is little chance of success for attempts limited to a national scope." As the late Marxist theoretician György Lukács noted,[3] much third world socialist language disguises an essentially nationalist impulse that is far removed from Marxist understandings of the revolutionary struggle. There is more than a hint in *A Theology of Liberation* that the nationalist impulse toward the Greater Latin America could result, as has happened elsewhere, in some kind of capitalist corporate state that would be quite capable of overcoming alienation through social solidarity. Thus it is possible that Gutiérrez's "Marxism" is more a matter of utilizing the language available among those who view themselves as engaged in the liberation struggle, and ought not, therefore, be interpreted in a literalistic fashion. If "the hope that is in" those whom he is addressing is framed in Marxist categories, then the "reason" for that hope must be similarly framed.

A passion for social solidarity can take many forms. In the utopia (not a perjorative term in Gutiérrez's vocabulary) toward which he presses, the "social appropriation of freedom" is, as we have seen, "definitive" for Gutiérrez. When anyone projects a "new order" it is always well to look carefully at what he says about freedom. There is, of course, the individualistic idea of freedom which is the bad joke of laissez-faire exploitation. That is the well-known freedom that both rich and poor have the right to sleep under bridges. There is the equally well-known "socialist freedom" of totalitarian states. This is the freedom of those enslaved to official and "scientific" definitions of the historical process. Rejecting both those perverse notions of freedom, one looks for the clear analysis and affirmation of freedom that nourishes the dialectic between individual and community, between the existent and the possible, between present and future. In *A Theology of Liberation* such clarity is distressingly absent. All the more distressing because one would suppose that in a theology of *liberation* the idea of freedom, or liberty, would receive particularly careful attention.

Gutiérrez, to be sure, frequently alludes to freedom, and the language of liberation marks almost every sentence. He cites Hegel to the effect that "world history is the progression of the awareness of freedom." The process of liberation, he says, is indebted to Marx, who advanced beyond Hegel in pointing the way "from awareness of freedom to real freedom." This real freedom is gained "through the dialectical process [by which] man constructs himself and attains a real awareness of his own being; he liberates himself in the acquisition of genuine freedom which through work transforms the world and educates man." The "man" in question seems always to be collective man. "The gradual conquest of true freedom leads to the creation of a new man and a qualitatively different society." Even Dietrich Bonhoeffer, whose resistance to collectivist pretensions about establishing "new orders" needs no comment, is quoted to the effect that "Being free means being free for the other, because the other has bound me to him. Only in relationship with the other am I free." When dramatically different statements on freedom are cited, Gutiérrez is not provoked to examine the contradictions; freedom is invoked rather than defined. Gutiérrez inveighs against older "political theologies" which sought to restore a "Christian state." Such ideas, he writes, are "repressive and authoritarian." He seems curiously indifferent to the repressive and authoritarian potentialities within other forms of the state which assert, with an authority of religious intensity, the establishment of "new orders."

Thus *A Theology of Liberation* comes close to providing carte blanche legitimation for joining almost any allegedly revolutionary struggle to replace almost any allegedly repressive regime. The absence of conceptual clarity in the statement of the goal is matched by a deep obscurity about the means by which the goal is to be achieved. It is still possible to hear complaints from Latin American prelates who accuse Gutiérrez and other liberation theologians of advocating violent revolution. No doubt Gutiérrez has opponents in high places who are profoundly conservative and understandably fearful of what he represents. Yet it is not possible, in the basis of *A Theology of Liberation*, to dismiss their criticisms as being motivated merely by conservative fear. There is in fact a deep and perhaps dangerous abstruseness about what precisely Gutiérrez is advocating.

There is no effort in *A Theology of Liberation* to weigh means and ends in the revolutionary struggle or to develop criteria by which the justice of a cause might be judged. I hold no ultimate brief for the "just war" criteria,[4] which no doubt have their limitations, but one does expect a theologian to at least suggest an alternative apparatus for critical ethical reflection. As it is, almost any struggle that fashions itself a liberation struggle is reinforced by Gutiérrez with all the moral warrants appropriate to Christ's work in the world.

The dialectic in Gutiérrez's argument might be strengthened by a stronger emphasis on the negative. Barrington Moore (*Reflections on the Causes of Human Misery*) writes on "the unity of misery and the diversity of happiness." He understands, in a way one misses in Gutiérrez, that radical efforts at social change are best directed toward the elimination of readily agreed upon miseries than toward the establishment of a much more elusive happiness. Projections of "a new man in a new society" are always deserving of the greatest suspicion. Relating this insight specifically to the church's mission in the world, Dom Helder Camara of Brazil has suggested that the church, in addressing itself to the social situation, must always say No. That is, the church must protest evil and be sophisticated in its analysis of the roots of evil, but never offer a blueprint for the new order, nor open-ended moral legitimation for those who might purpose such a blueprint.

In this way the Christian community is captive neither to the prevailing order nor to those who would overthrow it. It neither keeps silent about injustice nor does it apotheosize particular manifestations of the revolutionary struggle. This is not to be confused with a course of neutrality or of standing above the battle. It is not a refusal to choose. It is clear choice against clear evil. It is courageous refusal, in view of the modesty appropriate to our placement in history, to absolutize any alternative to the kingdom, anything short of the kingdom. *A Theology of Liberation* on the other hand, comes very close to being an indiscriminate apotheosis of diverse revolutionary struggles, at least in Latin America.

It must be said, in fairness to Gutiérrez, that he seems to sense this danger, and his writing reflects a certain uneasiness about being misunderstood. On one page he makes statements of absolutist rigidity, but then, a few pages on or perhaps in a footnote, he urges the reader to keep in mind the variety of ways in which God may be working today in history. Ringing "Lo heres" in the text are frequently tempered by "maybes" in the footnotes. At times the struggle for the control of the means of production is unequivocally equated with faithfulness to Christ, but then we are cautioned that the new society cannot yet be defined and, at one point, that the just society is not, in any case, the same thing as the kingdom. There seem almost to be two Gutiérrezes. The one quotes Fanon and Che Guevara almost as Scripture, proclaiming we are on the edge of "revolutionary anthropophany" in which historically inexorable forces are creating "the new man in the new society" (the slogan appears with distressing regularity). The second Gutiérrez comes out of the closet in the notes, carefully positioning his arguments in relation to the larger theological and political discourse both of the past and of the international community. He cautions the reader against understanding what he has just said as what he has just said.

In criticizing another thinker, Gutiérrez says at one point: "We believe that the danger is not averted simply by noting its presence." It is an astute observation, and one that is applicable to Gutiérrez's own writing. Gutiérrez's qualifications of his own pronouncements are reassuring in that they anticipate the reader's objections to some of his more sweeping generalizations, but adding qualifications is not enough. It reveals the author's intelligent ambivalence about simple assertions on complex topics, but it does not result in the systematic achievement that the author intended and others have claimed to find in *A Theology of Liberation*.

Such a systematic treatment requires a much more searching examination of the presuppositions in current, usually Marxist, languages of liberation. The reason for Gutiérrez's frequent failure to undertake such an examination is perhaps to be discovered in what might be called his pastoral intention in *A Theology of Liberation*. He clearly believes the revolutionaries hold the cards that will shape the Latin American future, and he may well be right. He is admittedly unhappy that many leaders of the liberation struggle are alienated from Christianity. He wants to offer them an explicitly Christian theoretical framework within which their revolutionary commitment might be understood, strengthened and communicated. Theology, we are told again and again, is a reflection on the *praxis* of the liberation process. Perhaps it is his pastoral desire to identify with that process that gets in the way of his offering a theology that exercises critical resources for evaluating and redirecting that *praxis.* The necessary tension between Christ and that part of culture that is the liberation struggle is relaxed, and sometimes completely collapsed.

When the pastoral intention leads to a collapse of tension, the result is the chaplaincy syndrome. Criticism is suspended in order better to "minister." The search for rapport distorts the perception of reality. The comfort/challenge dialectic of the Christian message can be diffused also when one is comforting the challengers. The chaplaincy syndrome, in its more advanced stage, is a late prelate ministering to U.S. troops in Vietnam, assuring them they are the "soldiers of Christ." It is the professional ethicist ministering to the medical researchers, offering situational legitimations for most anything they can get a financial grant to do. To be sure, the church has usually provided chaplains to comfort the comfortable. That *A Theology of Liberation* might help right the imbalance is no little merit. But the real need is to break out of the chaplaincy syndrome.

Gutiérrez, a former chaplain to the National Union of Catholic University Students, does not intend by this book simply to call more Christians to chaplaincy on the other side of the barricades. He calls rather for the church as such to position itself in the lines of the liberation struggle. Obviously, any call to radical commitment will be divisive, disturbing the suprahistorical tranquillity that many look for in the life of the church. A healthy Christian community is one in which different and often conflicting views and commitments are not only openly admitted but celebrated. Within the sure bond of Christ a restless community interacts around disparate and always provisional sightings of the kingdom's coming. This is the lively interaction that too many churchmen fear and try to mute in the name of Christian unity.

Yet Gutiérrez too seems to fear the radical disparity within Christian perceptions of God's purposes in history. The tensions are collapsed, the conflicts resolved, by calling the church to choose one side. Gutiérrez, too, appeals to Christian unity. Real unity, he writes, requires division; it means pressing the class struggle in order to "build a socialist society, more just, free, and human, and not a society of superficial and false reconciliation and equality." Is there not, however, something "superficial" and "false" about a recon- ciliation that is merely a reconciliation among radicals? Of course a merely formal unity that seeks to contain conflicting elements can be profoundly dishonest. But there is nothing superficial or false about Paul's vision of the church, where in Christ Jesus "There is neither Jew nor Greek, there is neither slave nor free, there is neither male nor female," and, we might add, there is neither bourgeoisie nor proletariat (Galatians 3:28). To welcome and celebrate the par- ticularity of each member, and yet to affirm that that particularity does not define or restrict one's stature in the community—that is the challenge to be the church and the answer to "superficial and false reconciliation."

Gutiérrez, on the other hand, suggests that the church can no longer be a meeting place where understanding can be sought, ideas shared and communion celebrated among those on opposite sides of the barricades. The church must decide, it must make an unam- biguously partisan commitment. "The Gospel announces the love of God for all people and calls us to love as he loves. But to accept class struggle means to decide for some people and against others." (It is not much help when "the second Gutiérrez" adds: "This is a challenge that leads the Christian to deepen his faith and to mature in his love for others.") One's impression is that Gutiérrez's vision is not that of the church renewed but simply that of the church switching sides.

Ten years ago, I predicted that *A Theology of Liberation* would be an important book and would no doubt be a major point of reference in the further development of liberation theologies, not only in Latin America, but also in other third world countries and in the United States. I also predicted that we could expect Gutiérrez's work to be put down by two apparently conflicting but symbiotic forms of condescension. The first is the arrogant condescension of North Americans and Western Europeans who applaud the new boy in the class who surprises everybody with his familarity with the literature and very scholarly critical apparatus. The second is the romantic condescension of those who have made a faith commit- ment to the proposition that "salvation comes from the third world" and therefore accept as the new gospel any militant echoes of their own vocal disillusionment with themselves and their culture. It would be as easy as it would be false to import theologies of liberation as adrenalin to stimulate the North American theological enterprise in its period of pervasive boredom. Neither condescension can respond adequately to Gustavo Gutiérrez and his search for theological restatement in a time of high confusion.

Several years ago, Daniel Berrigan remarked that, unlike many who see themselves as radicals, he has no taste for nurturing or exporting anti-Americanism. "In my sympathy with liberation struggles elsewhere, I never forget that I am an American and a Christian. I want to be as indigenous to my culture as they are to theirs." It is an exercise in false consciousness for North American Christians to parrot liberation theologies that are born, through much suffering, from situations dramatically different from our own. Our task, inspired by thinkers such as Gustavo Gutiérrez, is to apply ourselves to the North American experience, trying to reshape it in a way that might result in a more fulfilling society here and a society that is less oppressive, if not liberating, for our brothers and sisters to the south. Reshaping the North American experience means breathing new life into culturally formative metaphors such as accountability to the poor, covenant responsibility, and an empathy that makes us vulnerable to the yearning of the oppressed. When the radically empathic Jesus of the rich encounters the revolutionary Jesus of the poor we may all be liberated from his cultural captivity— and ours.

NOTES

1. In his 1925 bestseller, *The Man Nobody Knows*, Barton portrayed Jesus as the world's greatest business organizer.
2. See *Worldview*, March, 1972.
3. See "The Failure of Marxist Theory," *Worldview*, May, 1972.
4. See my "The Thorough Revolutionary" in *Movement and Revolution*.

CONCLUSION

CONCLUSION

CONCLUSION

While it is not the purpose of this book to provide the last word about liberation theology, it does aim to draw attention to questions and problems that liberation theologians need to address, issues that they have to this point ignored. Liberation theologians themselves have told us that theirs is a theology in transition and that it will take time for them to develop their position in a complete, unambiguous and systematic way. While this excuse may have carried weight ten or fifteen years ago, one must begin to wonder if liberation theologians ever will address their problems.

Almost without exception, the contributors to this volume have applauded the sincere motives of liberation theologians. Liberation thinkers have helped draw attention to problems that might otherwise have gone unheeded for years. But life seldom affords us the luxury of judging others exclusively on the basis of their motives. Antonio Martino warns:

> It cannot be denied that advocates of "social justice" are quite often motivated by lofty ideals. Such is the case, for example, of those who are genuinely concerned about poverty and the need to do something about it. Their sincere compassion for the poor is undoubtedly a noble sentiment, and it deserves respect and admiration. However, their belief that the way to help the poor is by remodelling the whole of society (according to their preferred general plan) is more likely to hurt everybody than to achieve their aim.[1]

Liberation theologians tell us that Christians should be on the side of the poor and oppressed because God is. As important as this truth may be, it is an empty formula that must be given content. What does it mean to be on the side of the poor and the oppressed? In what ways should my concerned action be channeled? As Quentin Quade observes, liberation theologians like Gutiérrez move "easily from the gospel's concern for the poor to specific political solutions: the poor 'are the oppressed, the exploited, the workers cheated of the fruits of their work, stripped of their being as men. The poverty of the poor is not therefore an appeal for generous action to relieve it, but a demand for the construction of a different social order.''[2] But, as Quade notes,

> A vast distance separates these two kinds of observations, that the Gospel teaches compassion for the poor and that compassion demands 'the construction of a different social order.' But the two are presented as equally derived from the Christian faith. Apparently Father Gutiérrez feels no obligation to explain how he knows political things—e.g., that it is time for radical change, or what a new and better order consists of and how it can be achieved. Addressing particular issues and structures, he offers no more defense than that 'we are in the presence of what is necessarily an offshoot of the Gospel.'[3]

It is Gutiérrez's utopianism, Quade believes, and not his understanding of the gospel that provides his bridge between his Christian compassion for the poor and his Marxist program. "Basically, Gutiérrez is a utopian; he believes man can make heaven on earth. He traces sin and evil to systems, not to human nature, and appears to believe that greed began with capitalism and will end with its demise."[4]

In his contribution to this book, Father James Schall describes liberation theology as an "impractical praxis." It is bound, Schall maintains, to be a cause of persistent underdevelopment. "Its eventual growth and success," he argues, will only "institutionalize in Latin America a life of low-level socialist poverty enforced by a rigid party-military discipline in control of economic enterprise and the movement of peoples." However noble its intentions, liberation theology will only succeed in impoverishing Latin America.

Liberation theology is deficient both in its diagnosis and its prescription. It fails to explain the real causes of poverty and thus it cannot hope to provide a cure since it misunderstands the nature of the disease. Liberation theology's analysis of the causes of Latin American poverty and oppression is simplistic and one-sided: all of the sins, in this view, rest in the first world nations, especially the United States. Liberation theologians seem most adept at blaming others for the problems of Latin America. But this should not surprise us since socialist systems thrive on blaming someone else for their economic miseries. As Michael Novak and other contributors to this book have pointed out, first world nations are not responsible for third world poverty which antedates capitalism and which, in fact, used to be far worse than it presently is. As Novak demonstrated, Latin America already has the resources needed to begin alleviating its poverty and destitution.

The liberation charge that colonialism (political dependence) was a major obstacle to the economic development of third world countries is contradicted by the evidence. According to William Scully, it is true that many weaker countries have been exploited by colonial powers.

> There is also no doubt that the colonies benefitted from such "exploitation." History shows that the areas that experienced the longest and/or most direct colonial control tend to be among the most developed, such as Malaysia, Nigeria, Singapore, and the Philippines. Other areas, under less direct colonial control, such as Laos or Bolivia, have proved more backward in economic development. Then, of course, those nations that have had little or no colonial involvement, as in the case of Afghanistan and Ethiopia, are found to be the poorest of all.[5]

Scully also answers the charge that the West is the major cause of worldwide poverty.

> Phrased in another way this accusation reads: the West was made rich at the expense of the poor. Actually, much of the developing world that has had contact with the West owes its economic development to such contact, which provided access to Western markets, Western enterprise, capital, and ideas. Today's poverty in the South is much more the result of domestic mismanagement and unsound domestic policies than of Western interference and domination. For example, the widespread collectivization programs in Kampuchea and Vietnam have caused far more severe economic and social dislocation than the war there ever did.[6]

Liberation theologians never talk about the formerly poor nations that have achieved rapid economic progress. Their silence may be due to the fact that these developing nations happen to have rejected socialism. Schall explains:

> a creative use of North American, European, Japanese, and ASEAN experiences, as opposed to dogmatic socialist models so often chosen for theoretical reasons by the liberation school, would better enable those nations of Latin America to alleviate their poverty, retain so much that is unique and valid in their culture, and protect the rights and duties of religion and public freedom. In spite of all protestations

to the contrary, it is precisely this approach that has not been considered by Latin American liberation thought. Paradoxically, what liberation thought seems most in need of is precisely a theory and practice of liberty.[7]

Because liberation theologians persist in ignoring economic models that have achieved the goals they seek and continue, on ideological grounds, to promote models that have led only to failure and/or tyranny, their promises of political and economic salvation are a mirage. What one sees from a distance seems to be paradise. But the oasis is always unattainable.

Because the movement we are considering is presented as a form of Christian theology, it must also be judged in terms of its faithfulness to the basic beliefs and practices of the Christian faith. It can certainly be faulted for its way of handling the biblical revelation. In the words of Bruce Demarest, liberation theology teaches "the Bible through the spectacles of Karl Marx." What Demarest means is that

> The Marxist-socialist critique of capitalist society wrongly forms the basis for the liberationist's interpretation of the Word of God. Instead of allowing its vision of the world to be shaped by the teachings of Scripture, liberation theology permits its understanding of Scripture to be shaped by analysis of the existing social order. The Christian's text must be the Word of God rather than the historical situation (Deut. 4:1-2, 5-6).[8]

Demarest, like many other critics of the movement, notes the weakness of biblical exegesis in liberation writings. He states that liberation theologians "are notably deficient in the area of exegesis. Biblical texts are commonly used as pretexts to justify pet economic and political theories. Gutiérrez and other liberationists often do little more than hang biblical window dressing on the framework of a sociological theory."[9] Liberation theology's peculiar hermeneutic coupled with the clear suggestion that many liberation thinkers have doubts about the normative character of the biblical revelation may explain the ease with which some of them are led to the brink of heresy. Some liberationists have blurred the distinction between the church (the company of redeemed believers) and the world. Some have suggested that the poor are saved simply because they are poor. Others imply that God cares more about the poor than he cares about

Conclusion

the rich.[10] It is heresy to state that God's love for people varies in proportion to their wealth. It is absurd to suggest that all the poor are good and all the rich are bad. Likewise when Jose Miranda dogmatizes that knowing God means nothing more than seeking justice for the poor, he is treading on extremely thin theological ice.[11]

Roman Catholic liberation theologians can also be faulted for their departure from the position their church has taken in this century on the political competence of the church which Quentin Quade summarizes in three propositions: "(1) Modesty or caution about any capacity to know what right political action is on the basis of religious perception alone. (2) Care in the terminology used when one is exhorting and prescribing. (3) Rigor in respecting the essential difference between church and state as human institutions."[12] The message of Pope John Paul II to the Third General Conference of Latin American bishops held in Puebla, Mexico in 1979 contained a clear warning to liberation theologians. He spoke of people who

> depict Jesus as a political activist, as a fighter against Roman domination and the authorities, and even as someone involved in the class struggle. This conception of Christ as a political figure, a revolutionary, as the subversive from Nazareth, does not tally with the church's catechesis . . . [But] Jesus . . . unequivocally rejects recourse to violence. He opens his message of conversion to all. . . . His mission . . . has to do with complete and integral salvation through a love that brings transformation, peace, pardon, and reconciliation.[13]

Robert Walton's chapter in this book may be the most forceful statement to date of the heresy implicit in liberation thought. Walton's basic assumption is that liberation theology is the very opposite of a movement which can advance the cause of true freedom because it refuses to recognize or deal with our Christian tradition. By this tradition, Walton means the amalgam of God's dealing with the church, the community which has been gathered by His Word, and the church's response to God's dealings. Christians are products of this tradition. But as C. G. Jung pointed out, men and women who are cut off from their own history and tradition are bound to become sick and can become violent both individually and collectively.[14] Liberation theology and its consequences provide an excellent demonstration of Jung's thesis. In Walton's view, liberation theology is a sickness which leads naturally to violence and

243

death. It is essentially destructive and in terms of the Christian tradition, it is heretical.

This may explain why liberation theologians are so selective in their social criticism. Walter Benjamin is one of many who wonder why liberation theologians focus their attention exclusively on Latin America and "are all but mute on totalitarianism in Eastern Europe."[15] After all, he points out, people in Eastern Europe are also oppressed and poor but no one, least of all liberation theologians, ever says a word on their behalf. "Whatever the reason, the near silence of liberation theology regarding Eastern Europe reveals ethical astigmatism.[16] Benjamin's censure of its exclusive preoccupation with oppression in Latin America is an important mark against liberation theology. People who profess concern about justice and freedom should condemn bondage wherever it exists including the Marxist states of the world. Ironically, Benjamin points out, there is also a modest revolution beginning in Eastern Europe; but it is a revolution *against* Marxism.

> Liberationists should be more ecumenical in their humanistic sympathy. Too often, victims of Soviet oppression and their Eastern satraps, Boat People, Afghan rebels, the Kurds and Bahaists of Iran, Cuban political prisoners and exiles, and black victims of black dictators in Africa are ignored because the choice of underdog is selective and rooted in ideological criteria. Some liberation theologians . . . cannot admit injustice or oppression in Vietnam because, by definition, socialist countries cannot oppress.[17]

Benjamin continues by noting how often Christians who are sympathetic to Marxism ignore or cover over the deficiencies and failures of socialist revolutions. He advises: "Liberation theology should give up the penchant to believe the worst about the United States. It is a mystery to me why some liberationists who prize an autonomous lifestyle are so enamored by masses of people in motion in closed societies . . . "[18]

Where is liberation theology, the Pied Piper of our generation, leading us? Father James Schall wonders if an entire continent "is not being led to commit itself to a system in which the presumed elimination of poverty will rather result in the elimination of freedom, with only a minimal attack on poverty. Such a liberation would be ironic indeed, especially in the name of God."[19] In his chapter in

Conclusion

this book, Michael Novak laments that in opting for the road to utopia, liberation theologians "seem to imitate the Grand Inquisitor, who out of pity for the people promised bread, not liberty." We must not keep silent in such a situation. Not only do the people desire bread, they also long for liberty. And as Novak concludes, "Not only is it possible to have both, the second [liberty] is the key to the first [bread]." To quote Schall for one last time, it is ironic that "what liberation thought seems most in need of is precisely a theory and practice of liberty."[20]

This book has laid out the reasons why socialism can provide neither bread nor freedom. The only way in which the poor of any nation can be delivered from poverty is through an economic system that first of all produces enough wealth so that all are capable of sharing. Economic systems that decrease or discourage production can never succeed in eliminating poverty; they can only make it worse. No workable economy is feasible that does not take account of the operations of the market. Any economy that violates those principles is doomed to failure and, even worse, bound to create conditions in which human liberation becomes less attainable.

NOTES

1. Antonio Martino, "The Myth of Social Justice," in *Three Myths* by Arnold Beichman, Antonio Martino and Kenneth Minogue (Washington: The Heritage Foundation, 1982) p. 24.

2. Quentin L. Quade, editor, *The Pope and Revolution* (Washington, D. C.: Ethics and Public Policy Center, 1982) p. 19.

3. Ibid., p. 14.

4. Ibid.

5. William L. Scully, "The Brandt Commission: Deluding the Third World," *The Heritage Foundation Backgrounder*, No. 182, April 30, 1982, p. 15.

6. Ibid., p. 16.

7. James V. Schall, S.J., *Liberation Theology in Latin America* (San Fransisco: Ignatius Press, 1982) p. 126.

8. Bruce Demarest, *General Revelation* (Grand Rapids: Zondervan 1982) pp. 214-5.

9. Ibid., p. 215.

10. See Enco Gatti, *Rich Church-Poor Church* (Maryknoll: Orbis, 1974) p. 43.

Liberation Theology

11. See José Miranda, *Marx and the Bible* (Maryknoll: Orbis, 1974) p. 44.
12. Quade, op. cit., p. 6.
13. John Paul II, "Opening Address at Puebla," in Quade, op. cit., pp. 53, 54.
14. See Jung's *Essay on Wotan.*
15. Walter Benjamin, "Liberation Theology: European Hopelessness Exposes the Latin Hoax," *Christianity Today*, volume 26, March, 1982, p. 21.
16. Ibid.
17. Ibid., p. 22.
18. Ibid., p. 23.
19. Schall, op. cit., p. 44.
20. Schall, op. cit., p. 126.

SELECTED BIBLIOGRAPHY

Selected Bibliography

The following bibliography contains a representative sampling of books and articles that expound, defend or criticize liberation theology. No attempt has been made to provide a complete bibliography. Most of the cited works refer to additional sources. Some works cited as either supportive or critical of liberation theology may overlap categories.

Books and Articles Supportive of Liberation Theology

Alves, Ruben. *A Theology of Human Hope* (Washington: Corpus Books, 1969).

Anderson, Gerald H. and Stransky, Thomas F., C.S.B., editors. *Mission Trends Number 4, Liberation Theologies in North America and Europe* (Grand Rapids: Eerdmans, 1979).

Anderson, Justice C., "The Church and Liberation Theology, *Southwestern Journal of Theology* 19 (1977) pp. 17-36.

Assmann, Hugo. *Theology for a Nomad Chruch* (Maryknoll: Orbis, 1975).

Berryman, Phillip E. "Latin American Liberation Theology," *Theological Studies* 34 (1973) pp. 357-395.

Bigo, Pierre. *The Church and Third World Revolution* (Maryknoll: Orbis, 1977).

Boff, Leonardo. *Jesus Christ Liberator* (Maryknoll:Orbis, 1978).

Brown, Robert McAffee. *Gustavo Gutíerrez* (Atlanta: John Knox, 1980).

Brown, Robert McAffee. *Theology in a New Key: Responding to Liberation Themes* (Philadelphia: Westminister, 1978).

Camara, Helder. *Church and Colonialism: The Betrayal of the Third World* (London: Sheed and Ward, 1969).

Dussel, Enrique. *History and Theology of Liberation: A Latin American Perspective* (Maryknoll: Orbis, 1976).

Eagleson, John, editor. *Christianity and Socialism* (Maryknoll: Orbis, 1975).

Eagleson, John and Scharper, Phillip. *Puebla and Beyond: Documents and Commentary* (Maryknoll: Orbis, 1980).

Ellacuria, Ignacio. *Freedom Made Flesh: The Mission of Christ and His Church* (Maryknoll: Orbis, 1977).

Ferm, Deane William. *Contemporary American Theologies: A Critical Survey* (New York: Seabury, 1981) pp. 59-76.

Fierro, Alfredo. *The Militant Gospel* (Maryknoll: Orbis, 1977).

Fiorenza, Francis P. "Latin American Liberation Theology," *Interpretation* 28 (1974) pp. 441-457.

Frei, Eduardo. *Latin America: The Hopeful Option* (Maryknoll: Orbis, 1978).

Freire, Paulo. *Pedagogy of the Oppressed* (New York: Seabury, 1970).

Garrison, Stephen. "Liberation Theology: A Challenge to the Church," *Crux* 16 (1980) pp. 20-23.

Gatti, Enco. *Rich Church - Poor Church* (Maryknoll: Orbis, 1974).

Geffré, C., and Gutiérrez, G., editors. *The Mystical and Political Dimension of the Christian Faith* (New York: Herder and Herder, 1974).

Gheerbrant, A. *The Rebel Church in Latin America* (London, 1974).

Gibellini, R., editor. *Frontiers of Theology in Latin America* (Maryknoll: Orbis, 1979).

Gutiérrez, Gustavo. *A Theology of Liberation* (Maryknoll: Orbis, 1973).

Gutiérrez, G. and Schaull, R. *Liberation and Change* (Atlanta: John Knox, 1977).

Haughey, John C. S.J., editor. *The Faith that Does Justice* (New York: Paulist, 1977).

Hennelly, Alfred, S.J. *Theologies in Conflict: The Challenge of Juan Luis Segundo* (Maryknoll: Orbis, 1979).

Herzog, Frederick. *Liberation Theology* (New York: Seabury, 1972).

Houtart, Francois, and Rousseau, Andre. *The Church and Revolution* (Maryknoll: Orbis, 1971).

Lehmann, Paul. *The Transfiguration of Politics* (New York: Harper and Row, 1975).

Selected Bibliography

MacEoin, Gary. "Puebla: Moment of Decision for the Latin American Church," *Cross Currents*, No. 1, Spring 1978.

MacEoin, Gary. *Revolution Next Door: Latin America in the 1970s.* (Maryknoll: Orbis, 1981).

McCann, Dennis P. *Christian Realism and Liberation Theology* (Maryknoll: Orbis, 1981).

McFadden, T. S., editor. *Liberation, Revolution, and Freedom* (New York: Seabury, 1975).

McGovern, Arthur F., S.J. *Marxism: An American Christian Perspective* (Maryknoll: Orbis, 1980).

Míguez-Bonino, José. *Christians and Marxists* (Grand Rapids: Eerdmans, 1976).

Míguez-Bonino, José. *Doing Theology in a Revolutionary Situation* (Philadelphia: Fortress, 1975).

Miranda, José Porfirio. *Communism in the Bible* (Maryknoll: Orbis, 1982).

Miranda, José Porfirio. *Marx and the Bible* (Maryknoll: Orbis, 1974).

Neely, Alan. "Liberation Theology in Latin America: Antecedents and Autochthony," *Missiology* 6 (1978) pp. 343-370.

Noel, Gerard. *The Anatomy of the Catholic Church: Roman Catholicism in an Age of Revolution* (New York: Doubleday, 1980).

Nunez, Emilio. "The Challenge of Liberation Theology,"*Evangelical Missions Quarterly* 17 (1981) pp. 139-146.

Ogden, Schubert M. *Faith and Freedom: Toward a Theology of Liberation* (Nashville: Abingdon, 1979).

Osborn, Robert. "Liberation Theology," *Perspectives in Religious Studies* 6 (1979) pp. 152-161.

Petulla, Joseph. *Christian Political Theology: A Marxian Guide* (Maryknoll: Orbis, 1977).

Ruether, Rosemary R. *Liberation Theology* (New York: Paulist, 1973).

Segundo, Juan Luis. *The Liberation of Theology* (Maryknoll: Orbis, 1976)

Sugundo, Juan Luis. *A Theology for the Artisans of a New Humanity* (Maryknoll: Orbis, 1974) 5 vols.

Sobrino, Jon. *Christology at the Crossroads: a Latin American Approach* (Maryknoll: Orbis, 1978).

Liberation Theology

Sölle, Dorothy. *Political Theology* (Philadelphia: Fortress, 1974).
Sölle, Dorothy. *Revolutionary Patience* (Maryknoll: Orbis, 1977).
Torres, S. and Eagleson, J., editors. *Theology in the Americas* (Maryknoll: Orbis, 1976).
Torres, Sergio and Fabella, Virginia, editors. *The Emergent Gospel* (Maryknoll: Orbis, 1976).
Vekemans, Robert. *Caesar and God* (Maryknoll: Orbis, 1977).
Wallis, Jim. *Agenda for Biblical People* (New York: Harper and Row, 1976).

Books and Articles Critical of Liberation Theology

Arrupe, Pedro, S.J. "Marxist Analysis by Christians," *Catholic Mind*, September 1981. pp. 58-64.
Benjamin, Walter W. "Liberation Theology: European Hopelessness Exposes the Latin Hoax," *Christianity Today*. March 5, 1982.
Demarest, Bruce. *General Revelation* (Grand Rapids: Zondervan, 1982) pp. 209-216.
Eppstein, John. *The Cult of Revolution in the Church* (New Rochelle, New York: Arlington House, 1974).
Henry, Carl F.H. *God, Revelation and Authority*, Vol.4 (Waco: Word, 1979).
Kirk, J. Andrew. *Liberation Theology: An Evangelical View from the Third World* (Atlanta: John Knox, 1980).
Lefever, Ernest W. *Amsterdam to Nairobi: The World Council of Churches and the Third World* (Washington, D.C.: Ethics and Public Policy Center, 1979).
Nash, Ronald. *Social Justice and the Christian Church* (Milford, Michigan: Mott Media, 1983).
Norman, Edward. *Christianity and World Order* (New York: Oxford University Press, 1979).
Novak, Michael, editor. *Capitalism and Socialism, a Theological Inquiry* (Washington, D.C.: American Enterprise Institute, 1979).
Novak, Michael, editor. *Liberation North, Liberation South* (Washington, D.C.: American Enterprise Institute, 1980).

Selected Bibliography

Novak, Michael. *The Spirit of Democratic Capitalism* (New York: Simon & Schuster, 1982).

Quade, Quentin L., editor. *The Pope and Revolution* (Washington, D.C.: Ethics and Public Policy Center, 1982).

Schall, James V., S.J. "The Weakness of Liberation Theology," *Christian Order*. April, 1983. pp. 239-246.

Schall, James V., S.J. *Liberation Theology in Latin America* (San Francisco: Ignatius Press, 1982).

Schall, James V., S.J. *The Church, the State and Society in the Thought of John Paul II* (Chicago: Franciscan Herald Press, 1982).

Trujillo, Alfonso Lopez. *Liberation or Revolution?* (Huntington, Indiana: Our Sunday Visitor, 1977).

Wagner, C. Peter. *Latin American Theology: Radical or Evangelical?* (Grand Rapids: Eerdmans, 1970).

Williamson, Rene De Visme. "The Theology of Liberation," *Christianity Today*. 19 (1975) pp. 7-12.

Other Books and Articles
Relevant to the Topic of Liberation Theology

Armerding, Carl E., editor. *Evangelicals and Liberation* (Phillipsburg, New Jersey: Presbyterian and Reformed, 1977).

Beichman, A., Martino, A. and Minogue, K. *Three Myths* (Washington, D.C.: The Heritage Foundation, 1982).

Bell, Daniel and Kristol, Irving. *The Crisis in Economic Theory* (New York: Basic, 1981).

Berger, Peter. *Pyramids of Sacrifice: Political Ethics and Social Change* (New York: Basic, 1974).

Bockmuehl, Klaus. *The Challenge of Marxism* (Downers Grove, Illinois: Intervarsity Press, 1980).

Brown, Susan Love, et al. *The Incredible Bread Machine* (San Diego: World Research Inc., 1974).

DeGeorge, Richard T. and Picheler, Joseph A., editors. *Ethics, Free Enterprise and Public Policy* (New York: Oxford University Press, 1978).

Friedman, Milton. *Capitalism and Freedom* (Chicago: University of Chicago Press, 1962).

Gilder, George. *Wealth and Poverty* (New York: Basic, 1981).

Hayek, Friedrich. *Law, Legislation and Liberty*, 3 vols. (Chicago: University of Chicago Press, 1973-79).

Hayek, Friedrich. *The Road to Serfdom* (Chicago: University of Chicago Press, 1944).

Hazlitt, Henry. "Understanding 'Austrian' Economics," *The Freeman*, February, 1981.

Hobbs, Charles D. *The Welfare Industry* (Washington: The Heritage Foundation, 1978).

Hospers, John. *Libertarianism* (Los Angeles: Nash, 1971).

Kirzner, Israel. "The Ugly Market: Why Capitalism is Hated, Feared and Despised." *The Freeman*. 24 (1974).

Mavrodes, George. "On Helping the Hungry." *Christianity Today*. December 30, 1977.

Meyer, Frank. *In Defense of Freedom* (Chicago: Henry Regnery, 1962).

Nash, Ronald. *Freedom, Justice and the State* (Lanham, Maryland: University Press of America, 1980).

Nash, Ronald. "The Economics of Justice." *Christianity Today*. 23 (1979).

Nash, Ronald. "Three Kinds of Individualism." *The Intercollegiate Review* 12 (1976).

Nozick, Robert. *Anarchy, State and Utopia* (New York: Basic, 1974).

Pasour, E.C., Jr. "On Economic Justice," *Modern Age*. 1981.

Petuchowski, Jacob J. "The Altar-Throne Clash Updated." *Christianity Today*. September 23, 1977.

Rawls, John. *A Theory of Justice* (Cambridge: Harvard University Press, 1971).

Reisman, George. *The Government Against the Economy* (Ottawa, Illinois: Caroline House, 1979).

Rogge, Benjamin. "Christian Economics: Myth or Reality?" *The Freeman*. Dec., 1965.

Sowell, Thomas. *Markets and Minorities* (New York: Basic, 1981).

Sowell, Thomas. *Race and Economics* (New York: David McKay, 1975).

Selected Bibliography

Sowell, Thomas. "The Uses of Government for Racial Equality,"
    National Review September 4, 1981.
Van den Haag, Ernest, editor. *Capitalism: Sources of Hostility* (New
    Rochelle: Epoch, 1979).
Wogaman, J. Philip. *The Great Economic Debate: An Ethical
    Analysis* (Philadelphia: Westminster, 1977).

Person Index